Current Approaches to Collective Burials in the Late European Prehistory

Edited by

**Tiago Tomé, Marta Díaz-Zorita Bonilla,
Ana Maria Silva, Claudia Cunha,
Rui Boaventura**

Archaeopress Archaeology

ARCHAEOPRESS PUBLISHING LTD
Gordon House
276 Banbury Road
Oxford OX2 7ED

www.archaeopress.com

ISBN 978 1 78491 721 0
ISBN 978 1 78491 722 7 (e-Pdf)

© Archaeopress, UISPP and authors 2017

COVER IMAGE: Structure 10.034 from PP4 Montelirio at Valencina de la Concepción. Courtesy of the Research Group ATLAS, University of Seville (Spain). Photograph: José Peinado Cucarella.

VOLUME EDITORS: Tiago Tomé, Marta Díaz-Zorita Bonilla, Ana Maria Silva, Claudia Cunha, Rui Boaventura

SERIES EDITOR: The board of UISPP

CO-EDITORS – CIAS – Research Centre for Anthropology and Health, University of Coimbra

SERIES PROPERTY: UISPP – International Union of Prehistoric and Protohistoric Sciences

Proceedings of the XVII World UISPP Congress, Burgos (Spain)
September 1–7 2014

KEY-WORDS IN THIS VOLUME: collective burials, late Prehistory, western Europe, bioarchaeology, funerary patterns

UISPP PROCEEDINGS SERIES is a printed on demand and an open access publication, edited by UISPP through Archaeopress

BOARD OF UISPP: Jean Bourgeois (President), Luiz Oosterbeek (Secretary-General), François Djindjian (Treasurer), Ya-Mei Hou (Vice President), Marta Arzarello (Deputy Secretary-General).

The Executive Committee of UISPP also includes the Presidents of all the international scientific commissions (www.uispp.org)

BOARD OF THE XVII WORLD CONGRESS OF UISPP: Eudald Carbonell (Secretary-General), Robert Sala I Ramos, Jose Maria Rodriguez Ponga (Deputy Secretary-Generals)

All rights reserved. No part of this book may be reproduced, or transmitted, in any form or by any means, electronic, mechanical, photocopying or otherwise, without the prior written permission of the copyright owners.
This book is available direct from Archaeopress or from our website www.archaeopress.com

Contents

List of Figures and Tables iii

In Memoriam Rui Boaventura (February 10th 1971 – May 28th 2016) vi
Ana Catarina Sousa, Tiago Tomé, Ana Maria Silva

Foreword to the XVII UISPP Congress Proceedings Series Edition ix
Luiz Oosterbeek

Introduction x
Tiago Tomé, Marta Díaz-Zorita Bonilla, Ana Maria Silva and Claudia Cunha

Tomb 3 at La Pijotilla (Solana de los Barros, Badajoz, Spain): A Bioarchaeological Study of a Copper Age Collective Burial 1
Marta Díaz-Zorita Bonilla, Charlotte A. Roberts, Leonardo García Sanjuán and
 Victor Hurtado Pérez

On the applicability of the assessment of dental tooth wear for the study of collective prehistoric burials 11
Luís Miguel Marado, Claudia Cunha, G. Richard Scott, Tiago Tomé, Hugo Machado and
 Ana Maria Silva

Cova de Can Sadurní (Begues, Barcelona). Towards the definition of a multiple funerary model inside caves during the middle Neolithic I in the northeast of the Iberian Peninsula 21
Manuel Edo, Ferran Antolín, Pablo Martínez, Concepció Castellana, Remei Bardera,
 María Saña, M. Mercè Bergadà, Josep Maria Fullola, Chus Barrio, Elicínia Fierro,
 Trinidad Castillo and Eva Fornell

Mora Cavorso Cave: a collective underground burial in Neolithic central Italy 33
Mario F. Rolfo, Katia F. Achino and Letizia Silvestri

Bioarchaeological approach to the Late Neolithic and Chalcolithic population of Cameros megalithic group (La Rioja, Spain) 41
Teresa Fernández-Crespo

Anthropological and taphonomical study of human remains from the burial cave of El Espinoso (Ribadedeva, Asturias, Spain) 55
Borja González Rabanal, Manuel Ramón González Morales and Ana Belén Marín Arroyo

Diet and ritual in the western Mediterranean Copper Age: human and animal stable isotopes from the collective burial at S. Caterina di Pittinuri (Sardinia, Italy) 67
Luca Lai, Ornella Fonzo, Elena Usai, Luca Medda, Robert Tykot, Ethan Goddard,
 David Hollander and Giuseppa Tanda

The artificial caves of Valencina de la Concepción (Seville) 79
Pedro M. López Aldana and Ana Pajuelo Pando

Multiple burials in pit graves from Recent Prehistory at Southwest of Iberia: The cases of Monte do Vale do Ouro 2 (Ferreira do Alentejo), Ribeira de S. Domingos 1 and Alto de Brinches 3 (Serpa) 91
Tânia Pereira, Ana Maria Silva, António Valera, Eduardo Porfírio

Bioarchaeological analysis at the Copper Age site of Valencina de la Concepción (Seville, Spain): The PP4-Montelirio sector 103
Sonia Robles Carrasco, Marta Díaz-Zorita Bonilla, Virginia Fuentes Mateo and Leonardo García Sanjuán

Assessing spatial dispersion of human remains in collective burials: A GIS approach to the burial-caves of the Nabão Valley (North Ribatejo, Portugal) 119
Tiago Tomé, Claudia Cunha, Ana Maria Silva, Luiz Oosterbeek and Ana Cruz

List of Figures and Tables

M. Díaz-Zorita Bonilla et al.: **Tomb 3 at La Pijotilla (Solana de los Barros, Badajoz, Spain): A Bioarchaeological Study of a Copper Age Collective Burial**

Figure 1. Map of La Pijotilla 2
Figure 2. Plan of Tomb 3 at La Pijotilla 3
Figure 3. *Cribra orbitalia* affecting the right orbit, grade 2 (ID 6887) 6
Figure 4. Dental abscess cavity (ID 10400) 7
Table 1. Radiocarbon dates for La Pijotilla 3
Table 2. Estimation of age at death at La Pijotilla 4
Table 3. Sex Estimation at La Pijotilla 5
Table 4. Stature calculation at La Pijotilla 5

L. Miguel Marado et al.: **On the applicability of the assessment of dental tooth wear for the study of collective prehistoric burials**

Figure 1. Tooth wear on different UI1 subsequently less affected by tooth wear 12

M. Edo et al.: **Cova de Can Sadurní (Begues, Barcelona). Towards the definition of a multiple funerary model inside caves during the middle Neolithic I in the northeast of the Iberian Peninsula**

Figure 1. Location of the sites mentioned in the text and site plan of Cova de Can Sadurní 22
Figure 2. East profile of the excavation area 22
Figure 3. Individual 1 (INH1) and Individual 2 (INH2) 24
Figure 4. Hypothetical reconstruction of the shroud of Individual 1 24
Figure 5. Radiocarbon dates based on human bone samples 26
Figure 6. Hypothetical reconstruction of the evolution of the funerary events in the cave 27
Figure 7. Materials associated to the burials or likely to be considered as funerary offerings 28
Table 1. Radiocarbon dates on human bone samples 26

M.F. Rolfo et al.: **Mora Cavorso Cave: a collective underground burial in Neolithic central Italy**

Figure 1. 1- The location of Mora Cavorso Cave in the Simbruini Mountains;
2- Plan of the cave with location of the archaeological test pits 34
Figure 2. 1, 3- The human bones found on the floor of the Lower Room;
2, 4- The human bones found on the floor of the Upper Room 35
Figure 3. Plan and Stratigraphy of the Lower Room (1) and Upper Room (2) 36
Figure 4. Archaeological remains from Upper Room (4-5) and Lower Room (1-3) 37

T. Fernández-Crespo: **Bioarchaeological approach to the Late Neolithic and Chalcolithic population of Cameros megalithic group (La Rioja, Spain)**

Figure 1. Map of Cameros region revealing the location of Late Neolithic
and Chalcolithic burial sites 42
Figure 2. Image showing the common fragmented, disarticulated and
commingled state of bones 43
Figure 3. Radiocarbon dates from the megalithic graves under study 44
Figure 4. Shape of mortality rates [q(x)] from Cameros megalithic graves 48
Figure 5. Evidence of spondyloarthritis or vertebral fusion from Peña Guerra II 49
Figure 6. Picture showing the positioning of a group of skulls by the orthostates of
the secondary chamber of Peña Guerra II 50
Table 1. Distribution by age of the individuals recovered from the Cameros mortuary sites
under study 47

Table 2. Distribution by sex of adolescent and adult individuals recovered from the Cameros mortuary sites under study 47
Table 3. Combined life table for the Cameros Late Neolithic/Chalcolithic population..................47

B. González Rabanal et al.: Anthropological and taphonomical study of human remains from the burial cave of El Espinoso (Ribadedeva, Asturias, Spain)

Figure 1. Geographic location of El Espinoso cave..................57
Figure 2. Plan of El Espinoso cave..................58
Figure 3. PCA results of *tali* collection..................61
Figure 4. Breakage of the long bones: type, angle, profile, edge and circumference of the fractures..................61
Figure 5. Comparison of the weathering stages between human and animal assemblages...................62
Figure 6. Grave goods of El Espinoso cave..................63
Table 1. Radiocarbon dates of human remains from burial caves in eastern Asturias..................56
Table 2. Radiocarbon dates for different phases of Cantabrian Bronze Age..................57
Table 3. Mathematical formulas to estimate the stature of individuals..................59
Table 4. Skeletal profile representation..................60

L. Lai et al.: Diet and ritual in the western Mediterranean Copper Age: human and animal stable isotopes from the collective burial at S. Caterina di Pittinuri (Sardinia, Italy)

Figure 1. Santa Caterina di Pittinuri. 1: location within the Western Mediterranean. 2: plan of the rock-cut tomb..................68
Figure 2. Santa Caterina di Pittinuri, rock-cut tomb. Isotopic and FT-IR values for paleodietary, paleoecological and diagenetic reconstruction..................73
Table 1. The two radiocarbon dates from the rock-cut tomb at Santa Caterina di Pittinuri..................70
Table 2. Santa Caterina di Pittinuri. All individual data, isotopic and FTIR values..................72

P.M. López Aldana and A. Pajuelo Pando: The artificial caves of Valencina de la Concepción (Seville)

Figure 1. Valencina location on the Iberian Peninsula..................80
Figure 2. Location of artificial caves in Valencina..................80
Figure 3. Location of artificial caves in southern Spain..................81
Figure 4. La Huera. Photo of Elena Méndez..................83
Figure 5. Estructura 48 calle Dinamarca 3-5..................84
Figure 6. Estructura 51 calle Dinamarca 3-5..................84
Figure 7. Estructura 28 calle Dinamarca 3-5..................85
Figure 8. Estructura 5 calle Dinamarca 3-5..................85
Figure 9. 1 and 2 individuals of the structure 5 calle Dinamarca 3-5..................86
Figure 10. Types and distribution of burials in Valencina..................87

T. Pereira et al.: Multiple burials in pit graves from Recent Prehistory at Southwest of Iberia: The cases of Monte do Vale do Ouro 2 (Ferreira do Alentejo), Ribeira de S. Domingos 1 and Alto de Brinches 3 (Serpa)

Figure 1. Geographic localization in the Iberian Peninsula of the studied area..................92
Figure 2. Pit 97 and 102 of Monte do Vale do Ouro 2..................93
Figure 3. Demographic profile of the individuals exhumed from pit 97 of Monte do Vale do Ouro 2..................94
Figure 4. Traces of fire on individuals 9701 and 9702 from pit 97 of Monte do Vale do Ouro 2..................95
Figure 5. Bone preservations of the individuals exhumed from pit 102 of Monte do Vale do Ouro 2..................95
Figure 6. Dental wear on occlusal and lingual surface of the two superior lateral incisors and a sulcus on the cement-enamel junction..................96

FIGURE 7. INDIVIDUALS ON PIT 1 FROM RIBEIRA DE S. DOMINGOS 1 97
FIGURE 8. PIT 691 OF ALTO DE BRINCHES 3 98
FIGURE 9. ILLUSTRATIONS OF THE ANATOMICAL CONNECTIONS THAT FORMS THE SKELETONS OF
INDIVIDUALS 1 (LEFT) AND 2 (RIGHT) FROM ALTO DE BRINCHES 3 99

S. Robles Carrasco et al.: **Bioarchaeological analysis at the Copper Age site of Valencina de la Concepción (Seville, Spain): The PP4-Montelirio sector**

FIGURE 1. MAP OF VALENCINA DE LA CONCEPCIÓN (SEVILLA) 104
FIGURE 2. MAP WITH STRUCTURES WITH AND WITHOUT HUMAN BONE REMAINS
AT THE PP4-MONTELIRIO SECTOR 104
FIGURE 3. LEH AT 21, INDIVIDUAL 2 FROM STRUCTURE 10.035 108
FIGURE 4. DILACERATION OF THE ROOT (TEETH 13) FROM STRUCTURE 10.003 109
FIGURE 5. UNUSUAL ALTERATION IN ENAMEL (TOOTH 21) AT STRUCTURE 10.055 110
FIGURE 6. POSSIBLE CASE OF 'DENS INVAGINATUS' ON TOOTH 22 FROM INDIVIDUAL 1
AT STRUCTURE 10.044. 111
TABLE 1. LIST OF STRUCTURES WITH BIOARCHAEOLOGICAL ANALYSIS 106
TABLE 2. LIST OF TEETH WITH LEH 108
TABLE 3. LIST OF TEETH WITH POSSIBLE 'DENS INVAGINATUS' 109
TABLE 4. LIST OF TEETH SHOWING ENAMEL ALTERATION 109

T. Tomé et al.: **Assessing spatial dispersion of human remains in collective burials: A GIS approach to the burial-caves of the Nabão Valley (North Ribatejo, Portugal)**

FIGURE 1. LOCATION OF CDV AND GRO 121
FIGURE 2. GLOBAL SPATIAL DISPERSION OF SKELETAL REMAINS 122
FIGURE 3. ADULTS *VERSUS* NON-ADULTS SKELETAL REMAINS DISTRIBUTION 123
FIGURE 4. SPATIAL DISPERSION BY SKELETAL REGION AT CDV 124
FIGURE 5. SPATIAL DISPERSION BY SKELETAL REGION AT GRO 124
FIGURE 6. DIFFERENTIAL DISPERSION PATTERNS FOR UPPER AND LOWER LIMB BONES AT GRO 124

In Memoriam
Rui Boaventura (February 10th 1971 – May 28th 2016)

RUI BOAVENTURA EXCAVATING AT QUINTA DO FREIXO IN 2012
(PHOTO BY GLEN JONES)

In 2014, Rui Boaventura was a member of the organizing committee of the XVII World UISPP Congress session that would ultimately result in this volume. Unfortunately, the condition that would lead to his premature demise manifested itself not long afterwards and he was unable to provide his precious help in the edition of this proceedings volume. For that reason, this volume is dedicated to his memory.

Despite his young age, Rui Boaventura was a well-known figure in the study of Prehistoric societies in Portugal. Having completed his undergraduate studies at the University of Lisbon in 1993, his early years would be dedicated to high-school teaching at several schools, along with the participation in archaeological excavations.

In the late 1990's, while working as an archaeologist in the Northern Alentejo, a region where he had distant family roots, his attention would be drawn to the Late Prehistoric communities of that area, particularly the ones at the 4th/3rd millennia BCE. On that context, he would develop research on the megalithic monuments of Rabuje, a relatively little known group of monuments originally included in the seminal works by Vera and Georg Leisner in the mid-XXth century. As an archaeologist working for the then newly-created Instituto Português de Arqueologia[1], he continued researching settlement sites of the same period in that area, one of which would constitute the theme of his 2001 Master dissertation at the University of Lisbon, under the coordination of Prof. Victor Gonçalves – published under the title '*O sítio Calcolítico do Pombal (Monforte). Uma recuperação possível de velhos e novos dados*'. This early work already revealed his focus on detailed analysis of archaeological information, as well as an understanding of the need to look at materials from older excavations with fresh eyes.

---

[1] Portuguese Institute for Archaeology, now extinct.

As of 2002, he moved to the Lisbon area, where he would continue his study of Neolithic-Chalcolithic societies, coordinating the excavation of several burial monuments in the region. Those works were the basis of his PhD research ('*As antas e o Megalitismo na região de Lisboa*', 2010). Once again this work was carried out under the supervision of Victor Gonçalves at the University of Lisbon. This would allow him to assess a territory where much more research on Late Prehistoric communities had been done, leading to richer, albeit more complex, interpretations. Thus, he dedicated efforts to studying collections from the Megalithic burials of the Lisbon area, curated at the Portuguese National Archaeological Museum and the Museum of the Portuguese Geological and Mining Institute. He also carried out a rigorous compilation of documents, cataloguing the Leisner Archive, kept at the Instituto Português de Arqueologia's facilities under an agreement with the Deutsches Archäologisches Institut and set up a wide range of collaborations aiming at interdisciplinary approaches, regarding absolute chronology and bioanthropological analysis.

This interest in interdisciplinary approaches resulted in the establishment of a research programme (Mega Osteology), led by the association Portanta, under which collaborations with Ana Maria Silva, Maria Teresa Ferreira (Research Centre for Anthropology and Health – University of Coimbra) and Maria Hillier (Max Planck Institute Leipzig) were developed. He would recognize quite early in his career the importance of Biological Anthropology's more recent methods to the interpretation of prehistoric collective burials.

Since 2011, he was a post-doctoral researcher with UNIARQ (University of Lisbon) and University State of Pennsylvania. Although his interests were diversified, his research kept focusing on megaliths and funerary practices on the 4th/3rd millennia BCE. With Ana Maria Silva he produced several studies, regarding funerary practices, mobility/migration and violence. On a colaboration in Carlos Odriozola's (University of Seville) project, along with Ana Catarina Sousa and Rodrigo Villalobos, he studied green stone adornments of Portuguese sites. With Katina Lillios (National Science Foundation), he cooperated in a project at the Sizandro Valley.

As of 2013, Boaventura coordinated the MEGAGEO project, funded by the Fundação para a Ciência e Tecnologia, partnering with geologists working at the Universities of Évora (Patrícia Moita, Jorge Pedro and Pedro Nogueira) and Aveiro (José Santos). This project aimed at the understanding of the geological provenance of stones used in building dolmens in Central and Southern Portugal, focusing on three regional case-studies: Monforte, Redondo (both on Northern Alentejo) and Lisbon (Lower Estremadura). He performed several excavations in cooperation with Rui Mataloto, namely at Redondo (Quinta do Freixo 4, Candieira, Godinhos), Monforte (Lacrau 2 e 3, Enxara de Cima 1) and Vila Franca de Xira (Monte Serves).

In 2014 he was one of the organizers of Session A25b of the XVII World UISPP Congress ('*Current Approaches to Collective Burials in the Late European Prehistory*'), held at Burgos (Spain). His name was an obvious choice for us ever since the first moment we thought about organizing this meeting. This volume is a result of that session and his contribution to the debates was quite relevant.

In November 2015, with Rui Mataloto, he organized Megatalks, an international congress held at Redondo, gathering researchers of megalithic sites from Britain, Sweden, France, Spain and Portugal.

His scientific interests were highly interconnected, including Neolithic and Chalcolithic funerary practices, mobility and migration, war and interpersonal violence, gender, Geoarchaeology, History of Archaeology, among others.

A researcher at UNIARQ, his work was characterized by an intense research activity, particularly at the National Archaeological Museum, but nevertheless keeping active collaborations with research centers both in Portugal (CIAS, University of Coimbra) and abroad (University of Louisville). He was also the coordinator of the Portanta association. His work was several times awarded with research grants from Fundação Ciência e Tecnologia, Calouste Gulbenkian Foundation, American Institute of Archaeology, Dorot Foundation and Deutsches Archäologisches Institut.

A member of the American Institute of Archaeology, Associação dos Arqueólogos Portugueses and Associação Profissional de Arqueólogos (of which he was a member of the directing board), Rui Boaventura was also an active voice in many moments related to the development of Archaeology in Portugal, such as the debate around the dismantling of government archaeological facilities in Portugal. He authored numerous publications, including two books, dozens of articles and book chapters, both in Portugal and abroad.

His was the cause of knowledge, but also the one of Humanism. This much was evident in the quotation by Albert Einstein with which he usually ended his e-mail messages: *'The ideals which have always shone before me and filled me with the joy of living are goodness, beauty, and truth'*. His tireless curiosity and enthusiasm about Late Prehistoric societies of the Iberian Peninsula would prove invaluable to the study of collective burials in Portugal. Portuguese Archaeology lost one of its most promising minds. Rui Boaventura was an accomplished archaeologist, a smart and provocative thinker, a gracious and open-minded debater and a great partner. But most of all, he was a loving father of three bright sons whom he taught his love for the Portuguese countryside and Archaeology. His many friends and colleagues will miss him deeply for the researcher and the human being he was. His family will miss a dedicated father, a loving son, brother, partner…

Ana Catarina Sousa, Tiago Tomé, Ana Maria Silva

Foreword to the XVII UISPP Congress Proceedings Series Edition

Luiz Oosterbeek
Secretary-General

UISPP has a long history, starting with the old International Association of Anthropology and Archaeology, back in 1865, until the foundation of UISPP itself in Bern, in 1931, and its growing relevance after WWII, from the 1950's. We also became members of the International Council of Philosophy and Human Sciences, associate of UNESCO, in 1955.

In its XIVth world congress in 2001, in Liège, UISPP started a reorganization process that was deepened in the congresses of Lisbon (2006) and Florianópolis (2011), leading to its current structure, solidly anchored in more than twenty-five international scientific commissions, each coordinating a major cluster of research within six major chapters: Historiography, methods and theories; Culture, economy and environments; Archaeology of specific environments; Art and culture; Technology and economy; Archaeology and societies.

The XVIIth world congress of 2014, in Burgos, with the strong support of Fundación Atapuerca and other institutions, involved over 1700 papers from almost 60 countries of all continents. The proceedings, edited in this series but also as special issues of specialized scientific journals, will remain as the most important outcome of the congress.

Research faces growing threats all over the planet, due to lack of funding, repressive behavior and other constraints. UISPP moves ahead in this context with a strictly scientific programme, focused on the origins and evolution of humans, without conceding any room to short term agendas that are not root in the interest of knowledge.

In the long run, which is the terrain of knowledge and science, not much will remain from the contextual political constraints, as severe or dramatic as they may be, but the new advances into understanding the human past and its cultural diversity will last, this being a relevant contribution for contemporary and future societies.

This is what UISPP is for, and this is also why we are currently engaged in contributing for the relaunching of Human Sciences in their relations with social and natural sciences, namely collaborating with the International Year of Global Understanding, in 2016, and with the World Conference of the Humanities, in 2017.

The next congresses of UISPP, in Melbourne (2017) and in Geneva (2020), will confirm this route.

Introduction

Tiago Tomé, Marta Díaz-Zorita Bonilla, Ana Maria Silva and Claudia Cunha

The present volume originated in session A25b ('Current Approaches to Collective Burials in the Late European Prehistory') of the XVII World Congress of the International Union of the Prehistoric and Protohistoric Sciences (UISPP), held in Burgos in September 2014.

Collective burials are quite a common feature in Prehistoric Europe, with the gathering of multiple individuals in a shared burial place occurring in different types of burial structures (natural caves, megalithic structures, artificial caves, corbelled-roof tombs, pits, etc.). Such features are generally associated with communities along the agropastoralist transition and fully agricultural societies of the Neolithic and Chalcolithic.

Over the last few decades, a renewed interest in the study of Prehistoric collective burials and specifically on the human skeletal remains they contained has emerged. Such interest is a consequence of biological anthropologists adopting methods focused on the understanding and reconstruction of the formation processes of funerary contexts, an increment in physicochemical analysis such as radiocarbon dating, ancient DNA and stable isotopes studies, as well as a growing collaboration between anthropologists and archaeologists. All this led to a larger integration of bioanthropological data within archaeological interpretation, eventually resulting in the emergence of a new disciplinary field, Bioarchaeology. This allows us to currently hold a deeper understanding of these communities, as well as of their funerary practices.

For a long time, human skeletal remains exhumed from collective burials were dismissed as valuable sources of information, their studies being limited mostly to morphological assessments and subsequent classification in predefined 'races'. They currently represent a starting point for diversified, often interdisciplinary, research projects, allowing for a more accurate reconstruction of funerary practices, as well as of palaeobiological and environmental aspects, which are fundamental for the understanding of populations in the Late Prehistory of Europe and of the processes leading to the emergence of agricultural societies in this part of the world.

The XVII World UISPP Congress venue (Spain) probably resulted in a greater focus of the contributions to this session on southern Europe. We believe, nonetheless, that this also reflects recent developments on this subject in southern European countries, with bioarchaeological studies becoming ever more common and in line with international practices.

The articles in this volume provide examples of different approaches currently being developed on Prehistoric collective burials of southern Europe, mostly focusing on case studies, but also including contributions of a more methodological scope:

Díaz-Zorita Bonilla *et al.* present a detailed bioarchaeological study of the remains recovered from the Tomb 3 of La Pijotilla, a key site to understand social dynamics in south-west Spain Copper Age mega-sites. This papers aims to contribute on how to record an extremely fragmented human assemblage with cutting edge techniques.

The contribution by Marado *et al.* is more of a theoretical and methodological proposal, on the importance of dental tooth wear assessment to the understanding of the communities buried on collective burials, based on Portuguese examples. Such methodological approaches are important in the sense that they are tools for understanding human behavior and the interaction between man and the resources provided by the environment.

Edo *et al.* present a detailed assessment of funerary treatment at a cave in northeastern Spain (Can Sadurní), where several individuals were deposited in tightly bound shrouds, along with votive offerings.

Rolfo *et al.* offer an overall description of the research developed on the burial cave of Mora Cavorso (central Italy), combining information from material culture and human remains, namely in terms of a paleobiological assessment and stable isotope studies.

Fernández-Crespo puts forward a general assessment of the human remains exhumed from a group of megalithic monuments in La Rioja, northern Spain, focusing on both paleobiological and funerary aspects.

González Rabanal *et al.* propose an approach that has become common over the last few decades: the reassessment, in light of modern methods, of skeletal assemblages previously recovered from El Espinoso cave, in Asturias (northern Spain).

Lai *et al.* provide us an insight into the diet of Copper Age Sardinia (Italy), through an isotopic analysis of remains recovered from the S. Caterina di Pittinuri burial.

López Aldana and Pajuelo Pando offer new information for another classic Copper Age site of southern Spain, Valencina de la Concepción, describing new burial structures, funerary practices and morphological features, as well as presenting aDNA data, crucial for our understanding of biological affinities within populations that occupied the region.

Pereira *et al.* develop an assessment of three different sites located in southern Portugal, where pits were used for multiple burials (adults and non-adults), spanning from the Late Neolithic to the Bronze Age. Among the more relevant data is the evidence of non-masticatory use of two teeth recovered from pit 102 of Monte do Vale do Ouro 2 and evidences of exposure to fire on individuals from pit 97 from the same site.

Robles Carrasco *et al.* also focus on Valencina de la Concepción, describing results from a bioarchaeological assessment of one of the site's excavated sectors.

The volume closes with a case-study by Tomé *et al.* on computer applications to the study of funerary contexts, through a GIS assessment of the spatial dispersion of human remains inside burial caves in central Portugal.

Diverse chrono-cultural contexts are included in this ensemble of texts – the oldest cases being the 6th millennium BCE depositions at Mora Cavorso and the 5th millennium BCE depositions at Can Sadurní, although the majority of collective burials discussed in this volume date to the 4th-3rd millennia BCE (Cameros megaliths, S. Caterina di Pittinuri, Valencina de la Concepción, Cadaval, Gruta dos Ossos). Some later cases are also presented, namely from the 2nd millennium BCE (El Espinoso, Monte do Vale do Ouro 2). Additionally, some sites reveal the presence of several collective burial periods (Peña Guerra II and Collado Palomero I in the Cameros megaliths or Monte do Vale do Ouro 2). This chronological diversity suggests that no single explanation can be put forward to the collective burial phenomenon as a whole – different symbolic realities must have existed, dependent upon spatial and temporal dimensions.

In summary, this volume represents an important contribution to the understanding of the funerary practices related to collective burials from the 6th up to the 2nd millennia BCE in Southern Europe. Not only funerary contexts of main archaeological sites from these periods are discussed, but also new approaches are suggested to deal with them. These include multi-disciplinary and cutting edge bioarchaeological analysis.

We believe that there is still much work to be done in order to understand the formation processes of these complex funerary contexts, but investigation is leading towards a wider approach, where Bioarchaeology is playing a major role. This includes the improvement on the excavation and exhumation strategies, the combination of more accurate methods of analysis of the osteological record and the application of several biochemical techniques such as radiocarbon, aDNA and stable isotope analysis. The next few decades will undoubtedly foment deeper knowledge on these Late Prehistoric societies, as well as more solid understanding of the diverse processes of agropastoralist transition.

Participants in the 'Current Approaches to Collective Burials in the Late European Prehistory' session of the 2014 UISPP Congress.

Tomb 3 at La Pijotilla (Solana de los Barros, Badajoz, Spain): A Bioarchaeological Study of a Copper Age Collective Burial

Marta Díaz-Zorita Bonilla[1], Charlotte A. Roberts[2], Leonardo García Sanjuán[3] and Víctor Hurtado Pérez[3]

[1] Institut für Ur- und Frühgeschichte und Archäologie des Mittelalters, Tübingen Universität
[2] Department of Archaeology, Durham University
[3] Departamento de Prehistoria y Arqueología, Universidad de Sevilla
marta.diaz-zorita-bonilla@ifg.uni-tuebingen.de

Abstract

This paper presents the results of the bioarchaeological analysis of La Pijotilla Tomb 3, which combines the application of standard methods in osteology and paleopathological analysis with the study of the funerary context. La Pijotilla is one of the most extensive Copper Age (c. 3200-2200 cal BC) settlements in Iberia, presenting a funerary complex with one of the largest human bone deposits available for the period, of which Tomb 3 is a prime example.

The human bone collection from Tomb 3 at La Pijotilla was commingled and highly fragmented, in spite of which each bone fragment and tooth was classified. The resulting MNI was 178 individuals, based on the analysis of 283,329 human bone and tooth fragments. An equal distribution of adult individuals by sex was identified, and most of the bone and tooth fragments corresponded to adult individuals, with little representation of subadults. The non-metric traits present suggested similarities with other prehistoric populations of the Spanish southwest. Most of the pathologies were related to joint and dental diseases, such as calculus and linear enamel hypoplasia.

Keywords

Bioarchaeology, Copper Age, Paleopathology, Human osteology, MNI

Résumé

Ce papier présente les résultats de l'analyse bioarchéologique de la Tombe 3 de La Pijotilla, qui combine l'application de méthodes standards en ostéologie et paléopathologie avec l'étude du context funéraire. La Pijotilla est un des plus importants gisements du Chalcolithique (3200-2200 av. J.-C. environ) de la péninsule Ibérique, avec un complexe funéraire qui a livré une des plus vastes accumulations d'os humains disponibles pour cette période. La Tombe 3 en est un exemple représentatif.

Chaque fragment d'os et de dent de la collection ostéologique de la Tombe 3 a pu être identifié malgré les processus de mélange et un fort taux de fragmentation. Le nombre minimum d'individus (NMI) qui en résulte est de 178, sur la base de l'analyse de 238,329 fragments d'os et de dent. Une répartition égale entre homme et femme a été déterminée; il a également été établi que la plupart des fragments osseux et dentaires se rapportaient à des individus adultes, avec une faible représentation des plus jeunes. Les caractéristiques non-métriques suggèrent des similarités avec d'autres populations du sud-ouest de l'Espagne. La majorité des pathologies correspond à des maladies articulaires et des paléopathologies dentaires comme la présence de tartre et d'hypoplasie dentaire.

Mots-clés

Bioarchéologie, Chalcolithique, paléopathologie, ostéologie humaine, NMI

Introduction

The first investigation at La Pijotilla was carried out about 40 years ago, in 1976 (Hurtado Pérez 1980), with excavation taking place between 1979 and 1984 (Hurtado Pérez 1999, 2000) and resuming in 1990 (Hurtado Pérez, 1990, 1991, 1995, 1997 and 2000; Hurtado Pérez and Mondéjar de Quincoces, 2009; Hurtado Pérez *et al.*, 2000; Hurtado Pérez, 2003, 2010; Hurtado Pérez and Odriozola Lloret,

2009). This site, covering approximately 80 hectares (Hurtado Pérez, 1986), represents one of the largest 3rd millennium BC settlements in Iberia. It is located in the municipality of Solana de los Barros (Badajoz, Spain) on the left bank of the Guadiana River, in the Middle Guadiana Basin (Figure 1).

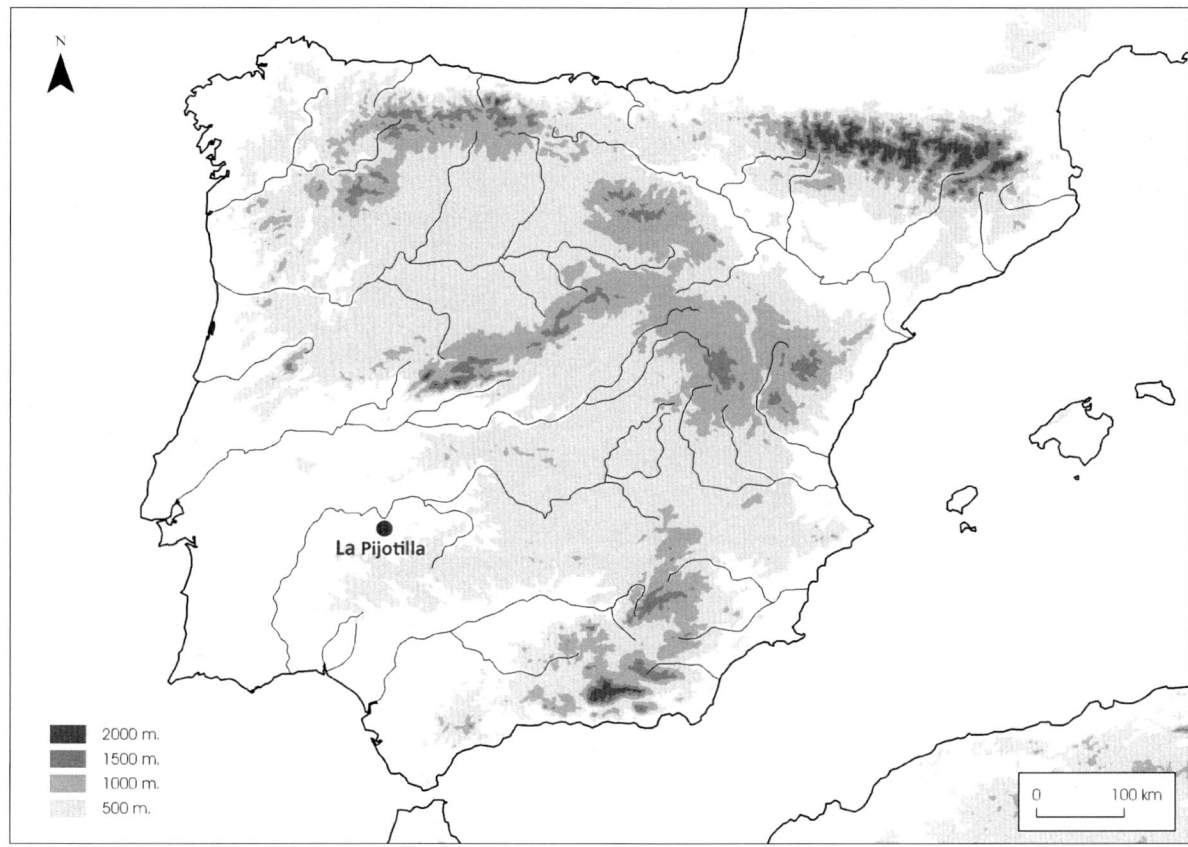

FIGURE 1. MAP OF LA PIJOTILLA.

La Pijotilla presents a host of structural and architectural elements, including a large circular ditch about 1 km in diameter that encloses a large number of pits and other negative features. In addition, various burial structures have been identified and excavated over the years, including two pits with individual inhumations as well as three collective burials: Tomb 1 (Minimum Number of Individuals (MNI)= 100), the so called 'circular tomb', Tomb 2 (MNI = 30), and Tomb 3, which this study is concerned with. With an overall length of 14 m (including an 11 m-long corridor and a 3.5 m-wide chamber), Tomb 3 is connected to Tomb 1, its corridor forming an angle of approximately 70° with the corridor of Tomb 1. Tomb 3 is basically cut into the ground, it is shallow depth in the outer part of the corridor but deeper (1.7 m) into the back of the chamber. No major slabs or uprights were used to line or roof either the corridor or chamber of Tomb 3, and the limited amount of smaller stones found inside the chamber's infill do not suggest a corbelled chamber ever existed, the roofing probably having been completed with a wooden or sun-dried mud structure. Based on field observations, the MNI of Tomb 3 was initially estimated at c. 300 (Hurtado Pérez *et al.*, 2002), a figure that this study has set more precisely at 178 (Figure 2). Two thermoluminescence (TL) dates (Odriozola Lloret *et al.*, 2008) and six radiocarbon dates (Hurtado Pérez *et al.*, 2002) suggest this tomb may have been in use between the 29th and 26th centuries BC (Table 1). Other published papers have dealt with the abundant material culture found in Tomb 3, including pottery (Polvorinos del Río *et al.* 2002a), stone

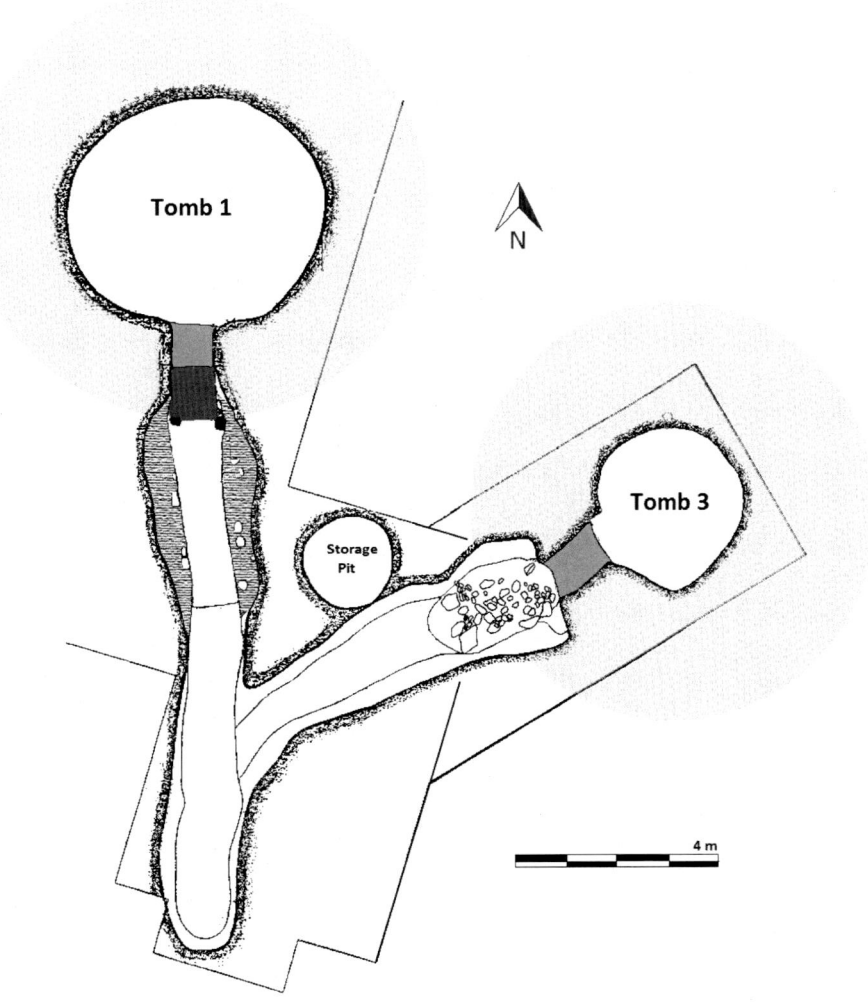

FIGURE 2. PLAN OF TOMB 3 AT LA PIJOTILLA.

Site	BP	BC (1 σ)	Lab ID	Context	Reference
La Pijotilla	4360±50	3077-2909	Beta-121146	E4. Organic material. At the base of the structure.	Hurtado Pérez, 1999; Odriozola Lloret et al., 2008
	4168 ±55	2870-2676	CNA-034	T3. Charcoal (UE 18)	Odriozola Lloret et al., 2008
	4130±40	2861-2625	Beta-121143	T3. Human bone (UE 15/16)	Hurtado Pérez, 1999; Odriozola Lloret et al., 2008
	4110±40	2854-2582	Beta-121147	E4. Organic material. Intermediate level of the structure.	
	4010±80	2836-2367	Beta-121145	E4. Organic material. Last use of the structure.	
	3860±80	2459-2212	BM-1603	E4. Re-use of the structure.	

TABLE 1. RADIOCARBON DATES FOR LA PIJOTILLA.

ornaments (Polvorinos del Río *et al.* 2002b), flint blades (Polvorinos del Río *et al.* 2008) as well as figurines and idols (Hurtado Pérez, 2010).

Tomb 3 represents one of the largest collections of human remains found in a single collective burial of the Iberian Copper Age, surpassed only, to our knowledge, by the Camino del Molino burial (Calatrava, Murcia), with an MNI estimated there of 1300 (Haber Uriarte *et al.*, 2013). In combination with the available funerary contextual data this collection of human remains provides an excellent basis for the study of social organisation in Copper Age Iberia. While the human remains from Tomb 3 were commingled and highly fragmented, some partial articulation was documented.

This paper presents a brief summary of the results obtained from the analysis of the human remains deposited in Tomb 3 at La Pijotilla. The specifics of the bioarchaeological methods applied and further relevant references are described in detail elsewhere (Díaz-Zorita Bonilla 2017: 37-51).

Material and Methods

La Pijotilla Tomb 3 yielded 283,329 human bone and tooth fragments. A comprehensive classification of each of them was made according to bone or tooth type, side, bone segment and completeness, sex and age at death.

The general age categories used were: fetal, I1 or infant 1 (birth-6 years), I2 or children (7-12), adolescents (13-17) for subadults (Scheuer and Black, 2000; Buikstra and Ubelaker, 1994; Ubelaker, 1989, and young adults (18-25), middle adult (26-35), mature adult (36-45) and old adult (>45), for adults (Lovejoy et al., 1985; Brooks and Suchey, 1990; Iscan et al., 1984; Iscan and Loth, 1986; Meindl and Lovejoy, 1985; Buikstra and Ubelaker, 1994; Brothwell, 1981, Smith, 1991). The sex categories used were female, probable female, adult indeterminate, male, probable male and subadult. In addition, metrical data, non-metric traits and enthesophytes, as well as pathological lesions, were recorded.

Results

The MNI was calculated based on the most frequent bone or tooth fragment occurring within the different age categories. The most frequent bone fragment was the petrous portion of the left temporal bone for adults and adolescents, and the mental protuberance of the mandible for subadults (aged >12); thus, the total MNI estimation for La Pijotilla was 178 individuals. Overall, there are at least five subadults belonging to the I1 category (birth-6 years old), another five to the I2 category (7-12 years old), 13 adolescents and 155 adults.

Estimation of age at death for the people buried in Tomb 3 was originally based on the full range of indicators for subadults and adults. However, due to extensive post-excavation fragmentation, adult ages were eventually estimated solely on preserved *os coxae* fragments, particularly the auricular surface and the pubic symphysis. It was possible to assess age based on 19 *os coxae*. The estimation of age at death for subadults was based on bone and tooth development; for this purpose, 25 bone fragments were assessed. However, there were five individuals whose age estimation was based only on tooth development. Results can be seen in Table 2.

Age	Category	N	%
Birth-6	I1	5	2.80
7-12	I2	5	2.80
13-17	AO	13	7.30
18-25	YA	8	4.49
26-35	MID	8	4.49
36-45	M	3	1.68
>45	OA	0	0
Adult	A	136	76.40
Total	-	178	100

Key to table: R=right; L= left; I1=birth-6 years old; I2=7-12; AO= adolescent 13-17; YA= young adult; MID= middle adult; M= mature adult; OA= old adult; A=adult.

TABLE 2. ESTIMATION OF AGE AT DEATH AT LA PIJOTILLA.

Due to the highly fragmented state of this assemblage, it was only possible to estimate sex for 45 of 178 bone fragments; of those 45, 18 fragments were female (9.47%) and 27 were male (14.21%). It must be noted that since we are dealing exclusively with bone fragments and not with complete skeletons, other bone elements from the same individual could not be examined and the presence of robustness in some of the available elements could have prompted an over-estimation of the number of fragments attributed to males. The overall sex distribution at La

Pijotilla based on bone fragments can be seen in Table 3.

Due to the high fragmentation, only five complete bones were found in Tomb 3: three adult *radii*, an adult fibula and a right adult ulna. Although the mean stature of this population cannot be estimated due to the lack of complete bones, the estimation based on the maximum length measurements available are shown in Table 4:

Sex	N	%
Female	18	9.47
Male	27	14.21
Subadult	23	12.92
Unsexed	110	61.79
Total	178	100

TABLE 3. SEX ESTIMATION AT LA PIJOTILLA.

Bag ID	Type of bone	Side	N	Trotter and Gleser 1958	
				Male	Female
2930	Radius	L	221	1.62 ± 4.32	1.59 ± 4.24
2968	Radius	R	221	1.62 ± 4.32	1.59 ± 4.24
1730	Fibula	L	351	1.72 ± 3.29	1.62 ± 3.57
5810	Ulna	R	234	1.60 ± 4.32	1.57 ± 4.30
7212	Radius	L	227	1.64 ± 4.32	1.62 ± 4.24

Key to table: N = maximum length of bone in millimetres; stature estimates given in metres ± standard deviation in centimetres.

TABLE 4. STATURE CALCULATION AT LA PIJOTILLA.

In Tomb 3 at La Pijotilla, a total of 20 non-metric traits were identified in the infracranial skeleton, mostly belonging to bones of the upper limbs, and none in the cranial bones. This reflects taphonomic factors affecting the skull, as well as overall fragmentation of the assemblage. The most common non-metric trait was the septal aperture ($n = 10$), followed by the vastus notch ($n = 3$). Unfortunately, no relationships could be established with respect to age or sex, as 9 of the 10 were classed as unsexed adults and one was from an adolescent. Regarding the non-metric dental traits, 16 of 2944 (0.54%) of the teeth presented non-metric traits. The most common trait was shovelling (8 of 16). Other traits included three dental *foramina* on the labial surface, two Carabelli traits, an interruption groove on the cingulum, a forked root and a dental gemination. All non-metric dental traits were found on adult teeth, except for one subadult I2, a 7-12-year-old.

A total of 14 enthesophytes were observed. In relation to the skull, only one individual presented a 'marker' at the insertion of the sternocleidomastoid muscle. There were six examples of enthesophytes in the upper skeleton (upper limb and vertebrae). One was identified on a left adult clavicle at the insertion of the subclavius muscle; there was also a radius showing hypertrophy of the *biceps brachii* insertion. The rest of the enthesophytes on the upper limb bone fragments are related to hypertrophy of the phalangeal flexors that inserted to a proximal 2nd metacarpal and a 3rd metacarpal. In relation to the ribs, an adult rib showed a prominent insertion area for the *iliocostalis cervicis*. With respect to the lower limbs, there were 9 bone fragments, two of which presented hypertrophy of the *linea aspera* on left and right adult femora; given that they were found in the same stratigraphic unit and their similar morphology, they could have belonged to the same individual. Concerning foot bones, two examples of an Achilles tendon enthesophytes were identified on left adult *calcanei*, and there was an enthesophyte related to the *extensor digitorum brevis* of an adult proximal 2nd metacarpal. There was also an anterior tibiofibular ligament enthesophyte, two *patellae* with enthesophytes on the superior part of the anterior facet, and another enthesophyte on the patellar tendon insertion on a left patella.

Due to the nature of this assemblage and the lack of complete skeletons, finding pathological changes and producing a diagnosis was expected to be very difficult. Bones and bone fragments showing pathological changes from Tomb 3 of La Pijotilla showed evidence of joint disease (N of fragments observed = 1711; N affected = 44 or 2.57%). Joint disease changes were observed in 44 fragments, mainly affecting the vertebrae (8.69%), hand bones (8%), long bones (6.06%) and foot bones (3.44%). The most frequently represented disease was osteoarthritis (24 of 44 bones) and most of the evidence was found in foot phalanges (15 in total).

At Tomb 3 of La Pijotilla, seven bones with evidence of trauma were documented (N of fragments observed = 623; N affected = 1.12%). At least five were rib fractures, all of them healed. According to Brickley (2006), rib fractures are among the better-represented traumatic lesions in the bioarchaeological record but, due to fragmentation of this assemblage, no further rib fractures were documented. Concerning other bone fragments, an adult fibula with a possible fracture of the diaphysis was recorded, as well as a second metatarsal.

There were a total of six bone elements with pathological changes consistent with metabolic disease (N of fragments observed = 84; N affected = 6 or 7.14%), porotic hyperostosis of the skull vault and *cribra orbitalia* on the orbital roof. In terms of *cribra orbitalia*, there were five orbits affected, four of them in the right orbit and one in the left orbit. There was one skull with bilateral *cribra orbitalia* (Figure 3).

FIGURE 3. *CRIBRA ORBITALIA* AFFECTING THE RIGHT ORBIT, GRADE 2 (ID 6887) (SCALE IS IN CM).

A total of 2,944 dental fragments (of tooth crowns or roots) were identified from Tomb 3. Some of these fragments showed evidence of dental disease; the most frequently found condition was *calculus* (N of teeth observed = 1866; N affected = 98 or 5.25%). This affected 99 of 2944 tooth fragments (3.36%), mainly on their labial/buccal surfaces and mostly of grade 1 (Buikstra and Ubelaker 1994: 56). *Calculus* affected 54 of 98 of the maxillary teeth (55.10%) and 42 of 98 of the mandibular teeth were also affected (42.85%).

Linear enamel hypoplasia (LEH) was the second most frequently represented dental disease at La Pijotilla (N of teeth observed = 697, N affected = 19 or 3.01%). Nineteen teeth were affected, primarily canines ($n = 11$), and less so for the premolars ($n = 5$), incisors ($n = 2$) and molars ($n = 1$). All individuals developed these defects in the teeth when they were between 2.7 and 5.6 years of age; some teeth had two or three hypoplastic defects. All the teeth with more than one hypoplastic defect were incisors and the individuals to whom these teeth belonged developed these changes when they were between 2 and 5 years of age.

There were nine teeth with evidence of caries at La Pijotilla Tomb 3; seven were molars, two were premolars and, of these, three were from the mandible and six from the maxilla; two premolars were also affected (N of teeth observed = 2944, N affected = 9 or 0.30%). There were also three examples of caries that had obliterated the entire tooth crown: both central upper incisor teeth and lower incisors, canines and premolars.

There were two examples of periapical lesions (in this case dental abscesses); the first one was on a partially preserved maxilla, near the upper right second premolar (15), approximately 4 mm in diameter (Figure 4). The other was found on a partially preserved mandible, measured 5.66 mm in diameter, and was located over the lower left second premolar (35), with reabsorption of the lower left second molar (37).

Dental wear was recorded for every tooth, showing wide-ranging results. In summary, of the 2,944 teeth found at La Pijotilla's Tomb 3, 143 teeth or tooth sockets were affected by dental pathology, representing 4.85%. *Calculus* was the best represented pathology (3.32%, 98 of 2944), followed by LEH (0.64%, 19 of 2944), AMTL (3.03%, 13 of 429), caries (0.30%, 9 of 2944), and dental abscesses (0.46%, 1 out of 429). *Ante mortem* tooth was visible in 14 tooth sockets.

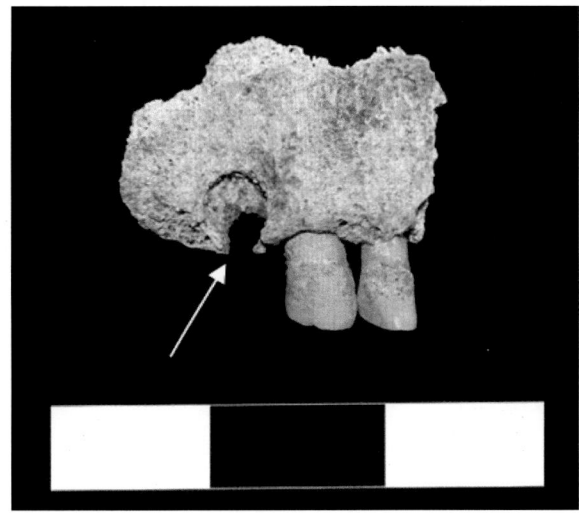

FIGURE 4. DENTAL ABSCESS CAVITY (ID 10400) (SCALE IS IN CM).

Discussion

Despite the high number of 'unidentified' bones/teeth fragments (those for which sex or age remain unknown because the complete skeletons were not analysed), there are sufficient data to describe the demographic profile of the human group buried at La Pijotilla Tomb 3. According to these data, the distribution of individuals by sex is as follows: 9.47% females (n = 18), 14.21% males (n = 27), 62% unsexed adult fragments (n = 110) and 12% unsexed subadult fragments (*n* = 23).

The interpretation of the distribution of this population within the age categories is problematic because of the difficulties of estimating age from bone fragments and individual teeth. However, the distribution by bone fragment for each age group showed that 136 fragments were aged as adult (76.40%), followed by adolescents (n = 13, 7.30%), young adults (n = 8, 4.49%), middle adults (n = 8, 4.49%), I2 (n = 5, 2.8%), I1 (n = 5, 2.80%) and mature adults (n = 3, 1.68%).

Despite the difficulty in recording these traits from fragmentary bones and teeth, the most common non-metric skeletal traits were the septal aperture and the vastus notch while the most common dental non-metric trait was shoveling, followed by dental *foramina* on the labial surface of teeth, Carabelli traits, and the interruption groove on the cingulum. These data could be used to infer biological distance between this and other Chalcolithic communities and also to investigate hidden heterogeneity (Wright and Yodder, 2003).

In what concerns health status, a few enthesophytes were recorded at La Pijotilla. These entheseal changes may be related to biomechanics which, found in association with pathological data such as joint disease, could suggest physical activity as an explanation for these bone changes (Hawkey and Merbs, 1995; Jurmain, 1999). Although in general, there is a very low percentage of bone disease, which could be interpreted as an indicator of good health, according to Wood *et al.* (1992) this also means high frailty where individuals could did not live long enough to develop those diseases. Oral pathologies included calculus, caries and LEH, are all directly related to diet, amongst other factors (Hillson, 2000).

Conclusions

The complete study and analysis of commingled human remains is not an easy task. This represents a major challenge for the understanding of 3rd millennium BC funerary patterns in Iberia. The recording and analysis of the MNI, sex and age of the skeletal assemblage found in Tomb 3 at La Pijotilla provides bioarchaeological data suitable for future comparative analysis in order to understand the demographic profile and social organisation of Copper Age populations. In this case, the MNI at La Pijotilla was 178, sex was more or less equally represented, and the age categories showed a predominance of adults (87.06%) when compared to subadults (12.94%). The reconstruction of health status suggests that most of the pathologies are related to joint disease, and the dental pathologies such as LEH; the latter related to stress episodes during development of the teeth (Infante and Gillespie, 1974; Sweeney et al., 1971).

Although the bioarchaeological analysis of commingled fragmented remains had its limitations, the combination of standard macroscopic analytical methods, along with biochemical analysis, will be in the future essential to reconstruct past behaviors of Copper Age communities, including comparison of data with other different populations.

Acknowledgements

The authors would like to thank Javier Escudero Carrillo for his help during data collection as well as several students from the University of Seville; special thanks go to Sonia Robles Carrasco, Milagros Sánchez Romero, María Gómez Martín, Luis Sevillano Perea, Pablo M. Santos Breval, María José Ramos Suárez, Eugenia Quirós Candelera, Reyes Ávila Gómez, Marta Moreno Martínez and Cristina Ávila Giménez. We would like also to thank Dr. Eva Alarcón García for processing the images.

References

Brothwell, D. (1981) – Digging up bones. London, British Museum (Natural History).
Buikstra, J.E.; Ubelaker, D.H. (eds.) (1994) – Standards for data collection from human skeletal remains: Proceedings of a Seminar at the Field Museum of Natural History Fayetteville: Archeological Survey, Research Seminar Series 44.
Brickley. M. (2006) – Rib Fractures in the Archaeological record: A Useful Source of Sociocultural Information?. International Journal of Osteoarchaeology 16, p. 61-75.
Brooks, S.; Suchey, J.M. (1990) – Skeletal age determination based on the os pubis: comparison of the Ascadi-Nemeskei and Suchey-Brooks methods. Human Evolution 5, p. 227-238.
Díaz-Zorita Bonilla, M. (2017) – The Copper Age in south-west Spain: a bioarchaeological approach to prehistoric social organisation. BAR International Series S2840. Oxford: BAR Publishing.
Haber Uriarte, M.; Avilés Fernández, J.; Lomba Maurandi, J. (2013) – Estudio antropológico preliminar de los restos humanos calcolíticos del enterramiento múltiple de Camino del Molino (Caravaca de la Cruz, Murcia). In Turbón, D., Fañanás, L., Rissech, C. and Rosa, A. (Eds.): Biodiversidad humana y evolución, Universidad de Barcelona: Barcelona. p. 236-242.
Hawkey, D.E.; Merbs, C. (1995) – Activity-induced musculoskeletal stress markers (MSM) and subsistence strategy changes among ancient Hudson Bay Eskimos. International Journal of Osteoarchaeology 5, p. 324-338.
Hillson, S. (2000) – Dental Pathology. In M.A. Katzenberg and S.R. Saunders (eds.), Biological Anthropology of the Human Skeleton. New York: Wiley-Liss.
Hurtado Pérez, V. (1980) – Los ídolos calcolíticos de la Pijotilla (Badajoz). Zephyrus XXX XXXI, p. 165-205
Hurtado Pérez, V. (1986) – El Calcolítico en la cuenca media del Guadiana y la necrópolis de La Pijotilla. In: Actas de la Mesa Redonda sobre Megalitismo peninsular (Madrid, 1984). Madrid: Asociación de Amigos de la Arqueología. p. 51-75.
Hurtado Pérez, V. (1990) Informe sobre las campañas de excavaciones en La Pijotilla (Badajoz). Extremadura Arqueológica I, p. 35-54.
Hurtado Pérez, V. (1991) – Informe de las excavaciones de urgencia en la Pijotilla. Campaña de 1990. I Jornadas de Prehistoria y Arqueología en Extremadura (1986- 1990). Extremadura Arqueológica II, p. 45-68.

Hurtado Pérez, V. (1995) – El Calcolítico a debate. Reunión de Calcolítico de la Península Ibérica. Seville, 1990. Sevilla: Junta de Andalucía.

Hurtado Pérez, V. (1997) – The dynamics of the occupation of the middle basin of the river Guadiana between the Fourth and Second Millennia BC: an interpretational hypothesis. In: Diaz Andreu, M. and Keay, S. (Eds.): The Archaeology of Iberia. The Dynamics of Change, London, Routledge: p. 98-127.

Hurtado Pérez, V. (1999) – Los inicios de la complejización social y el campaniforme en Extremadura. Spal. Revista de Prehistoria y Arqueología 8, p. 47-85.

Hurtado Pérez, V. (2000) – El proceso de transición a la Edad del Bronce en la Cuenca Media del Guadiana. Ruptura o continuidad. Actas do 3º Congresso de Arqueologia Peninsular. Volumen 4. Porto. p. 381-398.

Hurtado Pérez, V. (2003) – Fosos y fortificaciones entre el Guadiana y el Guadalquivir en el III milenio AC: evidencias del registro arqueológico. In Jorge, S.O. Recintos Murados da Pré-História Recente. Porto-Coimbra. p. 241-268.

Hurtado Pérez, V. (2010) – Representaciones simbólicas, sitios contextos e identidades territoriales en el Suroeste peninsular. In Cacho, C., Maicas, R., Galán, E. and Martos, J.A. (Coord.) Ojos que nunca se cierran. Ídolos en las primeras sociedades campesinas. Madrid. Museo Arqueológico Nacional. CD and web resource MAN. p. 137-198.

Hurtado Pérez, V.; Mondéjar De Quincóces, P.; Pecero Espín, J.C. (2000) – Excavaciones en la Tumba 3 de La Pijotilla. Homenaje a Elías Diéguez Luengo. Extremadura Arqueológica VIII, p. 249-266.

Hurtado Pérez, V.; Odriozola Lloret, C. (2009) – Landscape, identity and material culture in 'Tierra de Barros' (Badajoz, Spain) During the 3rd millennium BC. In R.B. Salisbury and T. Thurston (Eds.): Reimagining Regional Analyses: The Archaeology of Spatial and Social Dynamics. New York, Cambridge Scholar Press. p. 265-290.

Hurtado Pérez, V.; Mondéjar De Quincoces, P. (2009) – Prospecciones en Tierra de Barros (Badajoz). Los asentamientos del III milenio a.n.e. In Cruz-Auñón Briones and Ferrer Albelda, E. (Eds.): Estudios de Prehistoria y Arqueología en Homenaje a Pilar Acosta Martínez. Sevilla: Universidad de Sevilla. p. 187-206.

Infante, P.F.; Gillespie, G.M. (1974) – An epidemiologic study of linear enamel hypoplasia of deciduous anterior teeth in Guatemalan children. Archives of Oral Biology 19, p. 1055-1061.

Işcan, M.Y.; Loth, S.R.; Wright, S.K. (1984) – Metamorphosis at the sterna rib end. A new method to estimate age at death in white males. American Journal of PhysicalAnthropology 65: 2, p. 147-156.

Işcan, M.Y; Loth, S.R. (1986) – Estimation of age and determination of sex from the external rib. In K.J. Reichs (ed.) Forensic osteology. Springfield: Charles C. Thomas. p. 68-89.

Jurmain, R. (1999) – Stories from the Skeleton: Behavioral Reconstruction in Human Osteology. London: Taylor and Francis.

Lovejoy C.O.; Meindl R.S.; Pryzbeck T.R.; Mensforth R.P. (1985) – Chronological metamorphosis of the auricular surface of the ilium: a new method for the determination of adult skeletal age at death. American Journal of Physical Anthropology 68, p. 15-28.

Meindl, R.S.; Lovejoy, C.O. (1985) – Ectocranial suture closure: A revised method for the determination of skeletal age at death based on the lateral-anterior sutures. American Journal of Physical Anthropology 68, p. 57-66.

Odriozola Lloret, C.; Hurtado Pérez, V.; Dias, M.I.; Prudêncio, I. (2008) – Datación por técnicas luminiscentes de la tumba 3 y el conjunto campaniforme de La Pijotilla (Badajoz, España). In: Rovira Llorens, S., García-Heras, M., Gener Moret, M. and Montero Ruiz, I. (Eds.): Actas del VII Congreso Ibérico de Arqueometría (Madrid, 8-10 de Octubre de 2007), CSIC: Madrid. p. 211-225.

Polvorinos del Río, A.; Hernández Arnedo, M. J.; Hurtado Pérez, V.; Almarza López, J. (2002a) – Arqueometría de cerámicas de la tumba 3 del yacimiento calcolítico de La Pijotilla (Badajoz). In: Roldan, C. (Ed.): Actas del IV Congreso Nacional de Arqueometría (Valencia 15-17 de Octubre de 2001). Valencia. Universidad de Valencia. p. 106-118.

Polvorinos del Río, A.; Hurtado Pérez, V.; Hernández Arnedo, M.J.; Almarza López, J. (2002b) – Caracterización mineralógica del ajuar del enterramiento calcolítico (Tumba 3) de La Pijotilla (Badajoz). In: Roldan, C. (Ed.): Actas del IV Congreso Nacional de Arqueometría (Valencia 15-17 de Octubre de 2001), Valencia. Universidad de Valencia, p. 315-321.

Polvorinos del Río, A.; Hernández Arnedo, M.J.; Almarza López, J.; Forteza González, M.; Castaing, J.; Hurtado Pérez, V. (2008) – Estudio arqueométrico de las láminas de sílex procedentes de la Tumba III del yacimiento de La Pijotilla (Badajoz). In: Rovira Llorens, S., García-Heras, M., Gener Moret, M. and Montero Ruiz, I. (Eds.): Actas del VII Congreso Ibérico de Arqueometría (Madrid, 8-10 de Octubre de 2007). Madrid. CSIC. p. 379-389.

Scheuer, L.; Black, S. (2000) – Development and ageing of the juvenile skeleton. In: Cox, M. and Mays, S. (eds.): Human osteology in archaeology and forensic science. London: Greenwich Medical Media. p. 9-21.

Smith, B.H. (1991) – Standards of human tooth formation and dental age assessment. In M.A. Kelley and C.S. Larsen (eds.). Advances in dental anthropology. New York: Wiley-Liss. p. 143-168.

Sweeney, E.A.; Saffir, A.J.; Leon, R.D. (1971) – Linear hypoplasia of deciduous incisor teeth in malnourished children. American Journal of Clinical Nutrition 24, p. 29-31.

Ubelaker, D. (1989) – Human skeletal remains. Excavation, analysis and interpretation. 2nd edition. Washington: Taraxacum Press.

Wood, J.W.; Milner, G.R.; Harpending, H.C.; Weiss, K.M. (1992) – The osteological paradox: problems of inferring prehistoric health from skeletal samples. Current Anthropology 33:4, p. 343-370.

Wright, L.E.; Yoder, C.J. (2003) – Recent progress in Bioarchaeology: approaches to the Osteological Paradox. Journal of Archaeological Research 11:1, p. 43-70.

On the applicability of the assessment of dental tooth wear for the study of collective prehistoric burials

Luís Miguel Marado[1], Claudia Cunha[2,3], G. Richard Scott[4], Tiago Tomé[3,5,6], Hugo Machado[7] and Ana Maria Silva[3,8,9]

[1] Lab2PT – Laboratório de Paisagens, Património e Território, Unidade de Arqueologia da Universidade do Minho, Braga, Portugal
[2] Programa de Capacitação Institucional MCTI/MPEG, Coordenação de Ciências Humanas, Museu Paraense Emílio Goeldi, Belém, Pará, Brasil
[3] Laboratório de Pré-História, CIAS – Departamento Ciências da Vida, Universidade de Coimbra, Portugal
[4] Department of Anthropology – University of Nevada Reno, United States of America
[5] Instituto de Filosofia e Ciências Humanas – Universidade Federal do Pará, Brasil
[6] GQP-CG, Grupo Quaternário e Pré-História, Centro de Geociências (I&D 73 – FCT)/ Instituto Terra e Memória, Portugal
[7] Independent researcher, Portugal
[8] UNIARQ – WAPS. Centro de Arqueologia da Universidade de Lisboa, Portugal
[9] Laboratório de Antropologia Forense, Centro de Ecologia Funcional – Departamento Ciências da Vida, Universidade de Coimbra, Portugal
luismarado@gmail.com

Abstract

Teeth are a very important resource in Biological Anthropology. One of their many uses is the evaluation of dental wear, which can document both masticatory and non-masticatory behavior. The objectives of this work are to 1) present a protocol for scoring evidence of non-masticatory activity applicable to all kinds of contexts (including commingled collective burials), 2) suggest interpretation tools, and 3) use simple, time-saving and accessible procedures.

Procedures addressing oral alterations, a new trait – cingular continuous lesions (CCL) – and statistical analysis are described. This method will complement archaeological knowledge on past populations' cultural, ritual or work-related tooth uses.

Keywords

Bioarchaeology; extramasticatory dental wear; teeth as tools; dental lesions

Résumé

Les dents sont très importantes pour l'anthropologie physique. Un de ses uses est l'usure dentaire, qui peut documenter les comportements masticatoires et non-masticatoires. Les objectifs de ce travail sont 1) la présentation d'un protocole de registre des évidences d'activités non-masticatoires applicables à contextes diverses (notamment les enterrements collectifs mélangés), 2) la suggestion de outils d'interprétation et 3) l'use des méthodes simples, accessibles et rapides.

Méthodes pour adresser les altérations orales, un nouvel trait – «cingular continuous lesions» (CCL) – et testes statistiques sont décrits. Cette méthodologie complément la connaissance archéologique de l'use dentaire en fonctions culturelles, rituelles et de travail.

Mots-clés

Bioarchéologie; usure dentaire extra-masticatoire; les dents comme outils; lésions dentaires

Introduction

Teeth are the most important resource in Paleoanthropology: 1) when dental tissues (almost entirely mineral) have matured, they do not remodel – so any changes in their shape are resultant of their use or of the lesions they suffered, which do not undergo biological reparative actions (Hillson 2005); 2) teeth are the most resistant of human tissues, and endure most taphonomic conditions (Hillson 2005, Scott 2008, Scott and Turner 1988, Silva 2002), hence they are a remarkable source of information on archaeological populations.

One of the most common ways tooth shape is changed is through dental wear, *i.e.* the progressive loss of superficial dental tissues as crowns are exposed to environmental agents. Wear is also one of the ways in which tooth use molds the evolution of dental characteristics (tissue qualities, anatomy, morphology) (Kaidonis 2008). Contact with other teeth (attrition); contact with food, tongue and cheeks or other objects (abrasion); and the chemical dissolution of tooth tissue (erosion) are forms of wear (Hillson 2005, Kaidonis 2008, Soames and Southam 2005), although erosion is not wear, *stricto sensu* (since the loss of tissue is related to chemical reactions, not mechanical contact: Molnar 2011). Wear can occur in any extragingival part of the tooth, such as on the occlusal or incisal parts (the most distant from the roots), on the interproximal facets (that directly contact neighboring teeth), on the lingual/palatal and buccal/labial surfaces (that face the interior and vestibular portions of the mouth, respectively), on the cervical portion, near or at the enamel-cement junction and, in cases when teeth suffer extreme tooth wear, the roots themselves will endure loss of its exposed surfaces as a result of tribological (relating to relative movement of teeth) forces (Figure 1).

From early on, tooth wear was studied in past populations to interpret dietary habits and, most commonly, to estimate age at death (Rose and Ungar 1998). Alongside other data from analyses of varying degrees of technological complexity and of oral lesions, dental wear is still used to help reconstruct past human diets (Forshaw 2014). However, dental wear does not solely result from masticatory activities, and can occur when teeth are used as a third hand or as tools in labor, cultural or ritual activities (Molnar 2011); this non-masticatory tooth use has also been studied for several decades (*e.g.*: Hylander 1977, Molnar 1972, Turner and Machado 1983).

The value of teeth and their capacity for conservation are both high (see above). However, the poor conservation of other elements – and, occasionally, of teeth themselves – in some archaeological contexts (like collective prehistoric burials with commingled remains) can still make researchers' jobs difficult. When human remains are no longer attributable to a set of anatomically connected bones and teeth, the paleoanthropological analysis is limited in several ways and requires specific approaches in order to collect bioanthropological data: estimation of minimum number of individuals (MNI), age at death, stature, sex, individual biological affinities, individual social status, systematic

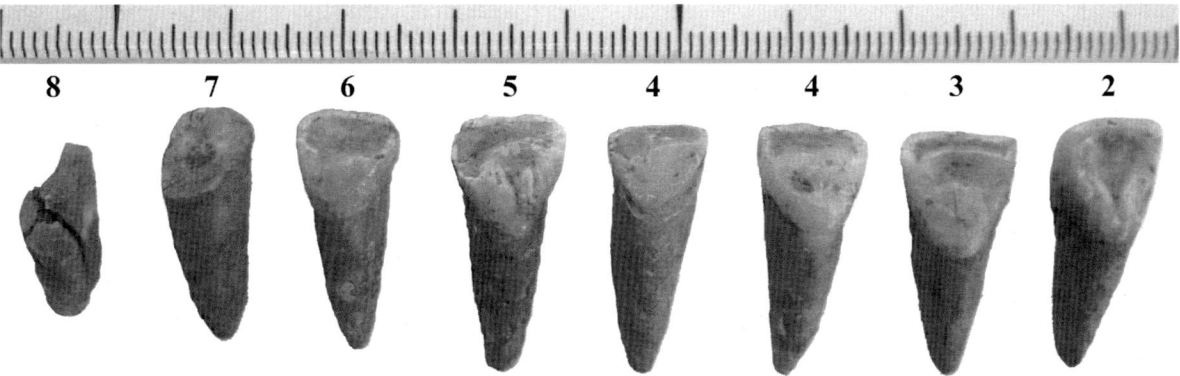

FIGURE 1. TOOTH WEAR ON DIFFERENT UI1 SUBSEQUENTLY LESS AFFECTED BY TOOTH WEAR, FROM WORN TOOTH ROOTS (AFTER COMPLETE CROWN OBLITERATION) TO SLIGHT ALTERATIONS CAUSED BY DENTAL WEAR. NUMBERS ABOVE EACH TOOTH CORRESPOND TO OCCLUSAL WEAR GRADES, ACCORDING TO MOLNAR (1971) AND SMITH (1984).

paleopathological analysis, association between characteristics on different skeletal or oral elements, etc. (see, for example, Silva 2002, Tomé 2011).

There are many examples of studies concerning patterns or traits of non-masticatory tooth wear in prehistoric (Fiorenza *et al.* 2011, Molleson 1994, Molnar 2008, Molnar 1971, 1972, Waters-Rist *et al.* 2010), historic (Scott and Jolie 2008, Scott and Winn 2011) and recent or contemporary (Berbesque *et al.* 2012, Clement *et al.* 2008, Wood 1992) samples. These studies of non-masticatory wear tend to focus on individuals; their application on loose teeth is rare and usually occurs in small samples or as a small part of a given sample (see Bonfiglioli *et al.* 2004, Liu *et al.* 2010, Minozzi *et al.* 2003, Pechenkina *et al.* 2002).

Molnar (2011) addresses the need for a standard methodology for scoring non-masticatory wear, which should include careful morphological characterization and description, as well as visual documentation. Despite this need for systematization, there is also the need for new methodology to enable and adapt to the study of loose teeth.

Molnar's (1971) attempt to standardize not only the scoring of occlusal wear, but also the recording of wear variations derived from non-masticatory tooth use, was the main influence for the presentation that originated this work.

The authors aimed at creating a laboratory protocol to: a) score dental wear on all exposed tooth surfaces, b) score specific wear signs related to non-masticatory tooth use, and c) other score alterations to teeth and/or bone that can be related to the application of massive occlusal forces or the use of teeth as tools (such as hypercementosis, chipping and bone exostoses). This method is applicable to both *in situ* and loose teeth, and only requires the use of 10x magnifying glass, when needed. Although designed to address commingled human remains, this approach could also be employed on large samples of individual inhumations.

The objectives of this study are 1) to present a methodological protocol for scoring non-masticatory dental wear (and other morphological or pathological alterations related to strenuous use of the dentition); 2) to suggest statistical approaches to assist the interpretation of the subsequent results; and 3) to accomplish the former objectives with simple, time-saving and accessible procedures.

Scoring methodology

1) Occlusal wear

Occlusal wear is scored using Smith's (1984) eight-graded scale, which has three versions for a) molars, b) premolars and c) incisors and canines. This method, despite its wide use and the schematization of the three different types of progressive occlusal wear patterns (also inspired by Molnar's 1971 work), is somewhat incomplete: Smith's scale does not account for possible wear inclinations, only for plane occlusal wear. This scale is very helpful – the thoroughly illustrated and described grades make this a relatively easy to apply method, which describes the general effect of occlusal wear (*e.g.*: Berbesque *et al.* 2012, Machicek and Zubova 2012) – but does not discern masticatory from non-masticatory wear and ignores the other tooth surfaces.

2) Non-masticatory wear

Following Molnar's 1971 intent to complement the scoring of occlusal wear, signs of wear most likely derived from non-masticatory activities are also contemplated, using a five-graded ordinal scale applied to all vertical tooth surfaces (buccal, lingual, mesial and distal), which are scored separately:

  1 – Wear is slight – the only physical effect is polishing of the surface and/or the obliteration of the natural and/or hypoplastic lines of enamel deposition;

2 – Significant loss of enamel – sometimes obliteration of morphological features such as the *cingulum* and/or *tubercula* occurs;
3 – Dentine is exposed on more than half of the surface;
4 – The pulp chamber is exposed by semi-vertical to vertical wear;
5 – The observed surface is destroyed by semi-vertical to vertical wear.

This kind of vertical wear has been found to be related with the use of teeth as tools (Liu *et al.* 2010, Molnar 2011, Pechenkina *et al.* 2002). The use of loose teeth impedes the verification of wear facets on antagonistic teeth or the exclusion of instances of malocclusion (as recommended by Sarig and Tillier 2014), which could demonstrate these wear patches' masticatory origin. This hindrance should however not be relevant when analyzing samples of sufficient size.

3) Curved/notched wear

Instances of curved (convex) or notched (concave) wear are commonly identified with non-masticatory tooth use (Bonfiglioli *et al.* 2004, Minozzi *et al.* 2003, Molleson 1994, Scott and Jolie 2008, Waters-Rist *et al.* 2010), since these are particular and unusual forms of dental wear. To characterize the variations within these forms of atypical wear (when present; in absence of convex/concave wear, the score for any tooth is 0), a nominal scale with four types was defined:

'Rou' – Rounded – tooth wear is convex on the occlusal/incisal surface;
'BL' – Bucco-lingual – tooth wear is concave on the occlusal/incisal surface. Direction of wear suggests the movement was from buccal to lingual;
'LB' – Linguo-buccal – tooth wear is concave on the occlusal/incisal surface. Direction of wear suggests movement was from lingual to buccal;
'MD' – Mesio-distal – tooth wear is concave on the occlusal/incisal surface. Direction of wear suggests movement was from mesial to distal (and/or vice-versa).

4) Cingular continuous lesions (CCL)

This type of lesion was not previously characterized or described, to the knowledge of the authors. It corresponds to a continuous lesion found around the most protruding part of the *cingulum* of upper incisors. The lesion is a usually narrow and shallow strip of missing enamel that arches between both lingual margins of the tooth. Sometimes this strip is enlarged towards the cement-enamel junction, presumably because of the strain put upon the remaining thin enamel band. The origin of this mark – that is tentatively named 'cingular continuous lesion' (CCL) – is abrasion, possibly through holding or processing fibers or thread. CCL was seen by one of the authors (AMS) in several Neolithic/Chalcolithic samples and was later scored by the authors on a Late Neolithic to Bronze Age sample.

CCL should be scored as present or absent at least on anterior teeth, although it may present itself on other teeth in future research.

5) Hypercementosis

Hypercementosis is the deposition of extra cement beyond the typical limits of the roots. This causes an alteration of the appearance of the root to the naked eye (greater root thickness, presence of nodules and rough appearance). Among its several possible etiologies (like continuous dental eruption, disruption of cementum deposition by cementicles, reaction to inflammatory processes and systemic factors) is stress caused by occlusal forces (Bürklein *et al.* 2012, Pinheiro *et al.* 2008).

Sometimes, the large occlusal forces that can cause hypercementosis can be associated to the use of teeth as tools (Hylander 1977, Waters-Rist *et al.* 2010). Therefore, hypercementosis' associations with other variables that could be related to non-masticatory wear will inform on its etiology and may provide further evidence on how large were the occlusal forces implemented on a given non-masticatory dental function. Hypercementosis should be scored as present or absent on every observable root.

6) Chipping

Enamel is hard and not very flexible, so it is a brittle material. Chipping results from applying force with a large hard object near the occlusal edge of a tooth (Constantino *et al.* 2010). It has been associated with either masticatory activities such as eating hard or frozen foods (Constantino *et al.* 2010, Scott and Winn 2011) and with the use of teeth as tools (Belcastro *et al.* 2007, Bonfiglioli *et al.* 2004). Scoring chipping and small fractures of teeth and testing these variables for associations with other non-masticatory activity lesions can further inform on their etiology and help understand both dietary habits and cultural, ritual or work-related use of teeth.

To score chipping, the number of small fractures on each tooth should be counted and registered.

7) Bone exostoses

Bone exostoses (mandibular, maxillary and palatine *tori*) can occur on either or both lingual and buccal aspects of the mandible and maxilla, and on the hard palate (Hauser and De Stefano 1989). The etiology for *tori* has been under debate and authors have proposed several different causes for this excessive bone growth. Genetic, environmental and functional etiologies have been proposed singly or in some combination as causative agents in the formation of *tori* (Halffman and Irish 2004, Hassett 2006, Hauser and De Stefano 1989). However, clinical and anthropological data (García-García *et al.* 2010, Halffman *et al.* 1992, Hassett 2006, Hylander 1977) suggest that multifactorial etiology might be involved in their development, once genetic predisposition for the development of this kind of morphological alteration is triggered by external environmental and/or functional factors (Hassett 2006). When strong masticatory forces are involved in the formation of *tori,* other symptoms might be observed in association with the bony outgrowth, namely: severe tooth wear, chipping and hypercementosis (Halffman *et al.* 1992, Hassett 2006, Hylander 1977).

Anthropological studies that link bone exostoses with non-masticatory dental use in past to contemporary samples are common (*e.g.*: Halffman and Irish 2004, Halffman *et al.* 1992, Hylander 1977, Pechenkina *et al.* 2002).

The presence of probable mandibular and maxillary *tori* should be registered (as two separate variables). The observation of adult individuals only is recommended, so as to limit cases to those most likely related to the use of strong masticatory forces. Associations with chipping, hypercementosis and, above all, non-masticatory tooth wear, will inform on the possible etiology of these bony outgrowths for each sample.

Statistical tests and interpretation

This section merely attempts to suggest how to approach the data in the statistical perspective. It is not the authors' intention to limit further analysis, or indicate there are no other possible valid and informative tests or approaches. The following ideas are meant as a simple guide to less statistically inclined researchers, to provide a start to statistical interpretation of the set of data collected.

It should be noted, before any analysis is undertaken, that there may be teeth or surfaces that will not be observable, due to destruction or obstruction. This impossibility should be properly annotated – with a number or symbol to correspond to the reason any surface or tooth could not be scored – and this data should be filtered out before any valid variable can be tested.

Data can be analyzed as occurrences per tooth, by tooth pair, by general sample, and by sections of the dentition: anterior, posterior, upper, lower, left and right dentitions. It may also be useful to separate these sections further (*e.g.*: superoanterior, lower left dentition) after possible patterns are detected.

To compare the results between samples or between sections of the dentition data are reported as averages (occlusal wear) and presence frequencies (CLL, hypercementosis, mandibular and maxillary *tori*), which in some cases (non-masticatory wear, curved/notched wear and chipping) need to be dichotomized (presence is defined as any grade above 0). Sometimes it may be useful to report grade frequencies for non-masticatory or curved/notched wear, or frequencies of chipping incidences, instead of dichotomizing those data. That allows associations between any given variable and a specific type of wear or number of chipping incidences to be tested.

The detection of statistically significant wear/lesion patterns, the use of two statistical tests is recommended. To detect different variable distributions between two dental sections, the chi-squared (χ^2) test for independence (a parametric test) is recommended. To determine if a dental section presents significantly higher variable values than another section (*e.g.*: anterior vs. posterior teeth), the Mann-Whitney U non-parametric test, a rank-sum statistic, is recommended. The two subsamples should be considered different if both these tests (χ^2 and Mann-Whitney U) provide a significant result between two sets of data for any variable.

The association between variables can be tested using Kendall's τ rank correlation coefficient. Data should not be dichotomized, since correlations will be more precise if the variation in the subsamples compared is fully documented. The resulting coefficients will be positive if the variables behave similarly (*e.g.*: the value in variable X tends to be high when the value in variable Y is high), negative if their variation is opposite (*e.g.*: the value in variable X tend to be low when the value in variable Y is high) and null if the variables are randomly distributed in relation to one another. Kendall's τ results between 0.25 and 0.4 (or -0.25 and -0.4) are recommended as moderate (positive or negative) correlations. Coefficients above 0.4 (or below -0.4) should be considered strong (positive or negative) associations.

The analysis of the data and statistical tests' results should take into account the archaeological context from which the sample hails and the known facts, as gathered from archeological (and/or historical) research. Ethnographic research and previously reported archaeological parallels are also valuable, as they can illustrate how certain tasks were realized and the part teeth could have played in those tasks. These sources can be very useful if the environmental and archaeological contexts are similar.

The patterns observed with the application of the proposed methods and statistical analyses should then be interpreted in light of the known limitations and possibilities. Contexts also provide useful questions to inform data interpretation (*e.g.*: did males or females perform a certain task?). Differences in the distribution of a given variable or the association between two variables can correspond to expected activities or merely generate further questions. Only further (preferably standardized) work on non-masticatory dental use wear and lesion patterns can help to continuously shed light into otherwise nearly invisible labor, cultural and ritual activities from past populations.

Conclusions

Past human and hominid populations have long used their teeth to help with their activities, in many occasions on a daily basis. Teeth can be used to hold pieces of string, a smoking pipe or a nail. Eskimos are known for towing large game (such as seals) by ropes using their teeth while their hands are used for rowing small boats. Teeth can process materials (like sinew or fibers), by chewing on, or cutting them. These and many other activities (and eating habits or needs) leave marks on teeth. The systematic study of these wear or lesion patterns (how they are distributed on a given dentition or on any sample) can be very informative on past populations and their relationship with the environment and with one another.

Bioarchaeologists often depend on inexpensive, fast to apply and easy to reproduce methods that can help put together and contribute to the information on a given site. The authors attempted to provide one such method. The proposed variables and tests can be entirely applied on commingled human remains from collective burials or on well identified, complete individual burials. This method can also be applied to populations from prehistory to near contemporaneity. In cases when the research hypothesis so dictates, some variables can be set apart and different (or no) statistical tests can be chosen.

The method introduced here is subject to changes as future research clears how non-masticatory tooth use affects some of the lesions included. The application of this approach in diverse archaeological contexts and the findings it provides will contribute to its amelioration. This method provides another way for anthropological data to support archaeology and the knowledge of past populations' non-alimentary dental use and, to some degree, their eating habits.

Acknowledgments

The authors thank to CIAS – Research Center in Anthropology and Health (Universidade de Coimbra) for continued support of result divulgation initiatives, including some of the authors' participations in UISPP 2014.

The first (LMM) and second (CC) authors were supported by grants from FCT – Fundação para a Ciência e a Tecnologia (Ministério da Educação e Ciência, Governo de Portugal) with the scholarship reference SFRH/BD/70183/2010 and and SFRH/BD/70183/2010, respectively.

References

Belcastro, G.; Rastelli, E.; Mariotti, V.; Consiglio, C.; Facchini, F.; Bonfiglioli, B. (2007) – Continuity or discontinuity of the life-style in central Italy during the Roman Imperial Age-Early Middle Ages transition: diet, health, and behavior. American Journal of Physical Anthropology. 132: 3, p. 381-394.

Berbesque, J.C.; Marlowe, F.W.; Pawn, I.; Thompson, P.; Johnson, G.; Mabulla, A. (2012) – Sex differences in Hadza dental wear patterns: a preliminary report. Human Nature. 23: 3, p. 270-282.

Bonfiglioli, B.; Mariotti, V.; Facchini, F.; Belcastro, M.G.; Condemi, S. (2004) – Masticatory and non-masticatory dental modifications in the epipalaeolithic necropolis of Taforalt (Morocco). International Journal of Osteoarchaeology. 14: 6, p. 448-456.

Bürklein, S.; Jansen, S.; Schafer, E. (2012) – Occurrence of hypercementosis in a German population. Journal of Endodontics. 38: 12, p. 1610-2.

Clement, A.; Hillson, S.; De La Torre, I.; Townsend, G. (2008) – Tooth use in Aboriginal Australia. Archaeology International. 11, p. 37-40.

Constantino, P.J.; Lee, J.J.; Chai, H.; Zipfel, B.; Ziscovici, C.; Lawn, B.R.; Lucas, P.W. (2010) – Tooth chipping can reveal the diet and bite forces of fossil hominins. Biology Letters. 6: 6, p. 826-829.

Fiorenza, L.; Benazzi, S.; Kullmer, O. (2011) – Para-masticatory wear facets and their functional significance in hunter-gatherer maxillary molars. Journal of Archaeological Science. 38: 9, p. 2182-2189.

Forshaw, R. (2014) – Dental indicators of ancient dietary patterns: dental analysis in archaeology. British Dental Journal. 216: 9, p. 529-535.

García-García, A.S.; Martinez-Gonzalez, J.M.; Gomez-Font, R.; Soto-Rivadeneira, A.; Oviedo-Roldan, L. (2010) – Current status of the torus palatinus and torus mandibularis. Medicina Oral Patología Oral y Cirugia Bucal. p. e353-e360.

Halffman, C.M.; Irish, J.D. (2004) – Palatine torus in the pre-conquest inhabitants of the Canary Islands. HOMO – Journal of Comparative Human Biology. 55: 1-2, p. 101-111.

Halffman, C.M.; Scott, G.R.; Pedersen, P.O. (1992) – Palatine torus in the Greenlandic Norse. American Journal of Physical Anthropology. 88, p. 145-161.

Hassett, B. (2006) – Torus Mandibularis: etiology and bioarcheological utility. Dental Anthropology. 19: 1, p. 1-14.

Hauser, G.; De Stefano, G.F. (1989) – Epigenetic variants of the human skull. Stuttgart: E. Schweizerbart'sche Verlagsbuchhandlung (Nagele u. Obermiller).

Hillson, S. (2005) – Teeth. New York: Cambridge University Press.

Hylander, W.L. (1977) – The adaptive significance of Eskimo craniofacial morphology. In Dahlberg, A.A.; Graber, T.M., eds. – Orofacial growht and development. Chicago, Illinois: de Gruyter. p. 129-169.

Kaidonis, J.A. (2008) – Tooth wear: the view of the anthropologist. Clinical oral investigations. 12 Suppl 1, p. S21-6.

Liu, W.; Zhang, Q.C.; Wu, X.J.; Zhu, H. (2010) – Tooth wear and dental pathology of the Bronze-Iron Age people in Xinjiang, Northwest China: Implications for their diet and lifestyle. HOMO – Journal of Comparative Human Biology. 61: 2, p. 102-116.

Machicek, M.L.; Zubova, A.V. (2012) – Dental Wear Patterns and Subsistence Activities in Early Nomadic Pastoralist Communities of the Central Asian Steppes. Archaeology, Ethnology and Anthropology of Eurasia. 40: 3, p. 149-157.

Minozzi, S.; Manzi, G.; Ricci, F.; Di Lernia, S.; Borgognini Tarli, S.M. (2003) – Nonalimentary tooth use in prehistory: an example from early Holocene in Central Sahara (Uan Muhuggiag, Tadrart Acacus, Libya). American Journal of Physical Anthropology. 120: 3, p. 225-232.

Molleson, T. (1994) – The Eloquent Bones of Abu Hureyra. Scientific American. 271: 2, p. 70-75.

Molnar, P. (2008) – Dental wear and oral pathology: possible evidence and consequences of habitual use of teeth in a Swedish Neolithic sample. American Journal of Physical Anthropology. 136: 4, p. 423-31.

Molnar, P. (2011) – Extramasticatory dental wear reflecting habitual behavior and health in past populations. Clinical oral investigations. 15: 5, p. 681-689.

Molnar, S. (1971) – Human tooth wear, tooth function and cultural variability. American Journal of Physical Anthropology. 34, p. 175-190.

Molnar, S. (1972) – Tooth Wear and Culture: A Survey of Tooth Functions Among Some Prehistoric Populations. Current Anthropology. 13: 5, p. 511-526.

Pechenkina, E.A.; Benfer, R.A., Jr.; Zhijun, W. (2002) – Diet and health changes at the end of the Chinese neolithic: the Yangshao/Longshan transition in Shaanxi province. American Journal of Physical Anthropology. 117: 1, p. 15-36.

Pinheiro, B.C.; Pinheiro, T.N.; Capelozza, A.L.A.; Sonsolaro, A. (2008) – A scanning electron microscopic study of hypercementosis. Journal of Applied Oral Science. 16: 6, p. 380-384.

Rose, J.C.; Ungar, P.S. (1998) – Gross dental wear and dental microwear in historical perspective. In Lukacs, J.R., ed., eds. – Human dental development, morphology, and pathology: a tribute to Albert A. Dahlberg. Eugene: University of Oregon Anthropological Papers. p. 349-386.

Sarig, R.; Tillier, A.M. (2014) – Reconstructing cultural behavior from dental wear studies: Is parafacets analysis approach scientifically valid? HOMO – Journal of Comparative Human Biology. 65: 3, p. 181-186.

Scott, G.R. (2008) – Dental morphology. In Katzenberg, M.A.; Saunders, S.R., eds. – Biological Anthropology of the human skeleton. New Jersey: Wiley-Liss. p. 265-298.

Scott, G.R.; Jolie, R.B. (2008) – Tooth-tool use and yarn production in Norse Greenland. Alaska Journal of Anthropology. 6: 1-2, p. 253-264.

Scott, G.R.; Turner, C.G. (1988) – Dental anthropology. Annual Review of Anthropology. 17, p. 99-126.

Scott, G.R.; Winn, J.R. (2011) – Dental chipping: Contrasting patterns of microtrauma in Inuit and European populations. International Journal of Osteoarchaeology. 21: 6, p. 723-731.

Silva, A.M.G. (2002) – Antropologia funerária e paleobiologia das populações portuguesas (litorais) do Neolítico final-Calcolítico. Coimbra: Universidade de Coimbra.

Smith, B.H. (1984) – Patterns of molar wear in hunter-gatherers and agriculturalists. American Journal of Physical Anthropology. 63, p. 39-56.

Soames, J.V.; Southam, J.C. (2005) – Oral Pathology. Oxford: Oxford University Press.

Tomé, T. (2011) – Até que a Morte nos Reúna: Transição para o agro-pastoralismo na bacia do Tejo e Sudoeste peninsular. Universidade de Trás-os-Montes e Alto Douro. 338 p.

Turner, C.G.; Machado, L.M.C. (1983) – A new dental wear pattern and evidence for high carbohydrate consumption in a Brazilian archaic skeletal population. American Journal of Physical Anthropology. 61, p. 125-130.

Waters-Rist, A.; Bazaliiskii, V.I.; Weber, A.; Goriunova, O.I.; Katzenberg, M.A. (2010) – Activity-induced dental modification in holocene siberian hunter-fisher-gatherers. American Journal of Physical Anthropology. 143: 2, p. 266-278.

Wood, S.R. (1992) – Tooth wear and the sexual division of labour in an Inuit population. Simon Fraser University. 167 p.

Cova de Can Sadurní (Begues, Barcelona). Towards the definition of a multiple funerary model inside caves during the middle Neolithic I in the northeast of the Iberian Peninsula

Manuel Edo[1], Ferran Antolín[2], Pablo Martínez[1], Concepció Castellana[1], Remei Bardera[1], María Saña[3], M. Mercè Bergadà[4], Josep Maria Fullola[4], Chus Barrio[1], Elicínia Fierro[1], Trinidad Castillo[1] and Eva Fornell[1]

[1] CIPAG. Col·lectiu per la investigació de la prehistòria i l'arqueologia del Garraf-Ordal
[2] CIPAG. IPAS (Integrative Prehistory and Archaeological Science), University of Basel
[3] Laboratori d'Arqueozoologia. UAB
[4] SERP. Seminari d'Estudis i Recerques Prehistòriques. UB
ferranantolin@gmail.com

Abstract

A series of burials dated to the second half of the Vth millennium cal BCE were discovered in Cova de Can Sadurní. These allow a first definition of a multiple funerary model that could have been practiced in several caves of the northeast of the Iberian Peninsula. The forced flexed position of the individuals indicates that the corpses must have been deposited inside a strongly-tied shroud. The bodies were not buried but deposited on the ground. It is estimated that this funerary episode lasted between 130 and 400 years.

Keywords
Multiple burial, Grave goods, Ritual, Postcardial, Molinot, Montboló

Résumé

Une série d'inhumations datées du seconde moitié du Vème. millenaire cal bC ont été découvertes dans la grotte de Can Sadurní. Elles ont permis une première définition d'un modèle funéraire collectif que on pourrait être pratiqué dans plusieurs grottes du nord-est de la péninsule Iberique. La position pliée des membres inférieurs indique que les corps ont été déposés dans la grotte fortement noués avec un linceul. Les individus n'ont pas été enterrés, mais placés dans le sol. On estime que cet épisode funéraire a duré entre 130 et 400 ans.

Mots-clés
Sépulture multiple, offrande funéraire, Ritual, Postcardial, Molinot, Montboló

Introduction

The early middle Neolithic in the northeast of the Iberian Peninsula is a transitional period between the early and the middle Neolithic, which, beyond the appearance of new pottery styles, is considered to reflect important changes in the productive and reproductive strategies of society. Among other novelties, larger sites with an increased amount of prestige goods that prove the existence of stable long-distance trade networks are known for the Middle Neolithic II period, along with the first large necropolises with individual or double burials (known as 'Sepulcres de Fossa') (for syntheses of the period see e.g. Martín and Villalba 1999; Clop 2010). Two pottery styles coexist during this phase in the northeast of the Iberian Peninsula: Molinot and Montboló (Blasco *et al.* 2005). Both have been used to name two cultural groups which would spread in this region before the development of the well-known 'Sepulcres de Fossa' culture (more or less contemporary to the French Chasséen culture), in the Middle Neolithic II. This phase could have an extent of 800 years (4800-4000 cal BCE).

The archaeological site of Cova de Can Sadurní is located on a slope overlooking a small and fertile plane, at c. 425 m asl, very close to the actual city of Barcelona, and includes both the deposits inside the cave and an external terrace of c. 200 m². A surface of around 50 m² was excavated inside the cave (Figure 1).

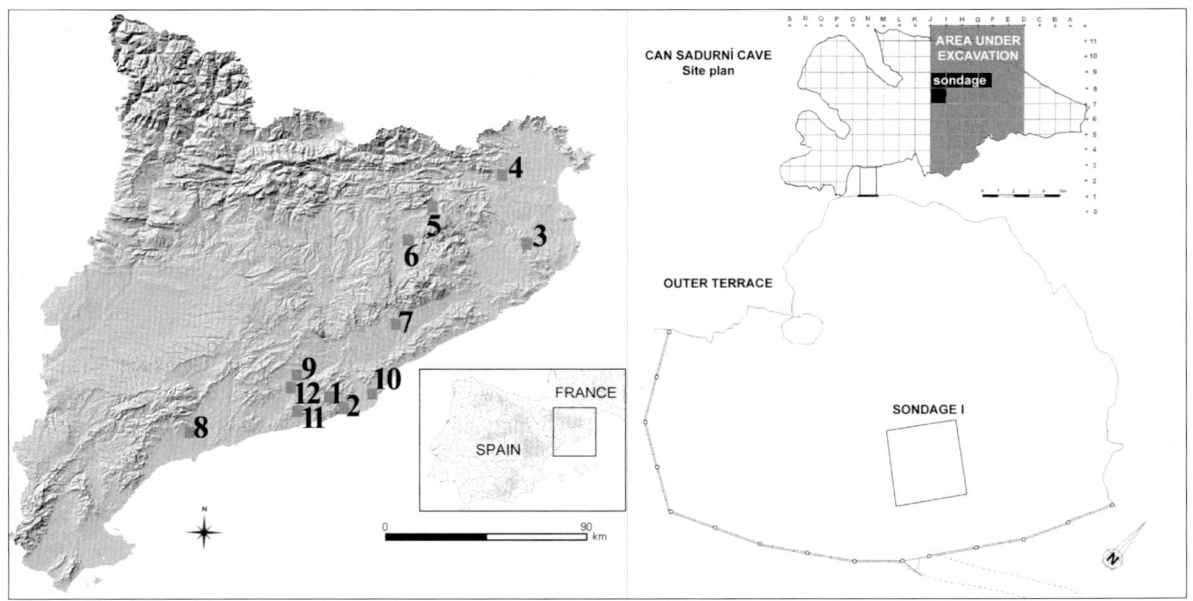

FIGURE 1. LOCATION OF THE SITES MENTIONED IN THE TEXT AND SITE PLAN OF COVA DE CAN SADURNÍ.
1- COVA DE CAN SADURNÍ, 2- MINES DE CAN TINTORER, 3- COVA DEL PASTERAL, 4- COVA DE L'AVELLANER,
5- COVA DE LES GRIOTERES, 6- MEGÀLITS DE TAVERTET, 7- CA L'ESTRADA, 8- TIMBA D'EN BARENYS,
9- HORT D'EN GRIMAU, 10- SANT PAU DEL CAMP, 11- PUJOLET DE MOJA, 12- POU NOU-2.

FIGURE 2. EAST PROFILE OF THE EXCAVATION AREA, WHERE THE DIFFERENT LAYERS
MENTIONED IN THE TEXT CAN BE OBSERVED. FOTO: CIPAG.

The cave is well known for its Holocene stratigraphy and the richness in archaeological materials, including several funerary episodes in recent Prehistory (Edo *et al*. 2011). Four different archaeological phases (from layer 11b to 9k1), dated to c. 4600-4000 cal BCE, being the earliest date 5790±40 BP (4763-4536 cal BC) and the youngest one 5279±31 BP (4232-3995 cal BC) (Edo *et al*. 2011)), each with a different use of the cave, have been identified within the middle Neolithic I. The stratigraphic description of the layers can be found in other works (Edo *et al*. 2011). We will focus in the phase *Neolític Postcardial 1(NP1)*, which has two distinct episodes: *NP1a*, which includes layers 11a5 and 11a4, and represents the use of the cave as a byre for ovicaprines, and *NP1b*, which includes layers 11a3, 11a2 and 11a1, during which the cave is used for funerary purpose. A more detailed description of these layers (Figure 2) and the funerary episode presented here can be found in Edo *et al*. (in press).

The funerary episode of the Middle Neolithic I of Can Sadurní. From the first findings to the 2013 field campaign

Research at the site started in 1978 and work is still ongoing. During the excavation of the Postcardial layers just above the NP1 phase, spare finds of human bones were observed. Some of them were dated to c. 4200-4000 cal BCE (see Table 1). These were the first signs that human burials dating to this period could have existed. In 2012, the first assemblages of human bones in anatomical connection were detected (INH-3; INH-5; INH-6). Moreover, in layer 11a1 possible offerings were found associated to the burials. Two hearths, potentially contemporaneous to these remains were also excavated.

In 2013 layer 11a2, a layer of small-sized stones, was reached. Once extracted, it was discovered that this layer was covering three burials (INH1-INH2-INH4) in complete anatomical connection. The layer had a natural origin, possibly a small collapse of the cave roof and it is very well visible in the profiles of the excavated area. INH1 and INH2 were completely excavated, but only the left foot of INH4 was found within the excavated surface (the rest of the body is presumably in the part of the site that will not be affected by our project). The individuals were longitudinally aligned, following the cave wall. They were deposited at an approximated distance of 1 m from each other and at around 60 cm from the wall. All burials appear in flexed position, over the right side of the body, oriented in direction W-E from head to feet, face towards the entrance of the cave and the back against the cave wall. INH-1 was dated to 5460±40 BP and INH-4 to 5568±34 BP (Table 1). At the same depth and only some metres away from these burials, a combustion feature (Structure XIII) dated to 5560±50BP was found. Its nature is difficult to state (soil micromorphology samples were taken), and so the contemporaneity between the hearth and the burial (the feature could in fact pre-date the burials and be connected to the previous use of the cave as animal byre). The burials were considered to represent a new layer or episode (11a3), while the rest of the sediment below the stone-layer 11a2 was labelled 11a4.

The soil micromorphological analyses of layer 11a4 in contact with the burials INH1 and INH2 show that it is formed of unlaminated colluvium and anthropic sedimentation, generated by animal stabling practices: disarticulated silica phytoliths, some faecal spherulites, charcoal fragments and sporadically, ovicaprine dung fragments partially burnt. Reworked traces are observed mainly due to trampling and biological activity which is accentuated due to the high content of organic matter in this horizon.

In short, we conclude that the burials were placed in a surface in which there is evidence of pastoral activity.

Description of the burials

The agents responsible for the sedimentary episodes that took place inside the cave after the burial phase were responsible for the disassembling and dispersion of most of the burials, which were progressively displaced towards the wall of the cave (like most of the archaeological material). Only INH1, INH2 and INH4 were excavated *in situ* in their primary position.

Concerning the findings recovered in layers 11a1 and 10b, these will be part of a more detailed and ambitious study in order to individualize the skeletal parts, although we will present some first results here. Until now, among the hundreds of bone fragments found, four non-adult individuals and three adults have been identified. Preliminary observations lead us to estimate that around 10 individuals were probably buried in the excavated area. Taking into consideration that only around 20% of the site has been dug, one could imagine that this number is probably much larger.

1) Individual 1 (INH1)

INH1 is a primary burial in right lateral decubitus position of an adult male (Fig. 3), found in anatomical connection and with bone fractures produced by postdepositional agents, probably the rock fall that constitutes layer 11a2. It is in a flexed position, with his vertebral column in a forward bent position. The lower extremities are hyper-flexed, with the knees next to the thorax. Both feet are in lateral-medial view and hyper-extended. The left arm lies in a position of natural fall, slightly

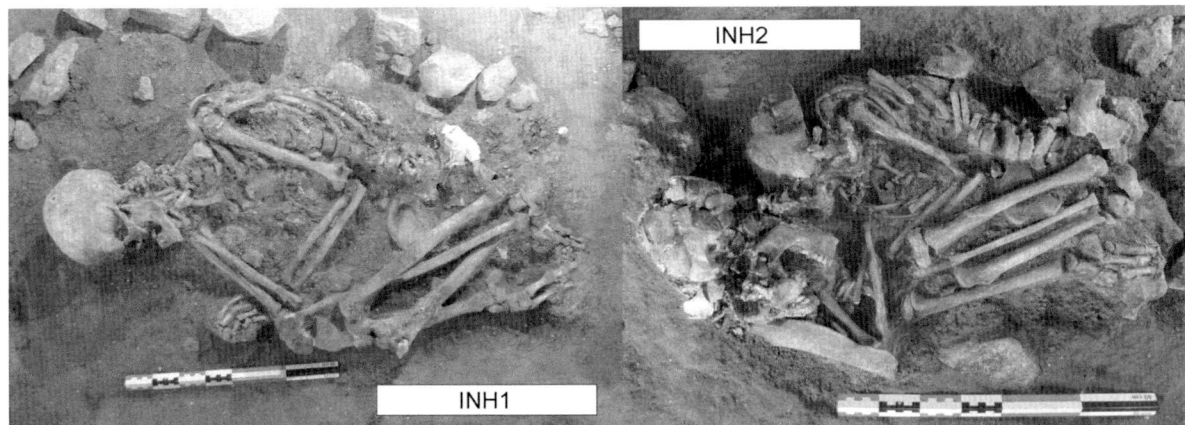

Figure 3. Individual 1 (INH1) and Individual 2 (INH2). Foto: CIPAG.

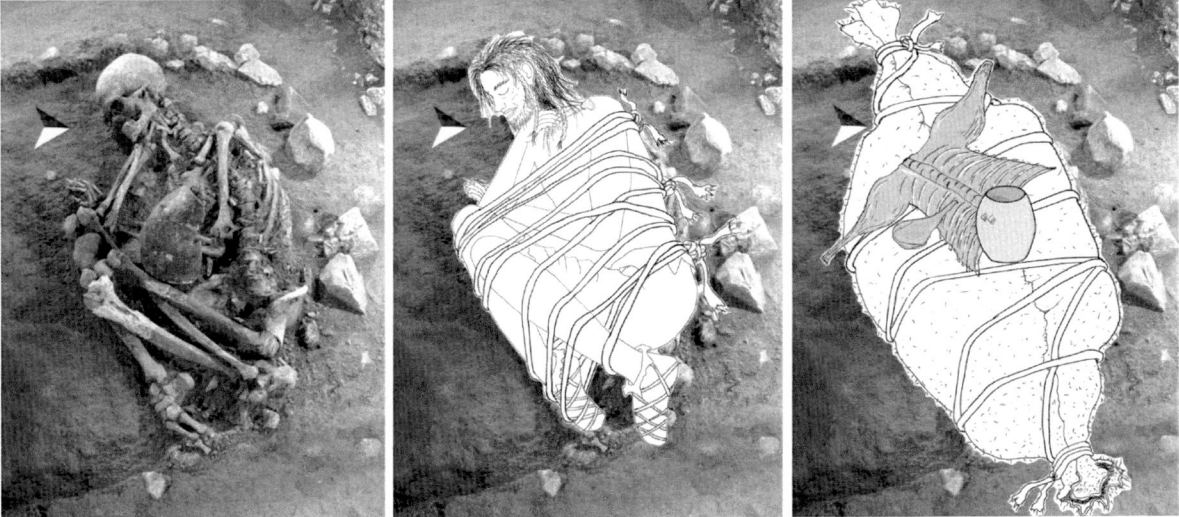

Figure 4. Hypothetical reconstruction of the shroud of Individual 1. CIPAG.

folded, with the hand at the level of the knees and under the right elbow. The right arm is totally folded on the chest and with the hand resting on the neck.

Its hyper-flexed position and the feet position indicate that the body was tied and probably wrapped in a shroud.

The offerings seem to have been deposited on the funerary shroud. A large fragment of an ovoid vase, with a black smooth burnished surface, of Montboló style, with two nipple-like handles in the upper part of the pot, was found on the lap of the individual.

On the chest, two selected portions of two goats (*Capra hircus*) were found. One was an adult animal with more than three years of age and the second one an infantile of five months.

The epiphysis and a large part of the diaphysis of a humerus of a young bovine (*Bos taurus*) of less than 15 months of age was found on the sternum of the individual. This element was radiocarbon dated to 5540±40 BP (4456-4335 cal BC), that is to say, c. 100 years older than the individual (INH1). This means that it could not be part of a consumption event related to the funerary ritual, but rather some kind of tool or symbolic element offered as a grave good (Figure 4).

2) Individual 2 (INH2)

This is a primary burial in right lateral decubitus position of a masculine infantile found in layer 11a3 (Figure 3). Sex identification was based on the measurements of the ilium and the mandible (following Krenzer 2006). Bones were found in anatomical connection. The cranium was highly fragmented and the bones of the breast and the dorsal spine were somewhat displaced backwards. The breakage and displacement was due to postdepositional processes, probably related to the rock fall identified as layer 11a2.

The body was in a hyper-flexed position. The right hand was on the chest while the left arm was in a position of natural fall. INH1 and INH2 were, in fact, in a very similar position.

The hyper-flexed position, like with INH-2, leads us to the conclusion that the individual had been tied. There was no associated apparel, although its head seemed to lie on a rib of a bovine.

3) Individual 3 (INH3)

This individual was identified from a number of infantile bones that were found in layers 10b and 11a1. It was not possible to recover all skeletal parts due to the permanent colluvium processes and the rock fall of layer 10b, which probably displaced or even destroyed them. There is no evident apparel linked to this individual.

4) Individual 4 (INH4)

This individual corresponds to a 5-6 year-old child, of unknown sex, that was found in layer 11a3 (see reference above for sex identification). Only the left foot was possible to recover, since the rest of the body probably lies in the unexcavated area of the settlement. In fact, the distal epiphysis of the tibia and the fibula were observed in the profile of the excavation, which makes us think that the whole skeleton is probably preserved in anatomical connection. The left foot was found in plantar view, like the left foot of INH1 and INH2. No grave goods could be connected to this individual.

5) Individual 5 (INH5)

It was found in layer 11a1. Despite the fragmentation and dispersion of the bones, it was possible to ascertain that it belonged to an adult individual. Two pottery fragments of Molinot style were spatially associated with them and considered as possible grave goods. One of the fragments was a fragment with a brushed surface (with a comb or a similar object) and four longitudinal ridges (*crestes*), both being characteristic of this pottery style. The second fragment still had the edge preserved, equally with a brushed surface and decorated with four ridges forming squares below the edge of the bowl: two ridges were perpendicular to the edge and two were parallel to it. The residue analyses of the latter fragment concluded that there were oxalates and phytoliths of barley, which lead to the interpretation that a fermented product of cereal origin had been produced in the pot, possibly some kind of beer product (Blasco *et alii*. 2008). If confirmed this would represent the oldest evidence of beer in Europe to date (Guerra-Doce 2014).

6) Individual 6 (INH6) and Individual 7 (INH7)

These skeletal parts were found in layer 10b, accumulated in the area of the northern wall of the cave as a result of the taphonomic processes already described.

The first one is a female individual (INH6) and the second is an infantile (INH7). The bones of the latter were surprisingly entirely preserved. Archaeological materials were found next to these remains but it is not possible to ascribe them to any of the individuals, since they are not in a primary position.

Radiocarbon dating of the individuals

There are six radiocarbon dates on human bone available for this funerary episode. Three of them were done in disarticulated bones since they were selected before the finding of the four individuals in anatomical connection. For each of the individuals INH1, INH2 and INH4, radiocarbon dates were carried out. The obtained results are presented in Table 1.

C14 Lab code	Inventory code	Date BP	Callibrated date 2 σ (95 %)
UBAR-1282	11CS-D10H11I11-10b	5260± 40 BP	4231–4193 and 4177–3979 cal BCE
Beta -197134	01CS-H9-IId-11-82	5290± 40 BP	4238-4036 and 4023-3994 cal BCE
Beta-210652	96CS-H9-Ig-10b-89	5340± 40 BP	4322-4292 and 4266-4048 cal BCE
Beta -363819	13CS-INH1-IIf-11a3-96/97	5460 ±40 BP	4368-4236 cal BCE
OxA-29640	13CS-INH2-IIf-11a3-1	5487±33 BP	4445-4261 cal BCE
OxA-29641	13CS-INH4-IIf-11a3-1	5568±34 BP	4459-4347 cal BCE

TABLE 1. RADIOCARBON DATES ON HUMAN BONE SAMPLES (CALIBRATIONS WERE DONE WITH OXCAL V4.2.4. (BRONK RAMSEY AND LEE 2013; REIMER ET AL. 2013).

Everything points towards the fact that during this period the cavity was used as a cemetery by the community or communities that inhabited the terrace in front of the cave. This seems to take place several times within a period of between 134 and 398 years, according to the available radiocarbon dates (Fig. 5).

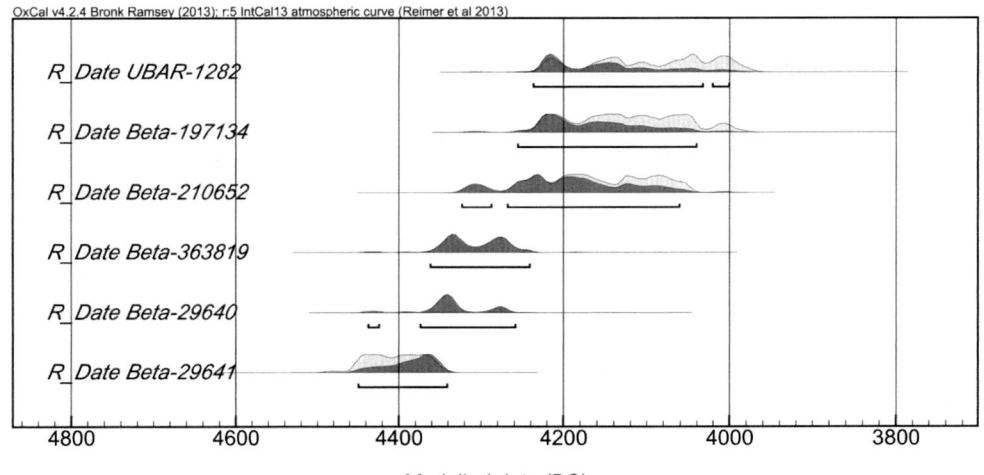

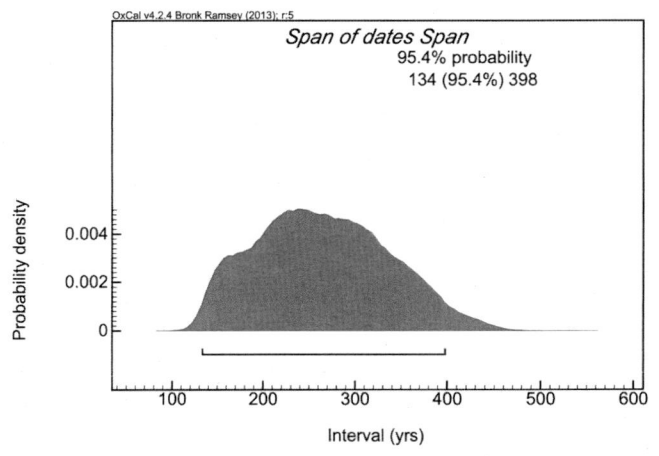

FIGURE 5. RADIOCARBON DATES BASED ON HUMAN BONE SAMPLES (CALIBRATION PERFORMED WITH OXCAL V.4.2.4. (BRONK RAMSEY AND LEE 2013; REIMER ET AL. 2013).

The individuals of layer 11a3 would belong to the earliest phase of the episode and it is our hypothesis, relying on the radiocarbon dates provided in Table 1, that the individuals (disarticulated bones) recovered in layers 11a1 and 10b could represent the later phase. It is not possible to know if the same funerary gestures were repeated in the second phase, since no *in situ* burials were found. Nevertheless, our hypothesis is that the same tradition was continued (Figure 6).

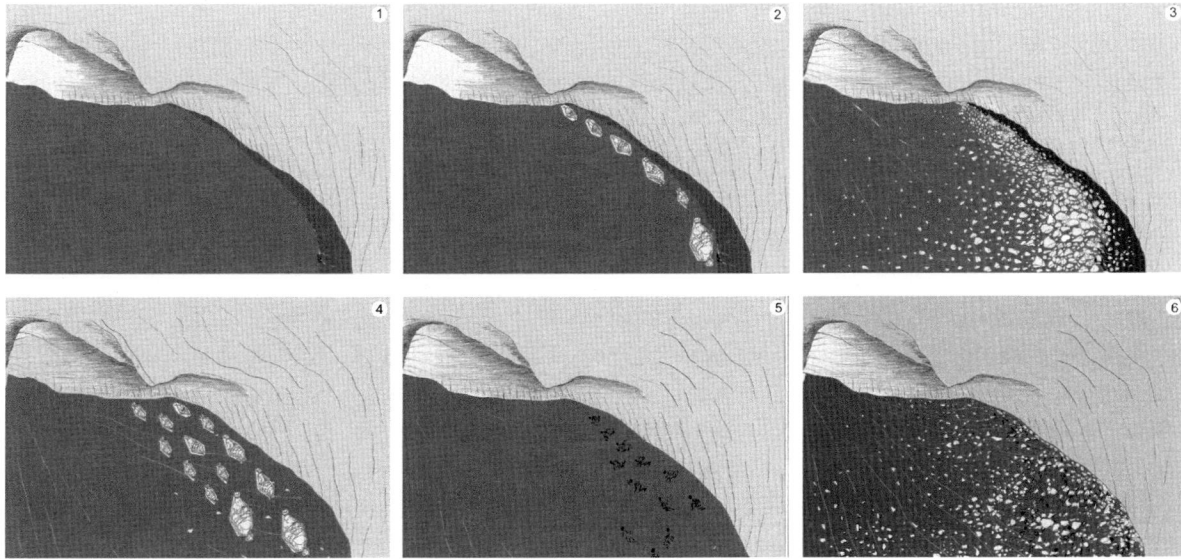

FIGURE 6. HYPOTHETICAL RECONSTRUCTION OF THE EVOLUTION OF THE FUNERARY EVENTS IN THE CAVE. CIPAG.

The treatment of the burials

As previously described, the positions of INH1 and INH2 are almost identical. The position of individuals INH3 and INH4 allow us to propose that they follow the same pattern, despite the fact that the skeletal parts are partly unconnected or only partly excavated.

The position of the feet of INH1, INH2 and INH4, and the hyper-flexed position of the extremities of the first two leads us to propose that ropes were used to keep a foetal position of the individuals. It is possible that a funerary shroud was also used.

Grave goods were only ascribed to two individuals. The fact that only fragments of the pots were recovered could be due to the fact that these pots were located outside the funerary shroud and suffered a stronger postdepositional displacement than the bones. Nevertheless, there are indicators that point to the fact that an important part of these offerings had to do with foods. The individual INH5 was connected to a vase containing a fermented beverage made with barley, while INH1 had selected portions of two goats in direct association with the burial. The presence of the fermented beverage is not only important for being an early find of this product, but also due to the investment of labour that it entails. One could speculate that beer could have been part of a feasting event linked to the burial. The goat extremities could suggest the same kind of episode, according to the archaeological indicators for feasts listed by Haydn (2001, Table 2.1). Feasts in connection to funerals are a well-known practice in anthropology and, as recently reviewed by Haydn (2009), they can be connected with social promotion or the creation of social networks within a community or with other communities. Large-scale funerary feasts already occurred in the early Neolithic, as demonstrated at the site of Kfar HaHoresh in Israel (Goring-Morris/Horwitz 2007). The finding of potentially unusual food products like beer in such a context gives some hint towards the significance of this event for the community.

Despite not having concluding evidence for the feast hypothesis, and still lacking a proper spatial evaluation of the findings, we do not exclude the possibility that the use of some of the hearths found in layer 11a1 could be related to the funerary ritual. More research is needed in this sense. These fires could have had a role during feasting events or a prophylactic effect against the smell of the decomposing bodies. Other elements need further research, like the finding of mandibles of goat between the burials INH4-INH2-INH1-INH3 or the potential content of the vessel fragment found with INH1, which has not yet been studied.

Furthermore, there are abundant materials in layers 10b and 11a1 which could be considered as potential grave goods, either due to their fine manufacture or because of their rarity (prestige goods) (Figure 7). We intend to focus in their study in the near future.

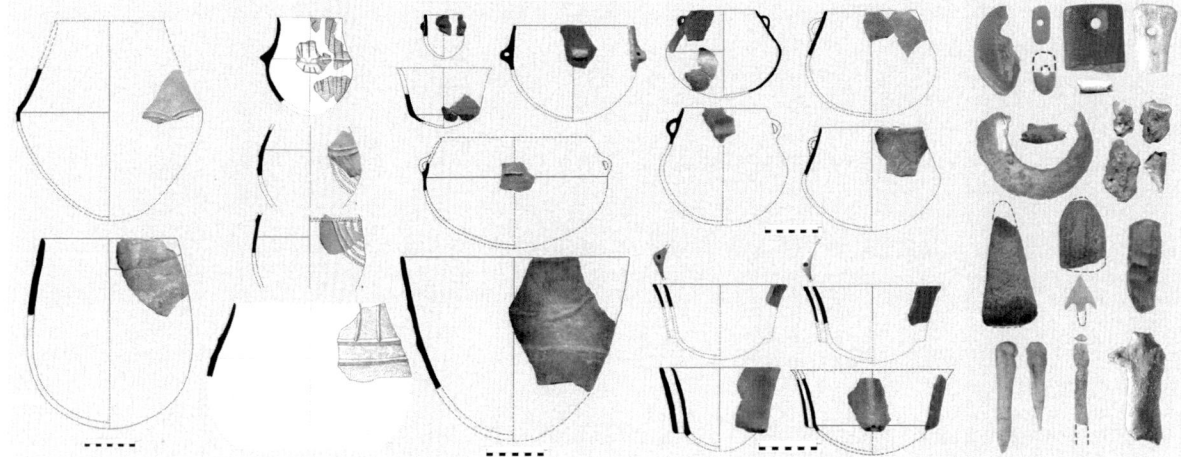

FIGURE 7. MATERIALS ASSOCIATED TO THE BURIALS OR LIKELY TO BE CONSIDERED AS FUNERARY OFFERINGS. TWO COLUMNS ON THE LEFT: CERAMIC OF MOLINOT STYLE; CENTRAL COLUMNS: CERAMIC OF MONTBOLÓ STYLE; RIGHT COLUMN: OTHER PRESTIGE GOODS FOUND IN THE STUDIED LAYERS. FOTO: CIPAG.

The funerary model of Can Sadurní in the context of the Northeast of the Iberian Peninsula and adjacent areas

The closest parallels to our case study are found at the other side of the Pyrenees, in south-eastern France. In relation to the funerary world of the early middle Neolithic in this area, Alain Beyneix said that 'in the Rossellon there is a will to gather together the cadavers. Funerary caves of the Montboló group (balma de Montboló, caune de Belestà, grotte de Montou) are true collective burials that gather members of the same group in a limited space and without any individual funerary structure. This behaviour expresses, without a doubt, close solidarity bonds between the living' (Beyneix 2002:631). This description gives a very similar picture to what was presented in this paper. Human remains were found at the shelter of Montboló (Guilaine 1974) and at the cave of Montou (Ponsich *et al.* 1990), both with Montboló pottery tradition. But the most interesting site from our point of view is the Caune de Bélesta (Claustre *et al.* 1993), with a collective burial in chamber VII. Around thirty individuals (15 adults, 13 children and 4 non-adults) were surrounded by a rich and homogeneous pottery assemblage that gave to the deposit a particular cultural specificity. The context is dated to 5640±120BP (4771-4261 cal BCE). From the available information (Claustre *et al.* 1993) we concluded that the individuals had their back against the wall of the cave and their faces oriented to the entrance of the cave. The position of the burials and their associated offerings seems to coincide with the findings recovered at Cova de Can Sadurní.

The funerary deposits found in the north-east of the Iberian Peninsula are diverse. Even though there are several multiple burials in caves, single burials were also found. Among the known cave contexts, one of the potentially oldest examples – although all these funerary deposits should be re-dated using AMS- is Cova de l'Avellaner (Girona). Charcoal remains from chamber 1 were dated to 5920±180BP (5292-4401 cal BCE) and human bones from chamber 2 to 5830±100BP (4934-4462 cal BCE) (Bosch and Tarrús 1991). Skeletal parts were disarticulated, although the authors mentioned that there were indicators towards a flexed position against the wall, similar to what has been described for our study site. A minimum of seven individuals lacking any type of significant grave goods were distinguished on the basis of aDNA analyses (Lacan *et al*. 2011). The authors suggest that this practice of multiple burials could have a Mesolithic tradition. Yet, given that multiple burials are found among incoming populations originally from the eastern Mediterranean (according to aDNA analyses) in the very first stages of the early Neolithic in an earlier phase (layer 18) of Cova de Can Sadurní (Edo *et al*. 2011; Gamba *et al*. 2011), this hypothesis should be rejected.

Another collective funerary space where 9 individuals (6 adults, 1 non-adult and 2 infantile) were buried was identified in chamber III of Cova del Pasteral (La Selva, Girona), dated to 5270±70BP (4315-3964 cal BCE) (Bosch 1985; Campillo *et al*. 1986; Bosch/Tarrús 1990).

As a last example, Gallery 11 of Cova de les Grioteres (Vilanova de Sau, Osona), was also used for funerary purposes for c. 20 individuals that were found very fragmented and dispersed. Many of the bones were burnt, like in Cova de la Pastora. Selected portions of fauna (sheep, goat, deer and cattle) were found as grave goods (Castany 1992), together with pots of Montboló style. The context is dated to 5300±180BP (4486-3711 cal BCE) (Castany 1995).

Other funerary models were found in this region. Funerary tumuli are known from the first half of the Vth millennium cal BCE in the area of Tavertet (Osona): Font de la Vena dated to 6190±100BP (5365-4851 cal BCE, on charcoal); Padró II dated to 5580±130BP (4723-4071 cal BCE), 5600±130BP (4771-4080 cal BCE), 5770±80BP (4824-4451 cal BCE) and 5870±100BP (4986-4501 cal BCE, all dates made on charcoal); Padró III and Collet de Rajols. These are the first manifestations of megalithism in the region, all linked with the pottery of Montboló tradition (Cruells *et al*. 1992).

Finally, individual burials were found in open-air sites, mainly in the central Catalan coast, where Cova de Can Sadurní is located, or close to it. One example is Ca l'Estrada (Canovelles, Vallès Oriental). Two individual burials were found in a flexed position and it was interpreted that the burials were tied. There is one radiocarbon date available: 5740±40BP (4696-4491 cal BCE) (Subirà *et al*. in press). This could be one of the earliest open-air necropolis in the area, and it could be considered a precedent to the well-known necropolis found towards the end of the Vth millennium cal BCE like in Timba d'en Barenys (5240±160BP, 4369-3700 cal BCE), with an individual burial in a silo pit; Hort d'en Grimau (5250±65BP, 4254-3957 cal BCE; 5270±65BP, 4260-3965 cal BCE), with burials in pits with tumuli made of stones (Mestres 1988-89); Sant Pau del Camp (5160±130BP, 4319-3697 cal BCE, on human bone), with twenty individual burials mostly in a similar position to the ones of Can Sadurní, and equally considered to have been wrapped in a funerary shroud (Chambon 2008) and potentially connected to multiple hearths (Molist *et al*. 2008); Pujolet de Moja (4990±70BP, 3946-3656 cal BCE)) (Mestres *et alii*. 1997) as well as Pou Nou-2 (Nadal *et al*. 1994) and burial 1 of Can Tintorer (Villalba *et alii*. 1986), without radiocarbon dating available but belonging to the same chronological framework. The predominant pottery tradition found in all these burials is of Molinot style.

Conclusions

The burials of the middle Neolithic I studied are organized as individual depositions of the bodies in a common space, to which the members of the community would have a more or less frequent access. A certain treatment of the body was observed and the potential existence of funerary feasts has been discussed. No differences in the funerary apparel among individuals were found. There seems to be a lack of significant prestige goods.

A review of the available data on funerary contexts of the region showed that the closest parallels to our case study are found in the Montboló region. The fact that both Montboló and Molinot pottery traditions are found in Cova de Can Sadurní might be relevant for several aspects. First it demonstrates that both styles were contemporary. In Can Sadurní however, both traditions co-exist within a funerary model that seems to be more frequent among the Montboló tradition. This would point towards the existence of important contacts with this region maybe representing the start of the social networks that are observed during the middle Neolithic II in this area when a circulation of prestige goods is observed on a large scale (Vaquer and Lea 2011). In fact, the later pottery productions of the 'Sepulcres de Fossa' culture that will develop in this region are a small evolution of the ceramic typology of Montboló tradition.

References

Bergadà, M.M; Cervelló, J.M. (2011) – Estratigrafia, micromorfologia i paleoambient de la cova de Can Sadurní (Begues, Baix Llobregat) des dels c. 11.000 fins els 5.000 anys BP. In Blasco, A; Edo, M.; Villalba, M.J., eds. lits.- Jornades '30 anys d'investigació arqueològica a Garraf'. Milan: Edar-Hugony. Milano. p. 95-108.

Blasco, A., Edo, M.; Villalba, M.J. (2005) – Cardial, epicardial y postcardial en Can Sadurní (Begues, Baix Llobregat). In Arias, P.; Ontañon, R.; Garcia-Moncó, C., eds. lits.- III Congreso del Neolítico en la Península Ibérica. Santander. p. 867-878.

Blasco, A.; Edo, M.; Villalba, M.J. (2008) – Evidencias de procesado y consumo de cerveza en la cueva de Can Sadurní (Begues, Barcelona). In Hernández, M.S., Soler, J.A.; López, J.A., eds. lits.- IV Congreso Neolítico Peninsular. Alicante. Vol. I p. 428-431.

Bosch, A. (1985) – La cova del Pasteral: un jaciment neolític a la vall mitjana del Ter. In Homenatge al Dr. Josep M. Coromines. Centre d'Estudis Comarcals de Banyoles, vol. II, p. 29-56.

Bosch, A.; Tarrús, J. (1990) – La Cova Sepulcral del Neolithic Antic de l'Avellaner (Cogolls, Les Planes d'Hostoles, La Garrotxa). Girona: Serie Monografica 11. 125p.

Bronk Ramsey, C.; Lee, S. (2013) – Recent and Planned Developments of the Program OxCal. Radiocarbon. 55:2-3, p. 720-730.

Campillo, D; Vives, E. (1986) – Estudi de les restes humanes de la cova de 'El Pasteral' (Girona). In Homenatge al Dr. Josep M. Coromines. Centre d'Estudis Comarcals de Banyoles, vol. II, p. 57-70.

Castany, J.; Guerrero Sala, L.A. (1992) – Població i antropología d'un nínxol d'inhumació col·lectiva i successiva del grup Montboló a Grioteres (Vilanova de Sau, Osona). In Estat sobre la investigació del Neolític a Catalunya. Andorra: IX CIAP, p. 153-154.

Chambon, Ph. (2008) – Alguns trets de les pràctiques funeràries del Neolític Postcardial. Quarhis. 4, p. 70-75.

Claustre, F.; Zammit, J.; Blaize, Y. (1993) – La Cauna de Bélesta: une tombe col·lective il y a 6000 ans. Centre d'Anthropologie des sociétes rurales et Cháteau-Musée de Bélesta, Toulouse et Belesta. 286 p.

Clop, X. (2010) – Le IVe millénaire avant notre ère dans le nord-est de la Péninsule Ibérique. In Lemercier, O.; Furestier, R.; Blaise, E., eds. lits.- 4e Millénaire. La transition du Néolithique moyen au Néolithique final dans le sud-est de la France et les régions voisines. Lattes: Publications de l'UMR 5140 / ADAL (Monographies d'Archéologie Méditerranéenne, 27). p. 249-259.

Cruells, W; Castells, J; Molist, M. (1992) – Una necròpolis de 'cambres amb túmul complex' del IV mil·leni a la Catalunya interior. In Estat de la Investigació sobre el Neolític a Catalunya. IX CIAP. Andorra, p. 244-248.

Edo, M.; Blasco, A.; Villalba, M.J. (2011) – La cova de Can Sadurní, guió sintètic de la prehistòria recent de Garraf. In Edo, M.; Blasco, A.; Villalba, M.J., eds. lits.- Jornades '30 anys d'investigació arqueològica a Garraf'. Milan: Edar-Hugony, p. 13-95.

Edo, M.; Antolín, F.; Barrio, M.J. (2012) – Can Sadurní (Begues, Baix Llobregat), de la captación de recursos abióticos al inicio de la minería de alumino-fosfatos (10500-4000 cal ANE) en el Macizo de Garraf. Rubricatum 4. p. 299-306. Congrés Internacional Xarxes al Neolític.

Edo, M., [et al.] (in press) – El episodio funerario del neolítico antiguo cardial pleno de la cueva de Can Sadurní (Begues, Barcelona). Estado actual de la cuestión. In Gibaja, J.F. [et al.], eds. lits.- Mirando a la Muerte: Las prácticas funerarias durante el neolítico en el noreste peninsular. Castellón: E-ditArx – Publicaciones Digitales.

Gamba, C. [et al.] (2011) – Ancient DNA from an Early Neolithic Iberian population supports a pioneer colonization by first farmers. Molecular Ecology. 21, p. 45-56.

Guerra-Doce, E. (2014) – The origins of inebriation: archaeological evidence of the consumption of fermented beverages and drugs in Prehistoric Eurasia. Journal of Archaeological Method and Theory. DOI 10.1007/s10816-014-9205-z.

Goring-Morris, N.; Horwitz, L.K. (2007) – Funerals and feasts during the Pre-Pottery Neolithic B of the Near East. Antiquity. 81. p. 902-919.

Guilaine, J. (1974) – La Balme de Montboló et le Néo!ithique de l'Occident Méditerranéen. Toulouse: Institut Pyrénéen d'Etudes Anthropologiques. 201 p.

Hayden, B. (2001) – Fabulous feasts. A prolegomenon to the importance of feasting. In Dietler, M.; Hayden, B., eds. lits.- Feasts. Archaeological and ethnographic perspectives on food, politics, and power. Alabama: University of Alabama Press. p. 23-64.

Hayden, B. (2009) – Funerals as feasts: why are they so important?. Cambridge Archaeological Journal 19: p. 29-52.

Krenzer, U. (2006) – Compendio de métodos antropológico forenses para la reconstrucción del perfil osteo-biológico. Tomo II. Métodos para la determinación del sexo. Guatemala: Centro de Análisis Forense y Ciencias Aplicadas (CAFCA).

Lacan, M. [et al.] (2011) – Ancient DNA suggests leading role played by men in the Neolithic dissemination. PNAS. 108, p. 18255-18259.

Martín, A., Villalba, M.J. (1999) – Le Néolithique moyen de la Catalogne, XXIVe Congrès Préhistorique de France-Le Néolithique du Nord-Ouest méditerranéen, Carcassonne 26-30 septembre 1994. Société Préhistorique Française. p. 211-224.

Martínez, P., Fortó, A. – Memòria científica de la intervenció arqueològica preventiva Ronda Nord de Granollers Tram II (Les Franqueses del Vall'es-Canovelles). Localització i excavació del jaciment de Ca l'Estrada (Canovelles) [Unpublished]. 2007.

Mestres, J. (1988-89) – Les sepultures neolítiques de l'Hort d'en Grimau (Castellví de la Marca, Alt Penedès). Olerdulae, Revista del Museu de Vilafranca. 1-4. p. 97-129.

Mestres, J. [et al.] (1997) – El Pujolet de Moja (Olerdola, Alt Penedès), Ocupació d'un territori durant el Neolític i Primera Edat del Ferro. Tribuna d'Arqueologia. 1995-96. p. 121-148.

Molist, M.; Vicente, O.; Farré, R. (2008) – El jaciment de la Caserna de Sant Pau del Camp: aproximació a la caracterització d'un assentament del Neolític antic. Quarhis. 4. p. 14-24.

Nadal, J.; Socias, J.; Senabre, M.R. (1994) – El jaciment neolític de Pou Nou-2 de Sant Pere de Molanta (Olèrdola). Gran Penedès. 38. p. 17-19.

Ponsich, P.; Treinen-Claustre, F. (1990) – Le gisement néolitjique de la galerie close de la grotte de Montou en Roussilon. In Autour de Jean Arnal. Laboratoire de Paléobotanique. Université des Sciences et Techniques du Languedoc. p. 101-122.

Reimer, P.J. [et al.] (2013) – IntCal13 and Marine13 Radiocarbon Age Calibration Curves 0-50,000 Years cal BP. Radiocarbon. 55:4. p. 1869-1887.

Vaquer, J., Lea, V. (2011) – Diffusion et échanges au Néolithique en Méditerranée nord-occidentale, In Blasco, A., Edo, M., Villalba, M.J. eds. lits.- La cova de Can Sadurní i la Prehistòria de Garraf. Recull de 30 anys d'investigació. Milan: Edar-Hugony. p. 265-291.

Villalba, M.J. [et al.] (1986) – Les mines neolítiques de Can Tintorer, Gavà. Excavacions 1978-1980. Barcelona: Generalitat de Catalunya. 203 p. (Excavacions arqueolgògiques a Catalunya núm.6).

Mora Cavorso Cave: a collective underground burial in Neolithic central Italy

Mario F. Rolfo[1], Katia F. Achino[2] and Letizia Silvestri[3]

[1] Department of History, Culture and Society, University of Tor Vergata, Roma (Italy)
[2] Quantitative Archaeology Lab (LAQU) – Department of Prehistory, Autonomous University of Barcelona, Bellaterra (Spain)
[3] Archaeology Department, University of Durham (UK)
katiafrancesca@libero.it

Abstract

Mora Cavorso Cave, located in South-Eastern Lazio, is a multi-tunnel cave displaying a complex stratigraphy. Its inner rooms revealed the presence of one of the most important funerary deposits of Early Neolithic central Italy. Around 30 individuals of all ages and both sexes, mostly chaotically piled for natural and anthropic reasons, were found along with grave goods and ornaments, whose materials come from different parts of Italy. This key deposit was object of a wide range of analyses, including isotopes and DNA studies, which helped unveil a sliver of life and death of the Neolithic communities of the Apennines.

Keywords

Italian Neolithic, Cave, Archaeology of death and burial, Bioarchaeology

Résumé

La Grotte de Mora Cavorso, située dans le Latium du Sud-Est, a une structure et une stratigraphie complexe. Ses chambres intérieures contenaient l'un des dépôts funéraires les plus importants du Néolithique ancien au centre d'Italie. Au moins 30 individus de tous âges et sexes, la plupart accumulés chaotiquement, ont été retrouvés ainsi que des mobiliers funéraires dont les matériaux proviennent de diverses régions d'Italie. Ce dépôt a été objet d'un large éventail d'analyses, y compris les isotopes et l'ADN, et a contribué au dévoilement d'un fragment de la vie et de la mort des communautés néolithiques des Apennins.

Mots-clés

Néolithique italienne, Grotte, Archéologie funéraire, Bioarchéologie

Introduction and description of the site

Mora Cavorso Cave is a multi-tunnel karst cave located on the right slopes of the Simbruini Mountains, in the Upper Aniene River Valley, South-Eastern Lazio (Figure 1.1), 715 metres above sea level, few kilometres from the village of Jenne (Province of Rome) and 195 metres above the Aniene River, along a particularly astonishing waterscape characterized by a small lake and waterfalls. This cave (Figure 1.2) is characterised by a 8 metre-wide, illuminated entrance with a sub-horizontal floor, whose ceiling lowers down drastically towards the end, leading into a 3 metre-long tunnel. This tunnel opens on the first inner chamber, 5 m wide, which terminates in another 5 metre-long passage leading to two chambers situated on different levels (the Upper and the Lower Room). The subsequent tunnels and chambers were of more difficult access and could not be extensively explored.

The discovery of the cave was made in early 2000s by Shaka-Zulu local speleological group. Archaeological excavations started in 2006 are still on-going. The archaeological importance of the cave became evident since its very first exploration as the speleologists immediately noticed the presence of human skulls concreted to the surface of one of the inner rooms (Figure 2). This stimulated the undertaking of systematic investigations by the University of Rome 'Tor Vergata', in agreement with the Soprintendenza per i Beni Archeologici del Lazio and the local municipality. The excavations undertaken over the last 9 years allowed to identify the complex stratigraphy of the site, ranging at least from the late Pleistocene to the Late Antiquity with a continuity of use up to

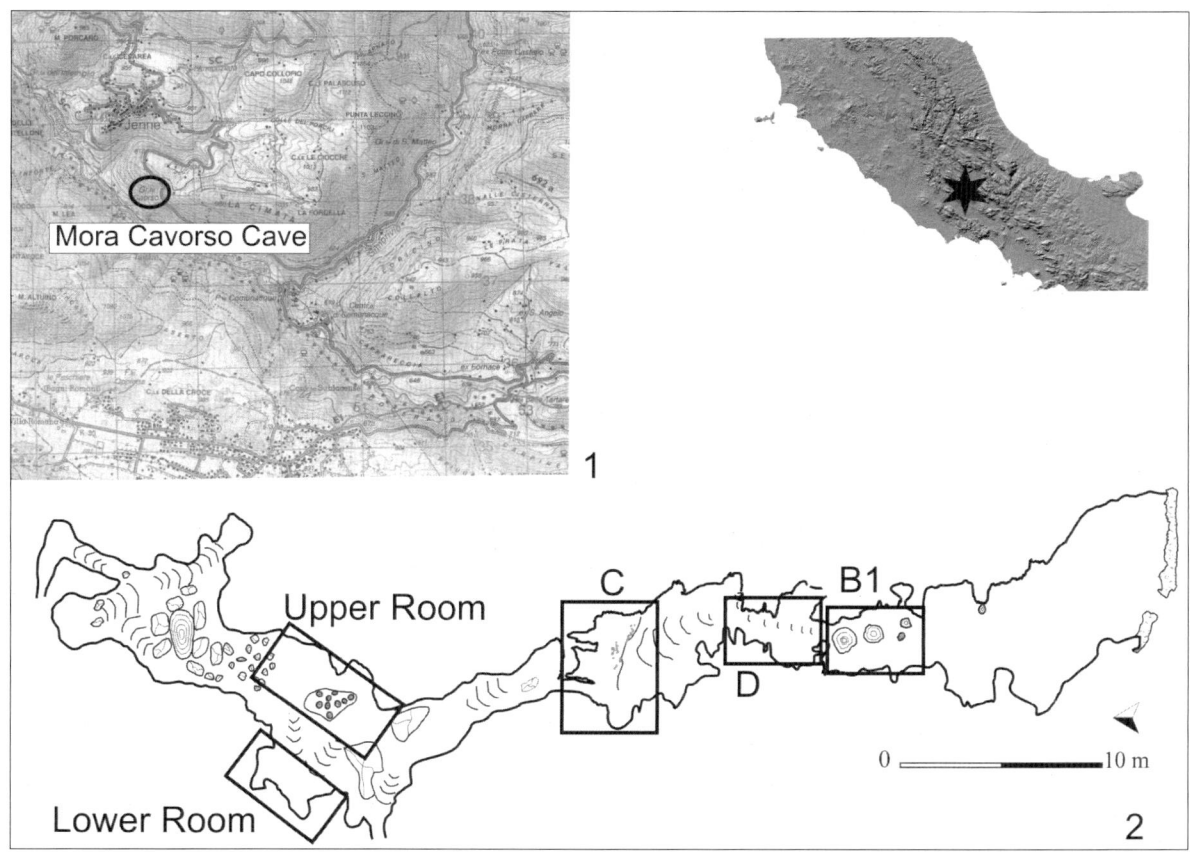

FIGURE 1. 1- THE LOCATION OF MORA CAVORSO CAVE IN THE SIMBRUINI MOUNTAINS;
2- PLAN OF THE CAVE WITH LOCATION OF THE ARCHAEOLOGICAL TEST PITS.

the 1950s (Rolfo *et al.*, 2009, 2010). The first ascertained attestation of human activity is presently dated to the Upper Palaeolithic, with a substantial increase of anthropic evidence over the Neolithic period. The Middle Bronze Age of the cave shows a more sporadic use, oriented towards a ritual and burial utilisation of the site. Human evidences of later phases are much more sporadic and of difficult interpretation, although ethnographic sources provided excellent information about the last phase of use of the site as a shepherd's stable and a war refuge over the last century (Achino *et al.*, 2013). The same ethnographic testimonies revealed that the entrance room was subject to anthropic modifications and soil removals over the last few decades, so that the top archaeological layers in the most accessible part of the chamber are now compromised. Analysis of the best preserved sectors of the site, however, enabled us to infer that the most intense frequentation of the cave occurred during the Early Neolithic, which is present in all the investigated rooms. In particular, the Upper and Lower rooms, very far from the only known entrance, were found to be holding hundreds of human bones. Although there seems to be no cultural relation or continuity between the burial use of Mora Cavorso Cave during the Neolithic period and the Middle Bronze Age, it is interesting to point out how caves of this region represented a key natural monument, connected with the sphere of death, over several millennia.

The Neolithic burials

The Neolithic collective burials were found in the inner rooms, called 'Upper' and 'Lower' due to their location on different levels. The Lower Room consists of a two-metre-wide chamber and held a chaotic accumulation of human bones. The stratigraphic analysis highlighted a 15-20 cm-deep-sequence consisting of stalagmite crusts, muddy layers and loose rocks (Figure 3.2).

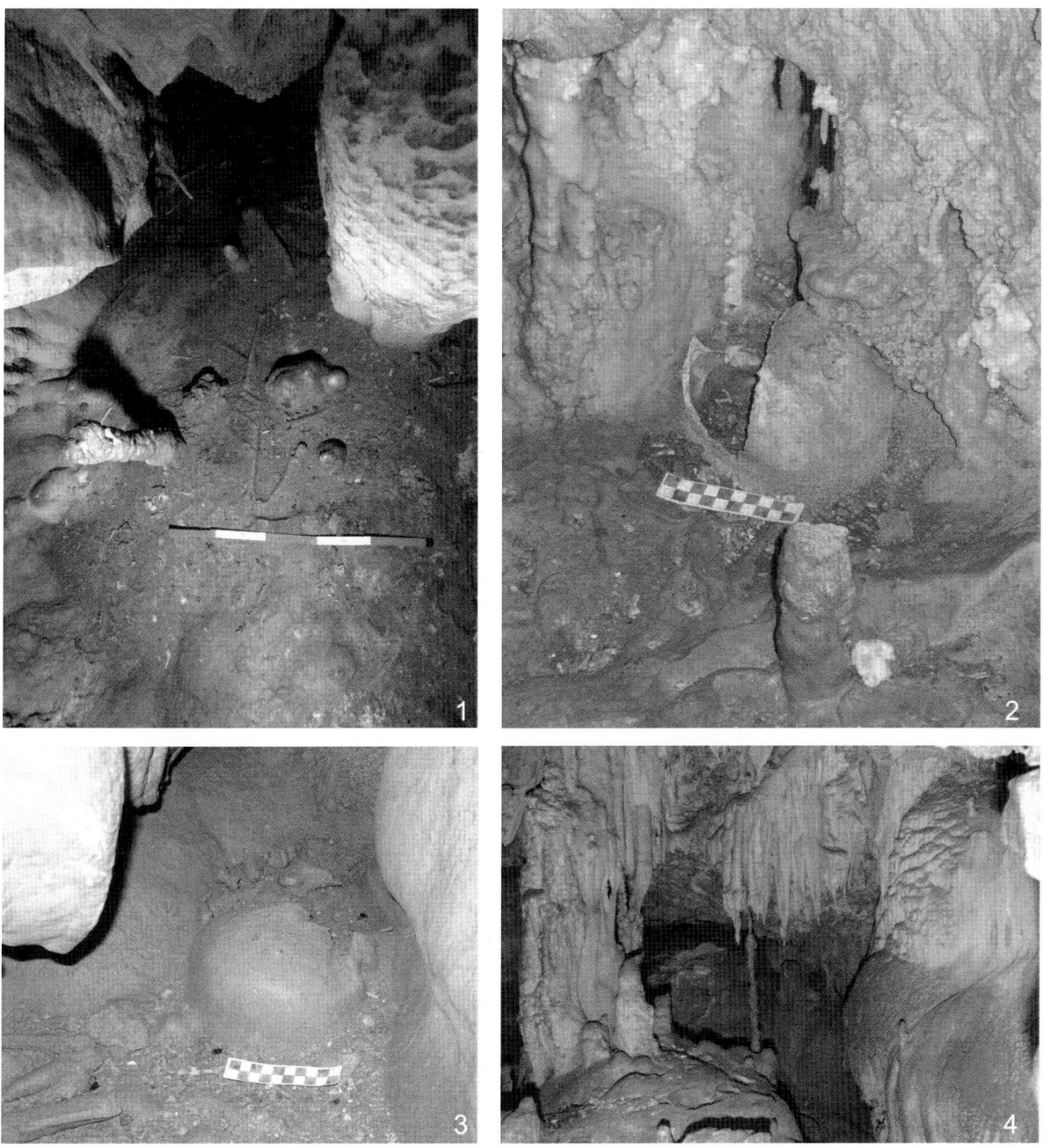

FIGURE 2. 1, 3- THE HUMAN BONES FOUND ON THE FLOOR OF THE LOWER ROOM;
2, 4- THE HUMAN BONES FOUND ON THE FLOOR OF THE UPPER ROOM.

Eleven beads, ten made of shell and one of grey calcareous stone, pottery and lithic industry were found in this room (Figure 4.1-3). The Lower Room is connected through a natural slipway with the much wider (15 square metres) Upper Room (Figure 3.1). Here, residues of primary burials were found laying directly on the stalagmitic crust, without any apparent delimitation of the funerary space. This mortuary practice was widespread in Neolithic Italy (Grifoni Cremonesi, 2002; 2006) as well as in the Mediterranean Europe (Beyneix, 2008, pp. 648-649). Limited skeletal connection and the association with archaeological artefacts characterized the Upper Room's human bones. The finds were completely sealed off by a thin stalagmitic veil and were located on the floor layer, which was rich in charcoal. Here, a polished sub-triangular green stone axe was found next to a right forearm, whereas a large pot portion and two retouched flint blades were found next to a right foreleg (Figure 4.4-5).

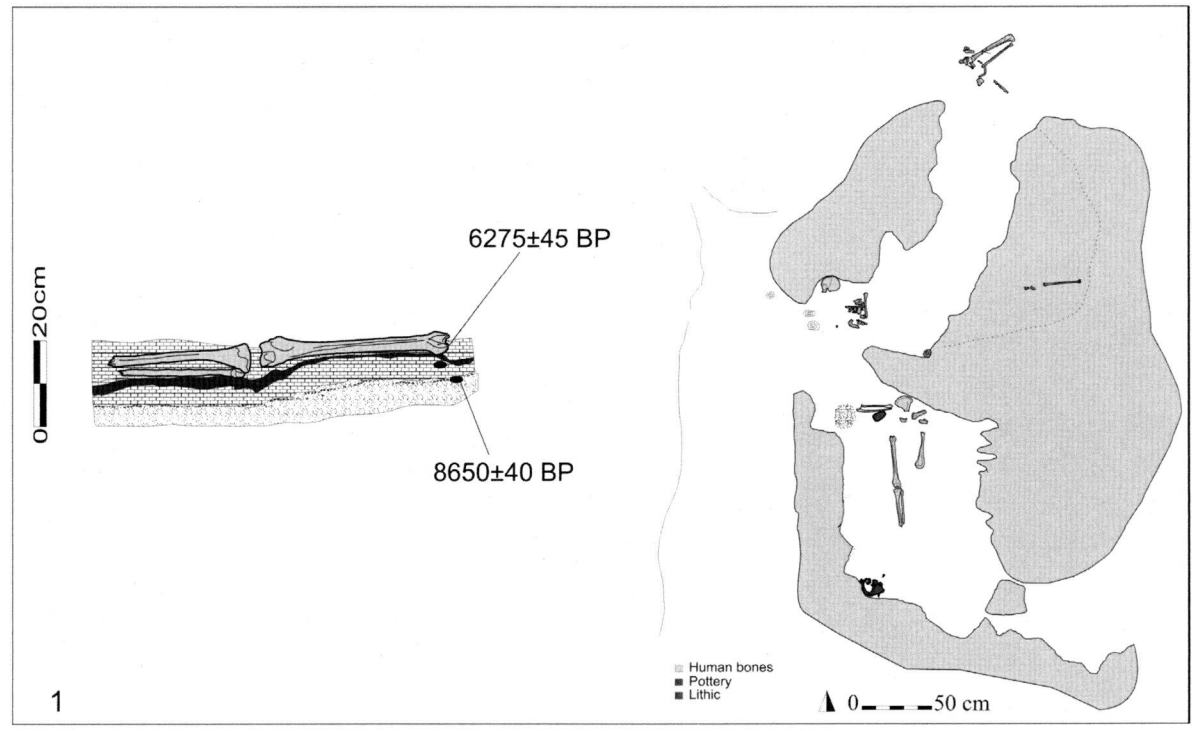

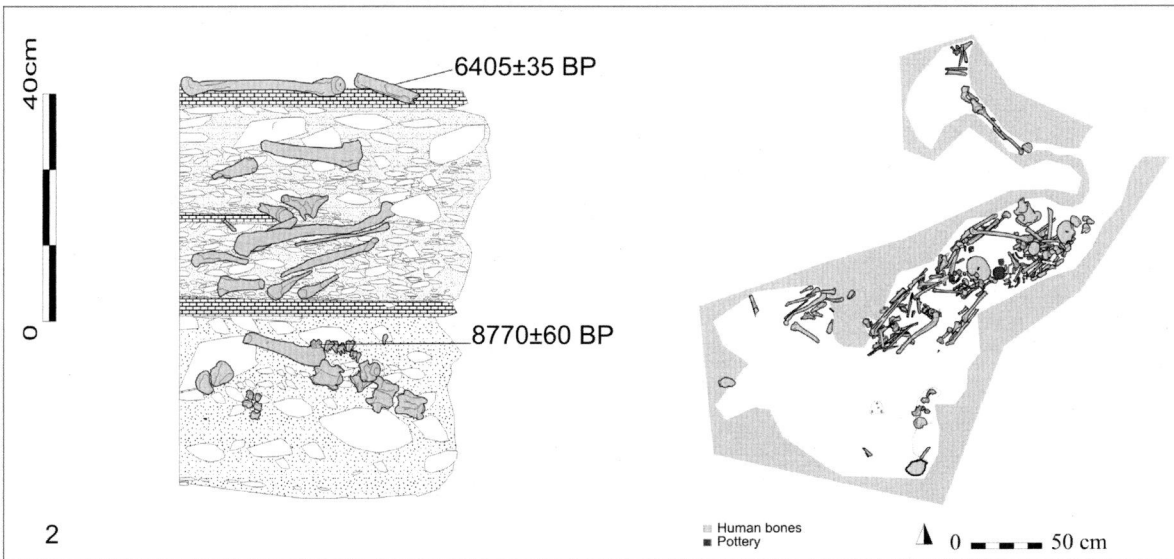

FIGURE 3. PLAN AND STRATIGRAPHY OF THE LOWER ROOM (1) AND UPPER ROOM (2).

According to the limited skeletal connection of the burials, the spatial distribution of both bones and artefacts and their proximity to each other, these archaeological finds can be interpreted as burial grave goods. C14 analysis from samples recovered in both rooms were carried out, in order to confirm and reinforce the assumed chronological framework, which was dated on a typological basis to the initial phase of Early Neolithic. Furthermore, below this last layer, an early Holocene C14 dated level, rich in faunal findings, is attested.

Bioarchaeological analyses: human osteology

Approximately 600 human bones have been recovered over three archaeological excavation campaigns in the contiguous Upper and Lower Rooms (Rolfo *et al.*, 2012). The remains of two individuals, still in partial anatomical connection, were identified in the Upper Room. The

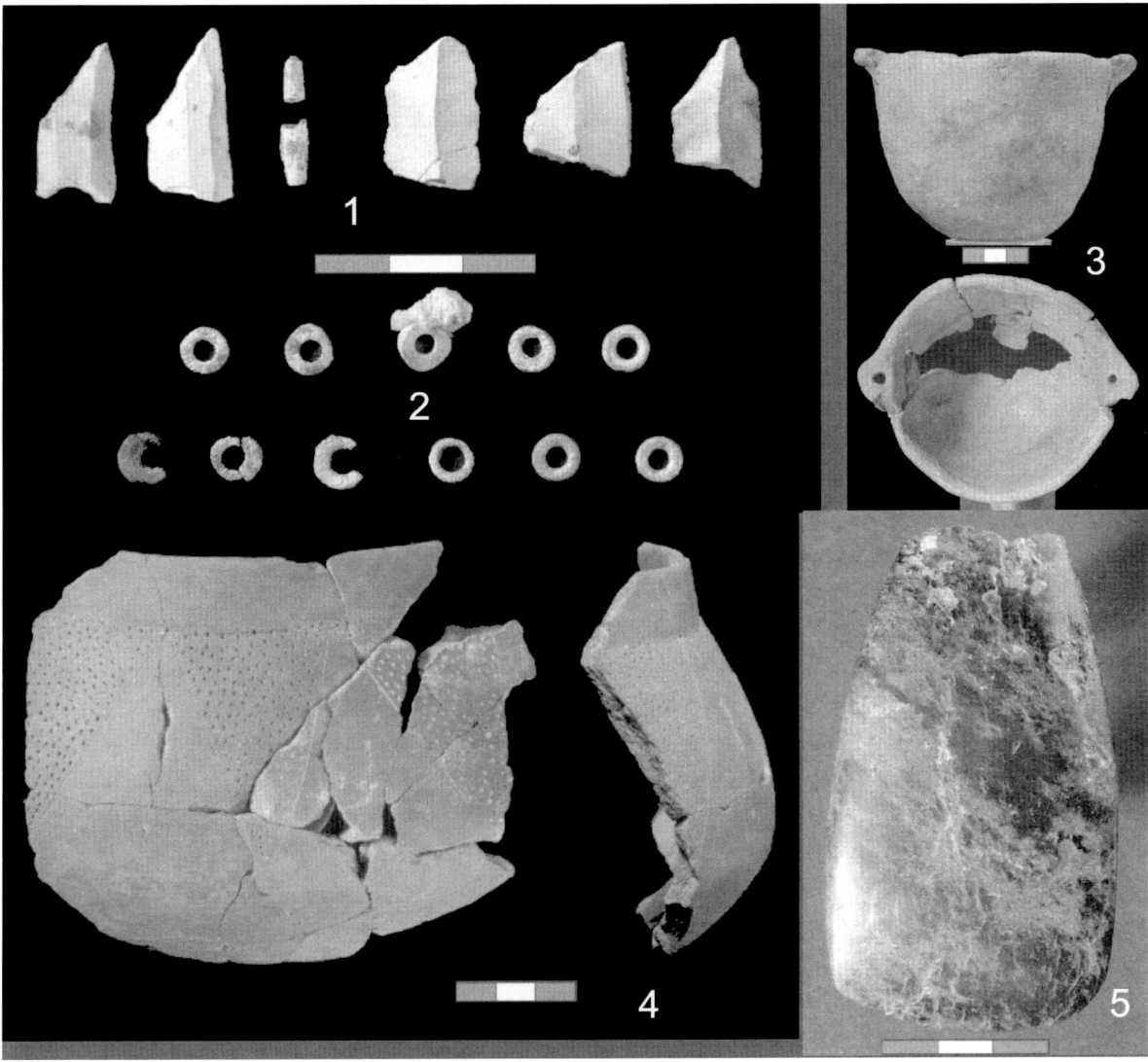

FIGURE 4. ARCHAEOLOGICAL REMAINS FROM UPPER ROOM (4-5) AND LOWER ROOM (1-3).

anthropological analyses revealed that there were 10 females and 7 males. In the central portion of the room a radio of a child and a group of at least 20 bones were found, whose study is in progress. In the Lower Room, the remains of at least 19 individuals were chaotically piled up in a 30 cm-deep-archaeological deposit located close to the natural slipway that connects the two rooms. According to this evidence, the paleosurface of the Upper Room, that was rich in charcoal and ashes, should have represented the primary burial surface. Analyses of the formation process of the deposit of human bones recovered in the Lower Room are on-going. The spatial distribution of the human bones could or could not be the result of an anthropic action carried out according to a different mortuary practice; in particular, the Lower Room could have hosted secondary burials of the remains which were pushed there from the Upper Room.

A preliminary morphological analysis on the diagnostic finds allowed to identify a demographic record consisting of 1 foetus, 1 perinatal, 9 infants (1-10 years), 7 young-adults (13-30 years) and 10 adults; a slight preponderance of females individuals is attested and the age at the death for the adult ranges between 25 and 35 years. Residual patches of the archaeological deposit in the Lower Room were excavated during the last excavation campaign, from which new bones were recovered. The study of these finds will certainly improve our understanding of the burial practices carried out at this site.

The faunal assemblage

The macrofaunal assemblage from the two inner rooms of Mora Cavorso Cave consists of c. 400 fragments, mostly attributed to domestic caprines, and secondarily to cattle, dog and red deer (Rolfo *et al.*, 2009, 2012). The preservation of most bones is rather poor, therefore the identification of species and body parts has been carried out on a small percentage of the complete sample (Rolfo *et al.*, 2009). However, preliminary information could be obtained: at least ten individuals (3 adults, 6 young or very young and 1 in perinatal age) were identified among the sheep/goats, represented with all the body portions. In addition, only one young cattle phalanx, an adult dog phalanx and two red deer upper teeth were recognized (Rolfo *et al.* 2012). The presence of young and very young individuals among the domesticates indicates the frequentation of the site during the warm season, possibly in relation to short-distance transhumance routes. The occurrence of red deer and forestal micromammals (present in the cave for natural reasons) points out to the existence of wet woodlands during the Neolithic. In addition, rodents such as *Arvicolidae* and hare inform about the presence of prairies at the time (Rolfo *et al.*, 2009, 2012). It is interesting to note that the Neolithic assemblage from the inner rooms of the caves, described in this paper, is very different to that found in the entrance room. This confirms the different use of the two areas and will offer an interesting input to further analyses and contextual interpretations.

On-going analyses

Archaeological investigations and the traditional study of the archaeological finds have been enriched by multidisciplinary analyses, such as molecular analyses of the human bones and the study of the speleothem. Isotopic analyses allowed to reconstruct the dietary habits of the Neolithic community buried in the cave (Scorrano *et al.*, 2015). In particular, analysis of the carbon and nitrogen stable isotopes revealed a high animal protein intake compared to a lower intake of cereal carbohydrates. This was not unexpected, given that the subsistence strategy of the community was most likely oriented towards sheep-farming. Mobility patterns are also being investigated, by looking at the oxygen isotopes of human and animal tooth enamel: assuming that the drinking water supply came from local sources, we would be able to infer whether the individuals had moved to the area or had been born and lived there.

Discussion and conclusions

The analyses of the Early Neolithic layers of Mora Cavorso Cave suggest that the site was frequented for funerary purposes. All the artefacts found in the inner rooms were identified as grave goods, although it can be assumed that the external rooms were used for more domestic purposes (fig. 1.2: B1). This hypothesis could not be proven by the stratigraphic deposit, which had been removed in historical times up to the Pleistocene contexts. However, the faunal record seems to show a seasonal occupation related to transhumance practices. The residual strips of this Neolithic deposit, 20 cm deep, held three hearths and related combustion areas, and a ritual pit. This indicates the cultic function of the area, also testified by its marginal position in the cave, next to the tunnel that leads to the inner burial chambers. The pathway that leads to the funerary rooms has not undergone substantial morphological modifications. The original walking pathway, rich in charcoals, was still preserved under few millimetres of carbonatic crust. It is likely that the dead were dragged along this path, which is still possible to go through, although in a difficult way and with a high energy expenditure rate.

The sacredness that characterises the cave from the entrance to the inner rooms is manifested in different ways in the different chambers. The Lower Room, a naturally bordered and marginal hollow, is suitable to bone accumulation; on the other hand, the Upper Room, wider and evocative, would work best as a primary burial place, as showed by the presence of individuals in partial skeletal connection.

The funerary frequentation of the cave in the Neolithic seems to be limited to a short period, ranging from 5460 to 4890 a.C., and is coherent with the Early Neolithic funerary customs of Central Italy, which were enacted mainly in natural caves. The most important evidences of this type were found in the Abruzzi caves: scattered human bones of at least 26 buried individuals were present in the 'ceramica impressa' layers of Grotta Continenza di Trasacco (L'Aquila), along with three cremated individuals identified in as many pots (Grifoni Cremonesi and Mallegni, 1978). Similarly scattered bones were also found at Grotta Sant'Angelo. At least six individuals, two adults (a male and a female) and four sub-adults, were found in its 'ceramica impressa' layers; three more individuals, a female adult, an infant and a foetus were also found in more recent layers (Di Fraia and Grifoni Cremonesi, 1996). The rituality at Grotta dei Piccioni di Bolognano is slightly different: here, only one individual with skeletal connection and no delimited burial space was found (Cremonesi, 1976).

The funerary framework of Lazio appears less rich, as much as the settlement evidence. This is most likely due to a research gap rather than an actual frequentation trend. Before Mora Cavorso Cave, only two funerary Neolithic caves were known in Lazio, *i.e.* Grotta Patrizi and Grotta delle Settecannelle. In the first site at least eight individuals dated to the Middle Neolithic were recovered, some of which were deposed in bordered areas (Grifoni Cremonesi and Radmilli, 2001). In the second one, eight individuals were found, seven of which scattered on the ground and one (a child's skeleton) delimited by stones. This last burial held evident traces of cults, such as the deposition of three hare's tibiae, pebbles and a millstone next to the skull (Gnesutta Ucelli, 2002).

Mora Cavorso Cave fits very well in this regional framework and is also similar to the Abruzzi collective cave burials. This is also supported by typological affinities of the artefacts, *e.g.* the 'Catignano' painted pottery. This ceramic style, born in the Abruzzi and Adriatic area, seems to spread towards the Tyrrhenian coasts through the inner Apennine valleys, where Mora Cavorso Cave is located. The burial phase in our site and all the other cited caves is characterised by skeletons in anatomical connection without bordered burial spaces and coeval bone accumulations. This suggests that the caves were no longer perceived and used as a 'container of graves', but rather as 'the grave' of the community itself.

Future developments

The archaeological deposit of Mora Cavorso Cave provides a wealth of opportunities to improve research in the upcoming years. First of all, it will allow us to undertake an up-to-date, critical intra-site analysis of the cave, as its Neolithic use appears to have been very different in each chamber of the cave (Entrance, Room 'C', Lower Room and Upper Room). This will follow, Ruth Whitehouse's (1992) work on Porto Badisco Cave, adding the key premises of a systematic and multidisciplinary archaeological investigation and documentation of the archaeological record to that interpretive approach. The chance to discuss the coexistence of domesticity and cult, as first introduced by Bradley (2005) and recently documented in the Grotta dei Piccioni and Grotta Sant'Angelo in Italy (Iaconis *et al.*, 2008), will be then tackled. Micromorphological analyses of the soils will enrich this discussion, by providing additional evidence of domestic and ritual uses of the entrance room. Spatial and taphonomical analysis will be crucial to draw reliable interpretations of the site biography. At the same time, surveys in the other caves of the Upper Aniene Valley's karst system will be carried out, as well as in the open-air territories of the area, allowing a much-needed contextualisation of the site in the archaeological landscape. Comparisons with earlier and later occupations of the cave will be undertaken, to investigate the changing uses of the site over time. Finally, with regard to the wider debate of the spread of the Neolithic in the Mediterranean, DNA analyses will certainly contribute to expand our understanding of the provenience of human groups populating central Italy in those critical centuries.

Acknowledgements

We would like to thank all the specialists involved in the study of this site, the Soprintendenza per i Beni Archeologici del Lazio, for the permission to investigate the site and the Ispettrici Annalisa Zarattini and Micaela Angle's for their active help. The Comune of Jenne and the Parco dei Monti Sibruini, for their support; the Shaka-Zulu speleological group for their priceless collaboration.

References

Achino, K.F.; Proietti, D.; Rolfo, M.F., Silvestri, L. (2013) – Oral sources and the Archaeological Data for the Study Case of the Mora Cavorso Grotto at Jenne. In Lugli, F.; Stoppiello, A.A.; Biagetti, S., eds. – Ethnoarchaeology: Current Research and Field Methods: Conference Proceedings (2010). London: B.A.R., p. 293-297. (BAR International Series; 2472).

Beyneix, A. (2008) – Mourir au Néolitique ancient en France méditerranéenne. L'Anthropologie. 112. p. 641-660.

Bradley, R. (2005) – Ritual and domestic life in prehistoric Europe. London: Routledge, 234 p.

Cremonesi, G. (1976) – La Grotta dei Piccioni di Bolognano nel quadro delle culture dal Neolitico all'età del Bronzo in Abruzzo. Pisa: Giardini, 349 p.

Di Fraia, T.; Grifoni Cremonesi, R. (1996) – La Grotta di S. Angelo sulla montagna dei fiori (Teramo) e il problema delle frequentazioni cultuali in grotta. Pisa: Istituto Editoriali e Poligrafici Internazionali, 392 p.

Gnesutta Ucelli, P. (2002) – Grotta di Settecannelle. In Fugazzola, Delpino M A; Pessina, A.; Tinè, V., eds. – Le ceramiche impresse nel Neolitico Antico. Italia e Mediterraneo. Roma: Istituto Poligrafico e Zecca dello Stato. p. 341-349.

Grifoni Cremonesi, R. (2002) – I culti e i rituali funerari. In Fugazzola, Delpino M A; Pessina, A.; Tinè, V., eds. – Le ceramiche impresse nel Neolitico Antico. Italia e Mediterraneo. Roma: Istituto Poligrafico e Zecca dello Stato. p. 209-219.

Grifoni Cremonesi, R. (2006) – Sepolture e rituali funerari nel Neolitico in Italia. In Martini, F., eds. – La cultura del morire nelle società preistoriche e protostoriche italiane, studio interdisciplinare dei dati e loro trattamento informatico, dal Paleolitico all'età del Rame. Firenze: Istituto Italiano di Preistoria e Protostoria. p. 87-107.

Grifoni Cremonesi, R.; Mallegni, F. (1978) – Testimonianze di un culto ad incinerazione nel livello a ceramica impressa della Grotta Riparo Continenza di Trasacco (L'Aquila) e studi dei resti umani cremati. Atti Della Società Toscana di Scienze Naturali. Pisa. 85, p. 253-279.

Grifoni Cremonesi, R.; Radmilli A.M. (2001) – La Grotta Patrizi al Sasso di Furbara (Cerveteri, Roma). Bullettino di Paletnologia Italiana. 91-92, p. 63-120.

Iaconis, M.A.; Boschian, G. (2008) – Geoarchaeology of the deposits of Grotta dei Piccioni and Grotta Sant'Angelo (Abruzzo, Central Italy). Atti Della Società Toscana di Scienze Naturali. Pisa. Memorie Serie A, 112, p. 181-188.

Rolfo, M.F.; Salari, L. (2009) – Nota preliminare sulle indagini archeologiche presso la grotta 'Mora di Cavorso'. Atti del V incontro di studio Lazio e Sabina. Roma. V, p. 15-22.

Rolfo, M.F.; Mancini, D.; Salari, L., Zarattini, A. (2010) – La Grotta di 'Mora Cavorso' a Jenne (Roma). Atti del VI incontro di studi Lazio e Sabina. Roma. VI, p. 11-17.

Rolfo, M.F.; Lelli, R.; Martínez Labarga, C.; Passacantando, D.; Scorrano, G.; Salari, L.; Rickards, O. (2012) – La comunità neolitica di Grotta Mora Cavorso a Jenne (RM): osservazioni deposizionali, paleobiologiche e faunistiche. Preistoria e Protostoria in Etruria. Atti del Decimo incontro di studi. Milano. X, p. 131-143.

Scorrano, G. *et al.* (2015) – Stable isotope analysis of human and faunal remains from an Early Neolithic Italian site: Mora Cavorso (Rome). In Rickards, O.; Sarti. L., eds. – Biological and cultural heritage of the Central-Southern Italian population through 30 thousands years. Proceedings of the PRIN 2010-2011 meeting held at Villa Mondragone, Monte Porzio Catone, Roma. p. 153-170.

Whitehouse, R.D. (1992) – Underground religion: cult and culture in prehistoric Italy. London: Accordia Research Centre, 216 p.

Bioarchaeological approach to the Late Neolithic and Chalcolithic population of Cameros megalithic group (La Rioja, Spain)

Teresa Fernández-Crespo[1,2]

[1] Departamento de Genética, Antropología Física y Fisiología Animal,
Universidad del País Vasco (UPV/EHU). 48940 Leioa. Spain
teresa.fernandezc@ehu.es
[2] Research Laboratory for Archaeology and the History of Art, University of Oxford.
South Parks Road. OX1 3QY Oxford. United Kingdom
teresa.fernandez-crespo@rlaha.ox.ac.uk

Abstract

The main aim of this paper is to look into the people buried and the funerary practices performed in the Late Neolithic and Chalcolithic megalithic graves of Cameros (La Rioja, northern Spain). To this end, four collections comprising a minimum of 92 individuals (Peña Guerra II, Collado del Mallo, Fuente Morena and Collado Palomero I) are studied.

Anthropological analyses reveal some demographic anomalies in age and sex distribution, a gracile constitution and medium stature, and a high incidence of arthrosic and degenerative signs.

The study of bone representation and manipulation shows the preeminence of primary burials but also a probable less frequent introduction of secondary assemblages into some monuments.

Keywords

Anthropological characterization, funerary practices, Cameros megalithic graves, northern Spain, Late Neolithic – Chalcolithic

Résumé

Le but de ce travail est de caractériser les gents enterrées et les pratiques funéraires utilisées dans les tombes mégalithiques de Cameros (La Rioja, Espagne) pendant le Néolithique Finale et le Chalcolithique (3500-1500 cal. BP). Quatre collections ostéologiques représentant un ensemble minimum de 92 sujets (Peña Guerra II, Collado del Mallo, Fuente Morena and Collado Palomero I) ont été choisies pour l'approche.

L'analyse anthropologique montre des anomalies démographiques dans la distribution á partir de l'âge et du sexe des individus, aussi bien qu'une complexion gracile et une stature moyenne et, finalement, la fréquence élevée des signes arthrosiques et dégénératifs.

L'étude de la représentativité et des différentes traitements des os indique une prédominance des enterrements primaires mais, en même temps, une probable introduction plus ponctuelle d'ensembles secondaires dans quelques tombes.

Mots-clés

Characterization anthropologique, pratiques funéraires, tombes mégalithiques de Cameros, Espagne du Nord, Néolithique Final – Chalcolithique

Introduction

Cameros region (Middle Ebro valley, north-central Spain) is known for preserving a rich archaeological record of Late Neolithic and Chalcolithic burial sites, particularly monuments. In the past twenty years, a dozen tombs were identified, the majority of them being excavated. Until recently, research on these sites mainly focused on chrono-cultural assessments, the architecture of monuments and the grave goods recovered from them, meaning that much less attention was paid to human remains, despite constituting the greatest part of the record available and being the most direct evidence of people from that period (López de Calle, 1993; Narvarte, 2005).

Against this background, a brief overview of the anthropological characterization of Cameros Final Neolithic and Chalcolithic communities and the funerary practices performed in their burial places is presented in this paper for the first time.

Context

The megalithic phenomenon in Cameros points out to a possible Portuguese and, more concretely, Spanish North Plateau origin, which may be evidence of a process of colonization and demographic input (Andrés, 2009: 19). After a peak of construction and use in the Late Neolithic, signs of interruption are detected in the beginning of the Chalcolithic in some megaliths, perhaps suggesting a movement of people or a change in the rituals. In the Late Chalcolithic, when funerary use of megalithic graves seems to decline, a relatively common phenomenon of Bell Beaker reuse is documented in some previously abandoned or sealed tombs (Andrés, 2005), as in other European areas.

With regard to the location, the graves are situated in a mountainous area (950-1240 masl), usually sharing a preference for hills related to high visibility, pathway control and close proximity to water streams (Figure 1). The finding of diverse archeological evidence (e.g. pottery, human bones) preceding the construction of some monuments also suggests the intentional selection of places that were traditionally frequented (López de Calle and Tudanca, 2005: 33-34).

Concerning the structure, Cameros group presents an important polymorphism. Simple tombs – Fuente Morena, Collado Palomero II –, passage tombs – Collado del Mallo, Peña Guerra I and Uñón –, double-chambered dolmens – Peña Guerra II –, dolmens with vestibule – Collado Palomero I –, as well as other non-monumental graves – La Hoyuela, Barranco de la Cadena I and II, Portillo de Los Ladrones, Peña Guerra III –, can be found in the area (Pérez Arrondo, 1983).

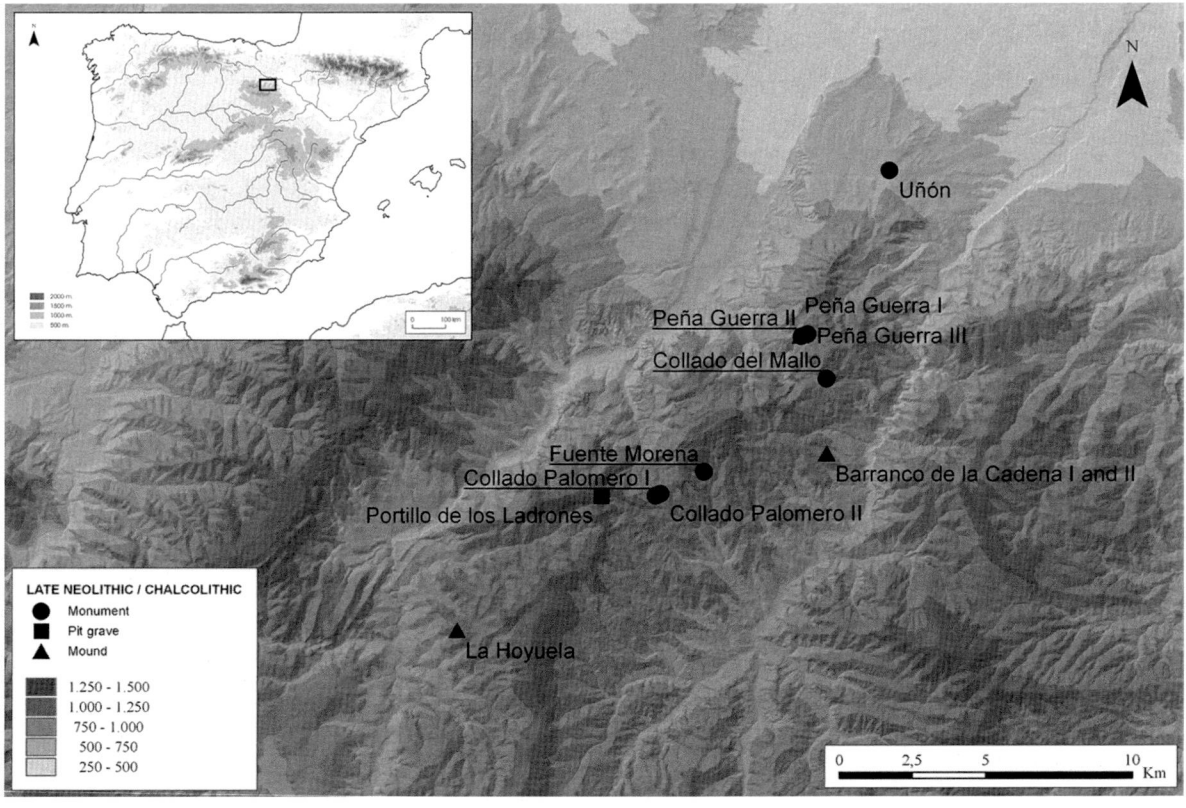

FIGURE 1. MAP OF CAMEROS REGION REVEALING THE LOCATION OF LATE NEOLITHIC AND CHALCOLITHIC BURIAL SITES. THE FOUR GRAVES UNDER STUDY ARE HIGHLIGHTED.

FIGURE 2. IMAGE SHOWING THE COMMON FRAGMENTED, DISARTICULATED AND COMMINGLED STATE OF BONES WHEN FACING NOT ONLY THE EXCAVATION BUT ALSO THE ARCHEOANTHROPOLOGICAL ANALYSIS OF THE COLLECTIONS FROM CAMEROS MONUMENTS. THE EXAMPLE CORRESPONDS TO THE INFERIOR LAYER OF THE MAIN CHAMBER OF PEÑA GUERRA II (PICTURE: C. LÓPEZ DE CALLE).

Their contents are also very diverse. It is difficult to establish a standard minimum of individuals for the graves, since the number of interred can vary from less than 10 to almost 50 individuals (Fernández-Crespo, 2012). Given the calcareous terrain of the area, the tombs contained relatively well preserved skeletal remains, even though most of them were commingled, disarticulated and fragmented due to different taphonomic and diagenetic factors as well as ritual practices (Figure 2).

The megalithic graves studied

The skeletal remains analysed come from the four megalithic tombs whose record is best known and therefore currently more representative of Cameros burial sites. Their funerary use spans local Late Neolithic and Late Chalcolithic periods, approximately from 3700 to 1500 cal. BC (Figure 3).

Collado del Mallo (Trevijano, La Rioja). The site was discovered in 1988 and excavated by C. López de Calle between 1994 and 1996 (López de Calle *et al.*, 2001). Radiocarbon dates suggest a funerary use of the site from the Neolithic to the Late Chalcolithic (ca. 3660-2050 cal. BC) (López de Calle and Tudanca, 1996). Despite the chaotic state of the human remains, the site has been predominantly interpreted as a primary deposit. The anthropological study allowed the identification of a minimum of 31 individuals (Fernández-Crespo, 2012).

Peña Guerra II (Nalda, La Rioja). The site was discovered in 1979, by means of a survey project. The excavation works, carried out in 1979 and 1980 by C. Pérez-Arrondo (1986), revealed a characteristic layout consisting of two chambers. The main chamber included two different layers split by a layer of stones, dating to the Late Neolithic (ca. 3635-3100 cal. BC) and to the Bell Beaker Chalcolithic (1886-1545 cal. BC). The secondary chamber provided evidence of clearly Neolithic use (3637-3382

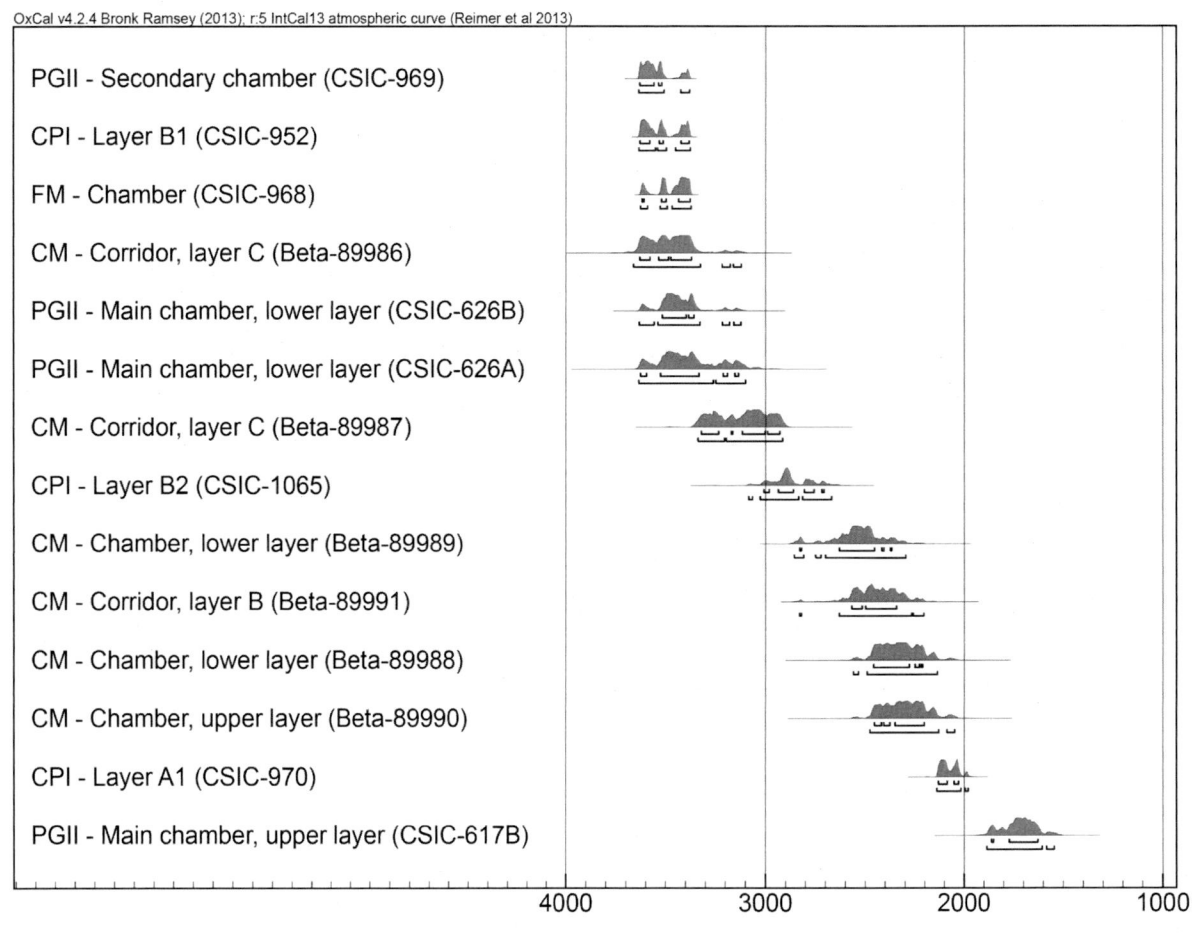

FIGURE 3. RADIOCARBON DATES FROM THE MEGALITHIC GRAVES UNDER STUDY (PÉREZ ARRONDO, 1986; LÓPEZ DE CALLE, 1993; LÓPEZ DE CALLE AND PÉREZ ARRONDO, 1995; LÓPEZ DE CALLE AND TUDANCA, 1996), CALIBRATED USING OXCAL V4.2.3.

cal. BC) (López de Calle, 1993). The grave was interpreted as a primary deposit considering the existence of some anatomical connections in all the sections. The anthropological study yielded a minimum of 41 individuals (Fernández-Crespo, 2012).

Collado Palomero I (Viguera, La Rioja). The tomb was discovered in 1981 and excavated in 1982, 1985, 1986 and 1987 by C. Pérez-Arrondo and C. López de Calle (López de Calle, 1993). The field works identified a partially previous pillaging in the chamber, but found both the corridor and the mound intact. The corridor yielded dates corresponding to two different episodes (López de Calle and Pérez-Arrondo, 1995): one assigned to the Late Neolithic/Early Chalcolithic (ca. 3635-2670 cal. BC); and the other to a Bell Beaker Chalcolithic (2139-1981 cal. BC). The anthropological analysis identified a minimum of 12 individuals (Fernández-Crespo, 2012).

Fuente Morena (Montalvo de Cameros, La Rioja). The site was discovered and excavated in 1986 in a single campaign led by C. Pérez-Arrondo (López de Calle, 1993). The burial is clearly assigned to the Late Neolithic/Early Chalcolithic according to the only radiocarbon date available (3627-3374 cal. BC). The presence of at least one partially connected skeleton could point to a possible primary deposit. The anthropological study yielded a minimum of eight individuals (Fernández-Crespo, 2012).

Methods

1) Minimum Number of Individuals

The method used to estimate the approximated population size was the Minimum Number of Individuals (MNI). It is calculated by sorting the bones by element and side and then taking the greatest number, adding to this estimation bones that do not match in age or morphology but avoiding counting the same individual twice (White and Folkens, 2005: 339).

2) Age and sex estimation

2.1) Age estimation

Classification of *non-adult individuals*. The recommendations of Ferembach *et al.* (1980) and the criteria established by Krogman and Iscan (1986) were followed to classify non-adult individuals by age groups. For non-adults under 12 years of age, dental development was the preferred criterion (Ubelaker, 1989), while the size of long bones was generally used as the secondary criterion (Brothwell, 1965; Scheuer and Black, 2000; Stloukal and Hanáková, 1978). For individuals over 12 years of age, the grade of ossification of post-cranial bones was prioritized when possible (Buikstra and Ubelaker, 1994).

Classification of *adult individuals*. Once again, the recommendations of Ferembach *et al.* (1980) were used to classify adult individuals. Unfortunately, the remains recovered were in great disorder and lacked anatomical connection, which made it difficult to use a multi-factorial approach for age estimation. The methods or criteria used were: the analysis of cranial suture obliteration (Acsádi and Nemeskéri, 1970), dental wear (Brothwell, 1965), morphological changes in the pubic symphysis (Krogman and Iscan, 1986; Meindl *et al.*, 1985) and metamorphosis of the auricular surface of the ilium (Lovejoy *et al.*, 1985).

2.2) Sex estimation

Given the difficulties involved in estimating sex in skeletally immature individuals and the lack of consensus regarding the methodology that should be applied, sexual diagnosis for infants and children was not undertaken. For adolescents and adults, sex estimation mainly focused on coxal bones, crania and mandibles, following W.E.A.'s international recommendations (Ferembach *et al.*, 1980) and Buikstra and Ubelaker's '*Standards for data collection from human skeletal remains*' (Buikstra and Ubelaker, 1994).

3) Paleodemography

An abridged life table, combined for both sexes, was created for each site following current methodological practice and using five-year age intervals. To solve the extensive standard error in the age estimation of some individuals, intervals were obtained using the principle of minimization of demographic anomalies or *principe de conformité* (Sellier, 1996). This method is based on the distribution of individuals who are located between age groups according to the greatest theoretical probability of belonging to a typical 'archaic' mortality regime (Ledermann, 1969: 138-155). The values of some non-adult mortality rates ($4q1$; $1q5$; $5q10$; $5q15$; $15q0$) and some population indices ($D5-9/D10-14$ and $D15-14/D20-x$) were used in non-adult distribution, whereas cubic interpolation after the model life table whose entry corresponds to the mortality rate previous to 15 years ($15q0$) was used in adult distribution (Fernández-Crespo and de-la-Rúa, 2015).

With regard to the analysis of sex composition among the population, the sex ratio was the index chosen. This rate expresses the proportion of males to females within a given population and, both in the animal world and human societies, tends to be around 100%, expressing a number of males similar to the number of females (Ledermann, 1969).

4) Morphology

Metrical data were recorded in adult bones and indices generated following Buikstra and Ubelaker (1994) and Brothwell (1965), when preservation allowed it. Stature was estimated based on the maximum lengths of adult long bones after the formulae of Trotter and Gleser (1958) for white males and females.

5) Paleopathology

Macroscopic examination of bones was the approach used for deepen the pathological condition of people interred in the monuments of Cameros (Aufderheide and Rodríguez-Martin, 1998).

6) Funerary practices

Some protocols based on the combination of both lab techniques (e.g. osteological profiles, bone refitting, record of taphonomic alterations) and the examination of the archaeological data (anatomical connection, bone selection and handling), were used to reconstruct the funerary practices once performed within the monuments (Duday *et al.*, 1990; Chambon, 2003).

Some demographic insights into Late Neolithic and Chalcolithic Cameros population

Anthropological analyses of the four collections led to identify a total sample of a minimum of 92 individuals, all the age classes and both sexes being represented among them (Tables 1 and 2). Although further inter-site and even diachronic intra-site approaches regarding the demographic composition of people interred can be done despite the low number of individuals identified in some layers or graves, as shown in a recent work (Fernández-Crespo and de-la-Rúa, 2015), both the combination of age data into a single life table and of sex data also are useful to achieve an overall paleodemographic profile of Cameros population.

1) Composition by age

The combined life table reveals some clear biases even after using the aforementioned *principe de conformité* (Sellier, 1996), (Table 3).

With regard to the mortality of infants, whether at group $1q0$ or $5q0$, Cameros population shows rates that are extraordinarily low as well as inconsistent with an 'archaic' mortality regime ($1q0 = 21.74$ and $4q1 = 77.78$). Thus, in the first case ($1q0$), with a 95% confidence interval, the values for Ledermann's model life tables (1969) should be placed between 460‰ (superior limit of $e°(0) = 25$) and 188‰ (inferior limit of $e°(0) = 30$). In the second case, ($5q0$), values should be placed between 789‰ and 345‰, respectively (Figure 4). This scarcity of infants under five years of age also explains the high life expectancy at birth ($e°(0) = 42.67$ años) provided by the table.

However, beyond the intervals of 0-1 and 1-4 years, the tendency is reversed and a regular over-representation of non-adult groups over five years of age becomes evident ($5q5 = 132.54$; $5q10 = 97.23$ and $5q15 = 92.31$). According to Ledermann (1969: 52), confidence intervals for $5q5$ range between 124‰ (superior limit of $e°(0) = 25$) and 38‰ (inferior limit of $e°(0) = 30$), for $5q10$ between 68‰ and 23‰ and for $5q15$ between 97‰ and 30‰.

Finally, adults are the leading age group in percentage terms (64%), but they also are under-represented when compared to model life tables. With regard to the internal sorting of adults, the lack of precision in age estimation prevents any reliable demographic information. But when considering the estimation previous to the implementation of the *principe de conformité*, young adults (56%) seem to dominate the sites, while mature individuals (29%) and especially senile adults (14%) have very low rates. However, the noticeable percentage of undetermined subjects (14%) must be taken

Cameros graves: distribution by age										
Site	Context/layer		Age group							Total
			Infant I (0-6)	Infant II (7-12)	Adolescent (13-19)	Young adult (20-39)	Mature adult (40-59)	Senile adult (>60)	Indet. adult (>20)	Layer	Site
Collado del Mallo	General		5	5	2	7	5	–	7	31	31
Peña Guerra II	Main chamber	Lower l.	1	1	1	4	4	1	–	12	
		Upper l.	–	1	–	2	–	–	–	3	41
	Secondary chamber		4	4	2	8	8	–	–	26	
Collado Palomero I	Vestibule	Layer A1	1	1	1	–	–	6	–	9	
		Layer B2	–	1	–	1	–	–	–	2	12
		Layer B1	–	–	–	–	–	1	–	1	
Fuente Morena	General		–	1	2	4	–	–	1	8	8
Total			11	14	8	26	17	8	8	92	

TABLE 1. DISTRIBUTION BY AGE OF THE INDIVIDUALS RECOVERED FROM THE CAMEROS MORTUARY SITES UNDER STUDY.

Cameros graves: distribution by sex of adolescent and adult individuals								
Site	Cotext/layer		Sex estimation				Total	
			Male	Female	Ambiguous	Indet.	Layer	Site
Collado del Mallo	General		10	5	–	5	20	20
Peña Guerra II	Main chamber	Lower l.	5	3	–	1	9	
		Upper l.	–	1	–	1	2	29
	Secondary chamber		6	7	2	3	18	
Collado Palomero I	Vestibule	Layer A1	–	–	–	7	7	
		Layer B2	–	–	–	1	1	9
		Layer B1	–	1	–	–	1	
Fuente Morena	General		3	1	–	3	7	7
Total			24	18	2	21	65	

TABLE 2. DISTRIBUTION BY SEX OF ADOLESCENT AND ADULT INDIVIDUALS RECOVERED FROM THE CAMEROS MORTUARY SITES UNDER STUDY.

Cameros population: life table. Distributed after *principe de conformité* (Sellier, 1996)							
Age interval	D (x)	d (x)	l (x)	q (x)	L (x)	T (x)	e° (x)
0-1	2	21.74	1000.00	22	989.13	42670.840	42.67
1-4	7	76.09	978.26	78	3760.860	41681.710	42.61
5-9	11	119.57	902.17	132	4211.925	37920.850	42.03
10-14	7	76.09	782.60	97	3722.775	33708.925	43.07
15-19	6	65.22	706.51	92	3369.500	29986.150	42.44
20-24	2.3	25.00	641.29	39	3143.950	26616.650	41.50
25-29	2.4	26.09	616.29	42	3016.225	23472.700	38.09
30-34	2.4	26.09	590.20	44	2885.775	20456.475	34.66
35-39	2.5	27.17	564.11	48	2750.550	17570.700	31.15
40-44	2.7	29.35	536.94	55	2611.325	14820.150	27.60
45-49	3.1	33.69	507.59	66	2453.725	12208.825	24.05
50-54	3.6	39.13	473.90	82	2271.675	9755.100	20.58
55-59	4.5	48.91	434.77	112	2051.575	7483.425	17.21
60-64	5.6	60.87	385.86	169	1777.125	5431.850	14.08
65-69	6.7	72.83	324.99	224	1442.875	3654.725	11.25
70-74	7.4	80.43	252.16	319	1059.725	2211.850	8.77
75-79	6.9	75.00	171.73	437	671.150	1152.125	6.71
80-84	5.3	57.60	96.73	595	339.650	480.975	4.97
85-89	2.8	30.43	39.13	778	119.575	141.325	3.61
>90	0.8	8.70	8.70	1000	21.750	21.750	2.50
Total	92	1000.00	–	–	42670.840	–	–

TABLE 3. COMBINED LIFE TABLE FOR THE CAMEROS LATE NEOLITHIC/CHALCOLITHIC POPULATION, WHERE INDIVIDUALS LOCATED BETWEEN SEVERAL AGE GROUPS ARE DISTRIBUTED ACCORDING TO P. SELLIER'S *PRINCIPE DE CONFORMITÉ* (SELLIER, 1996).

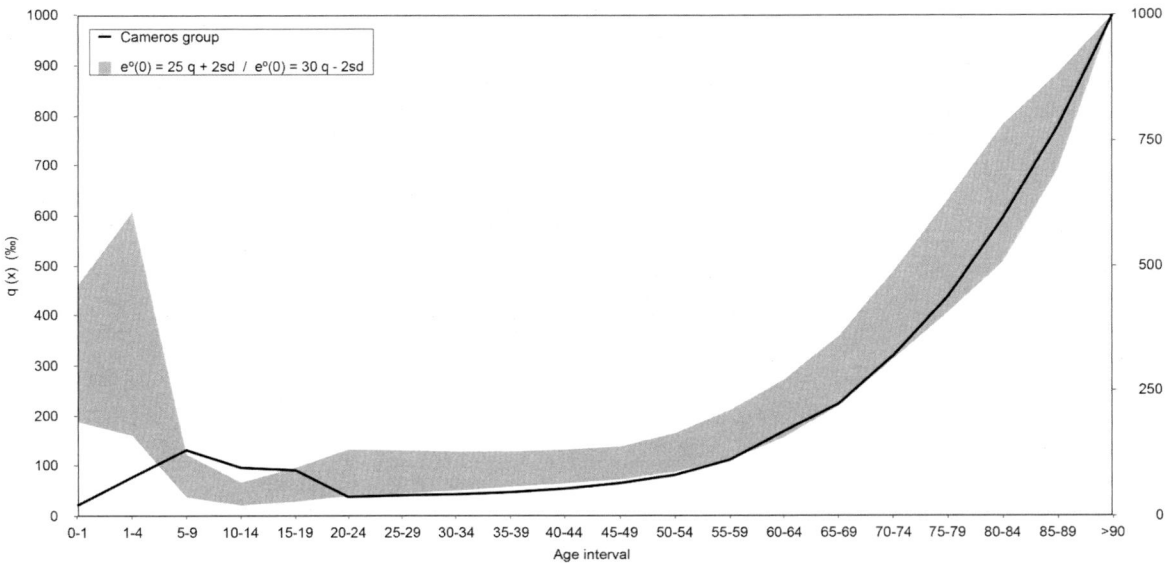

FIGURE 4. SHAPE OF MORTALITY RATES [Q(X)] FROM CAMEROS MEGALITHIC GRAVES COMPARED WITH 95% CONFIDENCE INTERVAL OF THE SUPERIOR LIMIT OF $e°(0) = 25$ AND THE INFERIOR LIMIT OF $e°(0) = 30$ FROM S. LEDERMANN'S MODEL LIFE TABLES (LEDERMANN, 1969).

into account, for they could belong to these older adult groups, as suggested through the distribution according to the aforementioned principle.

In summary, despite the percentage predominance of adults, the presence of non-adults between five and 19 years is noteworthy. It could be due both to a greater social recognition of these non-adults, to certain factors linked to their way of life (risky work activities, poor diet) or, more probably, to a reverse effect of the lack of adults. By contrast, the general exclusion of infants under five is clear and may be connected to the existence of unknown funerary treatments reserved to them outside the common funerary space (since poor preservation and/or the lack of the exhaustiveness of the excavations and their protocols for conservation are not applicable, at least in absolute terms, to these contexts), as might also be the case for the considerable number of adults that seems to be missing in the graves (Fernández-Crespo and de-la-Rúa, 2015).

2) Composition by sex

The combined distribution of adolescent and adult individuals by sex also provides traces of possible demographic irregularities, for it shows a predominance of male subjects in the megaliths (24 males, 18 females and 23 subjects of unknown sex), being the global sex ratio 133.33%. However, any cultural explanation of sex imbalances in favor of males, despite being a repeated trend in other northern Spanish coeval monuments (Delibes, 1995; Rojo, 2014), should be taken very carefully since no statistical significance is found (Fernández-Crespo and de-la-Rúa, 2015) and other possibilities, such as the existence of either a bias in the method of sex estimation -mainly adapted to the recognition of male individuals- or of bio-cultural imbalances (e.g. infanticide or poligamy) among the population, need to be further explored.

General aspects on morphological characterization

Metrical data recorded in adult bones provide some general traits on the body constitution of people interred in Cameros graves. Thus, the length of the few long elements that could be measured (due to the high fragmentation of bones) tends to be short to medium and the minimum perimeters are generally are medium, which provides weak or moderate robusticity indices.

According to the main indices, femora show platymeria, this is, a considerable anterior-posterior flatenning (X = 75.24, n = 26), whereas tibiae show mesocnemia or moderate flattening (X = 62.28, n = 17) (Fernández-Crespo, 2012). These features generally comply with those from other coeval and even contemporary societies. Nevertheless, flattening on the lower limb is interesting because it is sometimes linked to several factors, such as an adaptation of the bones to support body weight, frequent kneeling positions, musculoskeletal stress (especially on femora) at early chilhood or even a deficit of calcium and vitamins in diet (López Martínez, 2002: 100); and because it can also be evidence of a moment prior to the full establishment of sedentism, which is usually considered to be the reason for a morphological change involving progressive decrease in the flattening of femora and tibiae (Silva, 2003: 59; Boaventura *et al.*, 2014).

Finally and with regard to the stature, values obtained for the maximum length of long bones are consistent with a medium tending towards upper-medium height for males, with an average of 166 cm (n = 6), and a medium height for females, with an average of 154 cm (n = 5).

Health and disease among Cameros people

Cameros skeletal remains provide some clear pathological signs that are the closest evidence of local people's health status and their exposure to disease. In this case arthropathies are the most common lesion, especially those located in lumbar vertebrae, which may be linked to repetitive activities implying some overstrain when flexing both the back and the upper limbs, like climbing or lifting, holding and carrying heavy loads (Rihuete, 2003: 449). Among them, two cases of spondyloarthritis (or vertebral fusion) identified at Peña Guerra II must be mentioned (Figure 5).

Besides vertebral arthrosis, similar bone changes are detected on other articular segments. Those located on shoulders (especially on scapular glenoid cavities), knees (particularly on patellae), hands and feet are noteworthy. On the contrary, such evidence is much less frequent on elbows (with some cases on the proximal epiphysis of ulnae and radii), wrists, hip joints (exostosis on both the acetabulum and pubic symphysis) and ankles.

Tendon and ligamentous ossification is also a common pathology in the collections analysed. Thus, it is noteworthy its high incidence in the lower limb, namely in the links between quadriceps muscle and patellae (17%, n = 36) and between the Achilles tendon and calcanei (27%, n = 44), which may also be a result of traveling through rough terrains. In the superior limb, the largest evidence is detected in the insertion of the brachial biceps muscle on the right radius (4%, n = 28), as expected for mostly right-handed populations. Brachial biceps is responsible for flexing the forearm over the arm, a movement that would be involved in activities like heavy weight transport or the use of bow (Jiménez-Brobeil *et al.*, 2004: 144).

With regard to oral diseases, their presence seems to be moderate, despite

FIGURE 5. EVIDENCE OF SPONDYLOARTHRITIS OR VERTEBRAL FUSION FROM PEÑA GUERRA II.

the low percentage of tooth decay (less than 1%) and the scarcity of plaque and dental abscess. Thus, considerable signs of periodontitis, affecting 19 adult maxillae from a total sample of 59, can be identified; whereas *ante mortem* tooth loss is observed in 2.5% of tooth alveoli (and in 17 of 59 maxillae).

Finally, the existence of other signs of disease is much less usual, as it is in other contemporary Iberian anthropological series. Among them, two cases of bone periostitis on a tibia and a humerus from Collado del Mallo can be mentioned. Moreover, an unpublished reference to a case of congenital dislocation on a hip joint and a possible intra-spinal osteochondroma in a cervical vertebra have recently been reported for Peña Guerra II (J. Martínez Flórez, pers. comm.). Surprisingly, traumas have not been recorded so far, despite the fact that they are common findings in nearby areas, even those related with violence (Fernández-Crespo, 2017).

On burial practices and ritual

Despite the commingled and fragmented nature of the osteological collections, the analysis of bone representation has been able to determine the mainly primary nature of the deposits (Fernández-Crespo, 2015). These are characterized by the presence of scarce but significant grave goods (bone carved idol-palettes in the initial phases of use and Bell Beaker pottery in the latest) and are sometimes covered in ochre, which physical-chemical analysis mainly defines as iron oxide (e.g. goethite in Peña Guerra II). At the same time, some specific practices for managing the funerary space have been revealed, such as the treatment and positioning of some elements (e.g. nests of skulls and bundles of long bones by the orthostates in Peña Guerra II and Collado del Mallo) (Figure 6), which would explain the frequent unconnected state of the skeletons and so prevent any inference on the original arrangement of bodies.

FIGURE 6. PICTURE SHOWING THE POSITIONING OF A GROUP OF SKULLS BY THE ORTHOSTATES OF THE SECONDARY CHAMBER OF PEÑA GUERRA II (PICTURE: C. LÓPEZ DE CALLE).

Secondary deposits and removal of bones may exist too but, considering both archaeological and anthropological data, it seems that these practices would not have been the rule in the graves analyzed. Although evidence of them is difficult to distinguish, this might be the case of the isolated introduction of a few cremated human remains with no associated sedimentological evidence of fire in some sites (Collado del Mallo, Collado Palomero I) (López de Calle, 1993).

With regard to the nature of the people interred, the existence of demographic biases which are inconsistent with an 'archaic' mortality regime has already been mentioned, namely the lack of adults and especially of infants and the probable male predominance in the series. In this respect, it would not be reasonable to explain an oft-repeated and common phenomenon, the imbalance among age and sex that also show the megaliths from the nearby Rioja Alavesa region (Fernández-Crespo, 2012) or the Spanish North Plateau (Delibes, 1995), in terms of a 'demographic accident' (Chambon, 2003: 228-229). That is why an intentional selection of the deceased, at least by age criteria, appears to be more convincing (Fernández-Crespo and de-la-Rúa, 2015).

Concluding remarks

Despite the fragmentation and lack of connection in human remains, relevant results can still be obtained on the Cameros megalithic population and funerary behaviors. The demographic anomalies detected prevent from considering the group of people interred in the monuments as a typical natural population. It seems that some access restrictions regarding age and sex may have ruled, especially to adolescent and adult males. This fact could be suggesting the existence of some conditions for depositing bodies into the graves, perhaps connected to status.

The few morphological data available show a gracile constitution and medium stature, whereas pathological signs are common among human groups whose lifeway is closely linked to farming activity and a rough environment.

With regard to the burial practices, primary deposits seem to be the rule according to bone representation. However, the identification of many other funerary treatments (bone rearrangement, ochre, some secondary deposits and cremations) suggests the existence of a complex ritual within Cameros graves.

Acknowledgements

I am indebted to Profs Ignacio Barandiarán and Concepción de la Rúa (University of the Basque Country) for their orientation as co-heads of the Doctoral Dissertation from which the present article is derived. I would also like to thank Dr Carlos López de Calle for the unpublished data. Finally, HUM2005-04236 and HAR2011-26956 (Spanish Ministry of Science and Education) and POS_2013_1_147 (Basque Government) research projects provided the funding for this work.

References

Acsádi, G.; Nemeskéri, J. (1970) – History of human life span and mortality. Budapest: Akadémiai Kiadó.

Andrés, M.T. (2005) – Concepto y análisis del cambio cultural: su percepción en la materia funeraria del Neolítico y Eneolítico. Monografías Arqueológicas 42. Zaragoza: Universidad de Zaragoza.

Andrés, M.T. (2009) – Comportamiento funerario en el Neolítico y Eneolítico: sociedad e ideología. In Santos, J., coor.- Los tiempos antiguos en los territorios pirenaicos. Vitoria-Gasteiz: Anejos de Veleia, p. 11-36 (Series Acta; 8).

Aufderheide, A.C.; Rodríguez-Martin, C. (1998) – The Cambridge encyclopedia of human paleopathology. Cambridge: Cambridge University Press.

Boaventura, R.; Ferreira, M.T.; Neves, M.J.; Silva, A.M. (2014) – Funerary practices and Anthropology during Middle-Late Neolithic (4th and 3rd millenia BCE) in Portugal: Old bones, new insights. Antropologie. LII/2, p. 183-205.

Brothwell, D.R. (1965) – Digging up bones. The excavation, treatment and study of human skeletal remains. Ithaca: Cornell University Press.

Buikstra, J.E.; Ubelaker D.H. (1994) – Standards for data collection from human skeletal remains, Proceedings of a seminar at the Field Museum of Natural History, organized by J. Haas. Fayetteville: Arkansas Archaeological Survey Press (Arkansas Archaeological Survey Research Series; 44).

Chambon, Ph. (2003) – Les morts dans les sépultures collectives néolithiques en France. Du cadavre aux restes ultimes. Paris: CNRS éditions (Supplément à Gallia Préhistoire; XXXV).

Delibes, G. (1995) – Ritos funerarios, demografía y estructura social entre las comunidades neolíticas de la submeseta norte. In Fábregas, R.; Pérez, F.; Fernández, C., eds.- Arqueoloxía da Morte na Península Ibérica desde as Orixes ata o Medievo. Xinzo de Limia: Concello de Xinzo de Limia, p. 61-94.

Duday, H.; Courtaud, P.; Crubezy, E.; Sellier, P.; Tillier, A.M. (1990) – L'Anthropologie de «terrain»: reconnaissance et interprétation des gestes funéraires. Paris: Bulletins et Mémoires de la Société d'Anthropologie de Paris. 2, p. 29-50.

Ferembach, D.; Schwidetzky, I.; Stloukal, M. (1980) – Recommendations for age and sex diagnosis of skeletons. Journal of Human Evolution. 9, p. 517-549.

Fernández-Crespo, T. (2012) – Antropología y prácticas funerarias en las poblaciones neolíticas finales y calcolíticas de la región natural de La Rioja (Unpublished PhD thesis). Vitoria-Gasteiz: Universidad del País Vasco.

Fernández-Crespo, T. (2015) – Aportación de la Arqueoantropología a la interpretación de la dinámica sepulcral de las tumbas megalíticas de Cameros (La Rioja, España). Trabajos de Prehistoria 72(2): 218-237.

Fernández-Crespo, T. (2017) – New evidence of Early Chalcolithic interpersonal violence in the Middle Ebro valley (Spain): two arrowhead injuries from the swallet of Las Yurdinas II. International Journal of Osteoarchaeology, 27:76-85. DOI:10.1002/oa.2445.

Fernández-Crespo, T.; De-La-Rúa, C. (2015) – Demographic evidence of selective burial in megalithic graves of northern Spain. Journal of Archaeological Science. 53, p. 604-617.

Jiménez-Brobeil, S.A.; Al Oumaoui, I.; Esquivel, J.A. (2004) – Actividad física según sexo en la cultura argárica. Una aproximación desde los restos humanos. Trabajos de Prehistoria. 61:2, p. 141-153.

Krogman, W.M.; Iscan, M.Y. (1986) – The Human Skeleton in Forensic Medicine. Springfield: CC Thomas.

Ledermann, S. (1969) – Nouvelles tables-types de mortalité. Paris: Presses Universitaires de France (Institut National d'Études Démographiques, Travaux et Documents; 53).

López de Calle, C. (1993) – Los sepulcros megalíticos de Cameros (La Rioja) (Unpublished PhD thesis). Zaragoza: Universidad de Zaragoza.

López de Calle, C. (1994) – Caracteres arquitectónicos y restos materiales del sepulcro megalítico de Collado del Mallo (Trevijano). Campaña de 1994. Estrato. 6, p. 9-15.

López de Calle, C.; Iriarte, M.J.; Zapata, L. (2001) – Análisis paleoambientales del dolmen de Collado del Mallo (Trevijano, La Rioja). Viabilidad y trabas de la paleoecología vegetal en estructuras dolménicas. Zubía Monográfico. 13, p. 65-96.

López de Calle, C.: Pérez-Arrondo, C.L. (1995) – Fechas de radiocabono y fases de ocupación en los sepulcros megalíticos de Cameros (La Rioja). Isturitz: Cuadernos de Sección. Prehistoria y Arqueología. 6, p. 343-360.

López de Calle, C.; Tudanca, J.M. (1996) – Excavaciones en el sepulcro megalítico de Collado del Mallo. Campaña de 1995. Informe preliminar. Estrato. 7, p. 14-24.

López de Calle, C.; Tudanca, J.M. (2005) – El Megalitismo. In Moya, J.G.; Arrúe, B., coors.,- Historia del Arte en La Rioja: de la Prehistoria a la Antigüedad Tardía. Logroño: Fundación Caja Rioja, p. 27-44.

López Martínez, B. (2002) – Los pobladores del antiguo Reino de León: Antropometría, Paleodemografía y Palepatología. León: Secretariado de publicaciones y medios audiovisuales de la Universidad de León.

Lovejoy, C.O.; Meindl, R.S.; Pryzbeck, T.R.; Mensforth, R.P. (1985) – Chronological metamorphosis of the auricular surface of the ilium. A new method for the determination of adult skeletal age at death. American Journal of Physical Anthropology. 68:1, p. 15-28.

Meindl, R.S.; Lovejoy, C.O.; Mensforth, R.P.; Walker, R.A. (1985) – A revised method of age determination using the os pubis, with a review and test of accuracy of other methods of pubic symphyseal aging. American Journal of Physical Anthropology. 68:1, p. 29-45.

Narvarte, N. (2005) – Gestión funeraria dolménica en la Cuenca Alta y Media del Ebro: Fases de ocupación y clausuras. Logroño: Instituto de Estudios Riojanos (Historia-Arqueología; 16).

Pérez-Arrondo, C. (1983) – La cultura megalítica en la margen derecha del Ebro. Cuadernos de Investigación: Historia. 13:1, p. 51-63.

Pérez-Arrondo, C.L. (1986): Algunos datos para el estudio de la Edad de los Metales en el valle del Ebro Medio. In Estudios en homenaje al Dr. Antonio Beltrán Martínez. Zaragoza: Universidad de Zaragoza, p. 267-283.

Rihuete, C. (2003) – 'Esqueletos humanos en la investigación arqueológica de la diferencia sexual'. In Molas, M.; Guerra, S., coor.,- Morir en femenino: mujeres, ideología y prácticas funerarias desde la Prehistoria hasta la Edad Media. Barcelona: Universidad de Barcelona, p. 17-50 (Breviaris; 7).

Rojo, M.A. (2014) – El Neolítico en las tierras del interior y septentrionales. In Almagro-Gorbea, M., ed.- Protohistoria de la Península Iberica: del Neolítico a la Romanizacion. Burgos: Universidad de Burgos and Fundación Atapuerca, p. 43-70.

Scheuer, L.; Black, S. (2000) – Developmental juvenile osteology. San Diego: Academic Press.

Sellier, P. (1996) – La mise en évidence d'anomalies démographiques et leur interprétation: population, recrutement et pratiques funéraires du tumulus de Courtesoult. In Piningre, J.F., ed.- Nécropoles et sociétéau premier Âge du Fer: le tumulus de Courtesoult (Haute-Saône). Paris: Maison des Sciences de l'Homme, p. 188-202.

Silva, A.M. (2003) – Portuguese populations of Late Neolithic and Chalcolithic periods exhumed from collective burials: an overview. Anthropologie. XLI:1-2, p. 55-64.

Stloukal, M.; Hanáková, H (1978) – Die Länge der Längsknochen altslawischer Bevölkerungen, unter besonderer Berücksichtigung von Wachstumsfragen. Homo. 29, p. 53-69.

Trotter, M.; Gleser, G. (1958) – A re-evaluation of estimation of stature based an measurements of stature taken during life and of long bones after death. American Journal of Physical Anthropology. 16, p. 79-123.

Ubelaker, D.H. (1989) – Human skeletal remains: Excavation, analysis, interpretation. Washington: Washington Taraxacum.

White, T.D.; Folkens, P.A. (2005) – The Human Bone Manual. San Diego: Academic Press.

Anthropological and taphonomical study of human remains from the burial cave of El Espinoso (Ribadedeva, Asturias, Spain)

Borja González Rabanal[1], Manuel Ramón González Morales[1] and Ana Belén Marín Arroyo[1]

[1] Instituto Internacional de Investigaciones Prehistóricas de Cantabria
Universidad de Cantabria
borjagrabanal@gmail.com

Abstract

During the Bronze Age in the Cantabrian region (northern Spain) the human groups buried their dead in the surface of narrow caves. This work focuses, for the first time, in the archaeological, anthropological and taphonomical study of the unpublished human remains found in 1993 in El Espinoso Cave, located in Ribadedeva (Asturias). The site constitutes the only collective burial known from the Bronze Age in Asturias. The taphonomical results show the high fragmentation of the remains due to concretions and water activities and a difference between high and low-density bones representation. Additionally, short bones (patella, calcaneus and talus) were used for the sex and stature determination by applying a new methodological approach.

Keywords

El Espinoso cave, burial cave, Bronze Age, Cantabrian Region, taphonomy

Résumé

Durant l'Âge du Bronze, à la région cantabrique (Nord de l'Espagne) les groupes humaines enterraient leurs défunts dans la surface des grottes étroites. Ce travail traite pour première fois des études archéologiques, anthropologiques et taphonomiques des restes humaines trouvés en 1993 à la grotte d'El Espinoso, à Ribadedeva (Asturies). Ce site constitue la seule tombe de caractère collective connue de l'Âge du Bronze des Asturies. L'analyse taphonomique indique une fragmentation élevée des restes à cause de le concrétion et la dissolution et une différence entre la représentation de haute ou basse densité osseuse. D'un autre côté, des nouvelles méthodologies sont utilisées pour la détermination du sexe et la stature des individus à partir d'os courtes comme la rotule, le calcanéum et le talus.

Mots-clés

Grotte d'El Espinoso, grotte funéraire, l'Âge du Bronze, région cantabrique, taphonomie

Introduction

During Cantabrian Late Prehistory, specifically during Chalcolithic (4300-3800 BP) and Bronze Age (3800-2650 BP), the Cantabrian human groups buried their dead on the surface of small caves (Arias Cabal, 1995; Arias Cabal and Armendáriz, 1998). However, there are sites with similar burial characteristic already during Neolithic and others even reach the Middle Ages (Noval Fonseca, 2014; Hierro Gárate and Gutiérrez Cuenca, 2012). In particular, burial caves are named to the set of small caves, sometimes-simple hollows in the limestone that give burial to a variable number of humans remains. Those sites are usually formed by small galleries, with low ceilings and difficult access. At times, they are located in limestone walls, where it is necessary to climb for accessing them, while in others the mouth of the cave is relatively reduced making difficult its access (Armendáriz and Etxeberría, 1983).

Inhumation consists, in most cases, in the simple deposition of the human bodies on the cave surface. Neither graves nor any type of perimeter structure or cover were made, as if the morphology of the cave was enough by itself (Armendáriz, 1990). In some cases, natural niches of limestone within these small 'protected' cavities are used to bury the dead.

In the Cantabrian region, more than 300 burial caves have been documented. In the Basque Country there are over 160, 180 in Cantabria and hardly a dozen in Asturias (Arias Cabal and Armendáriz, 1998). It is significantly appreciated that the core of the burial tradition in caves is consolidated in the Basque Country and Cantabria. However, once it moves westward along the Cantabrian Region, the number of burial caves decreases. It seems to be some kind of cultural barrier in the borderline between current Cantabria and Asturias provinces. Nevertheless, many of these caves have been recently placed in the Bronze Age while other sites remain unexcavated or have been excavated imprecisely in the central decades of the twentieth century. Thus, the attribution to the Bronze Age of all them is unlikely.

In Asturias, the known burial caves are El Bufón, El Cuélebre, Sulamula, Trespando, El Toral III, La Llana, Fuentenegroso and El Espinoso. All of them are located in eastern Asturias with dates between 4700-2500 BP and cultural attribution from Neolithic to Iron Age. Radiocarbon dates have only been performed in four of those sites (Table 1): El Toral III, La Llana, El Espinoso and Fuentenegroso (Arias Cabal et al., 1986; Ontañón, 2003; Barroso et al., 2007; Noval Fonseca, 2014). El Espinoso has a radiocarbon date of 2960±40 BP. Also, there are other vague and very old references of human remains findings in four Asturian caves where metallic and ceramic materials were recovered. These are Cueva Fenoyal, Cueva del Palacio, Cueva de Valdediós and El Abrigo de Valle. They are located in different areas of central Asturias. Unfortunately, the vast majority of them is unknown the exactly location of the provenance of their materials. Most of them consists simply in decontextualized and isolated findings, while other materials were lost during the fire that destroyed the University of Oviedo in 1934 (Blas Cortina, 1983).

Site	Cultural attribution	Ref. Laboratory	Date BP	Date cal. BC 1σ	Material
El Toral III	Neolithic	UGAMS-5399	4690 ± 30 BP	3460 ± 60 cal. BC	Bone
La Llana	Bronze Age	UGAMS-9083	3300 ± 25 BP	1576 ± 35 cal. BC	Bone
El Espinoso	Bronze Age	ICA-14T/0804	2960 ± 40 BP	1189 ± 66 cal. BC	Tooth
Fuentenegroso	Iron Age	BETA-166077	2550 ± 40 BP	690 ± 92 cal. BC	Bone

TABLE 1. RADIOCARBON DATES OF HUMAN REMAINS FROM BURIAL CAVES IN EASTERN ASTURIAS. CALIBRATED WITH CALCURVE: CALPAL_2007_HULU.

Furthermore, human remains were also found in other Asturian contexts. These belong to the prehistoric copper mines of El Aramo and El Milagro. These mines, dated to the Bronze Age, might have been also related to the tradition of burying the dead miners in their working place (Blas Cortina, 1996).

Therefore, two conclusions can be drawn from the phenomenon of burial caves in Asturias: there is a limited archaeological record and the available qualitative data are rather poor. The location of some human remains is unknown, while other human materials have not been studied anthropologically (only El Bufón in ancient times and Fuentenegroso recently), and above all, the number of funerary cavities at Late Prehistory is reduced compared to Cantabria and the Basque Country provinces. The existence of a possible funerary tradition in eastern Asturias during the Bronze Age is represented by the El Espinoso cave. The results of the anthropological and taphonomical analyses of the human remains are presented here. The different preservation rate between long and short bones might indicate several reuses of the cave with cleaning activities for introducing more human bodies, although the extraction of long bones and skulls for secondary burials should be discarded. Both sexes and a wide age range were identified among this sample.

Materials and Methods

1) El Espinoso Cave

El Espinoso cave is located in the center of Cantabrian Region (Northern Spain), in the east of Asturias province, 100 km east from Oviedo (Figure 1). It rises on a 20 m high limestone wall, which dominates a closed valley, near the mouth of the river Cabra, only 200 m from the present shoreline. The entrance of the cave is oriented towards SW and its access is nowadays difficult due to the slope that characterizes the karstic surroundings (González Morales, 1995).

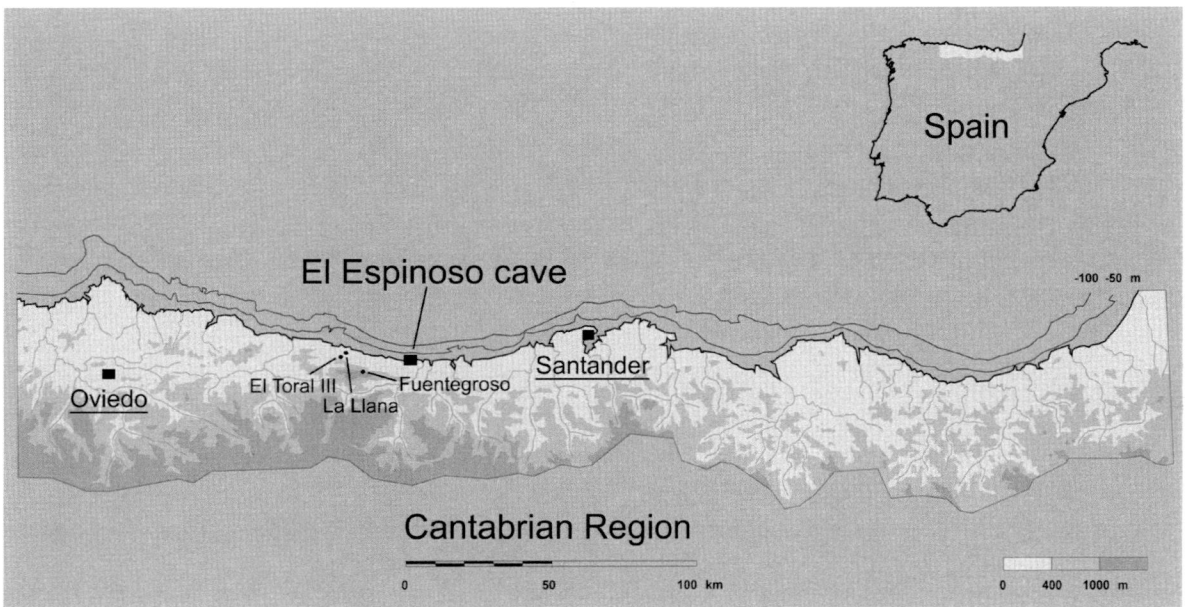

FIGURE 1. GEOGRAPHIC LOCATION OF EL ESPINOSO CAVE.

At the entrance of the cave an important archaeological site was discovered in 1978 by Manuel González Morales and his team. During 1979 and 1980 two small excavations were conducted. Field seasons provided lithic materials and some pieces of bone industry, terrestrial fauna such as red deer and ibex, and numerous *Patella vulgata* shells of large dimensions. Two radiocarbon dates were performed, which provided the dates of 17,460±50 BP and 17,310±40 BP, placing the Paleolithic site in the final stages of the Cantabrian Solutrean/early Magdalenian (Cuenca Solana, 2013). Additionally, at the end of the cavity, in a narrow and small area, abundant human remains distributed over the entire surface were documented. These human remains, discovered in the called Sala de los Muertos, are the subject of this work. In 2014 a human incisive was dated (Table 1) placing the site in the Late Bronze Age (Table 2). Therefore, Sala de los Muertos responds to a use of the cavity completely different to that of the Palaeolithic occupation found at the entrance of the cave (Figure 2).

Human remains of El Espinoso cave were found in 1979. However, it was not until 1993 when the site was excavated. The human bones were deposited on the surface of a small area of 40 m² at the end of the cave. Bones were found

Cultural attribution	Date BP	Date cal BC
Early Bronze Age	3800-3350	2200-1600
Middle Bronze Age	3350-3000	1600-1250
Late Bronze Age	3000-2650	1250-750

TABLE 2. RADIOCARBON DATES FOR DIFFERENT PHASES OF CANTABRIAN BRONZE AGE (ARIAS CABAL AND ARMENDÁRIZ, 1998).

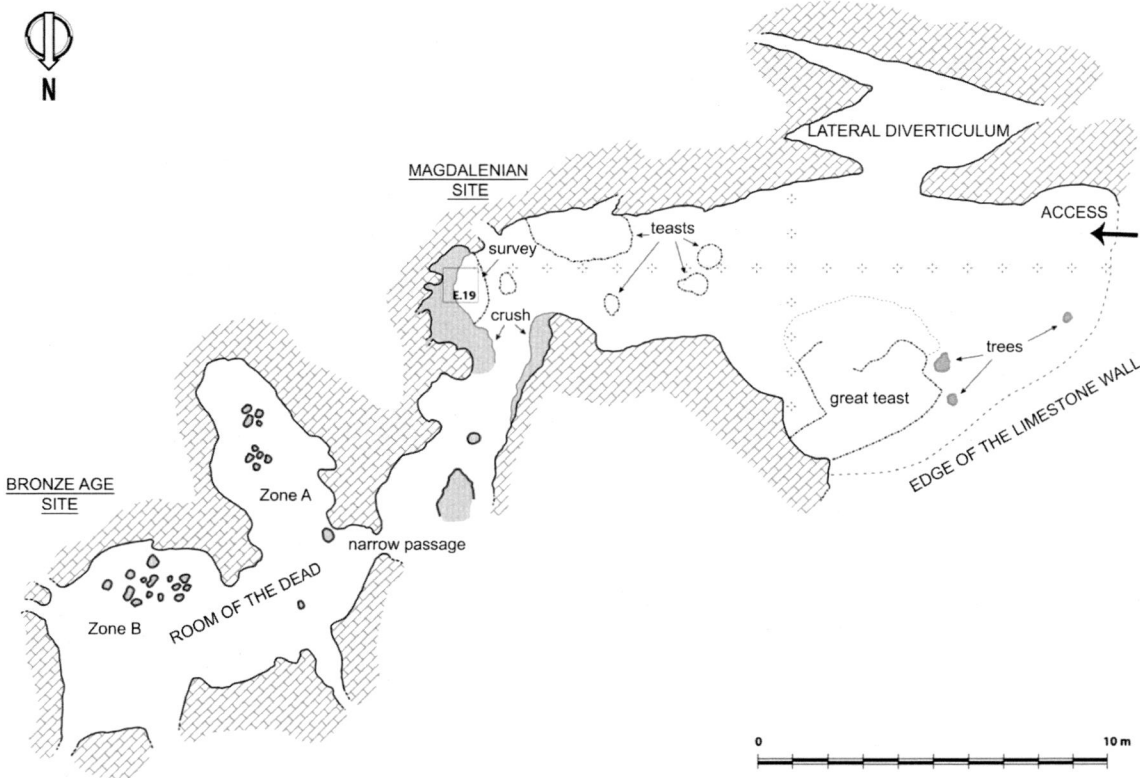

FIGURE 2. PLAN OF EL ESPINOSO CAVE.

scattered, without any apparent anatomical connection. Remains are very fragmented due to post-depositional processes. Although no grave goods were recovered during the excavation, the presence of three bronze bracelets, one ring and one pendant is known to have been discovered in the cave by plunderers. The cave was known by the local treasure seekers who did some holes within the deposit and removed some materials when they were looking for those metallic items (González Morales, 1995).

2) Methods

Firstly, an anatomical and taxonomical identification of the human remains was conducted at the Laboratory of Bioarchaeology of the Instituto Internacional de Investigaciones Prehistóricas de Cantabria (IIIPC), based at the University of Cantabria. Human bones were separated from the few faunal ones. Conservation of the remains was rather poor, so when it was possible identifiable bones were studied with the help of anatomical atlas (White and Folkens, 2005; Scheuer and Black, 2000; Schmid, 1972; Pales and García, 1981; Campillo and Subirà, 2004) and the comparative reference collection of the laboratory. Unidentifiable bones were divided into three different categories: epiphysis remains, shaft fragments and fragments of flat bones.

Secondly, several quantification indices were calculated: Number of Remains (NR), Minimum Number of Individuals (MNI) and the Minimum Number of Elements (MNE) (Lyman, 1994). In addition, to determine the degree of fragmentation and assemblage preservation, two other indices were applied: Fragmentation Rate (FR), which is obtained through the relation between NR and MNE. FR is measured around the value 1. The higher the result, the higher the fragmentation rate (Marín-Arroyo, 2010). And finally, the Index of Anatomical Preservation (IAP) was calculated to estimate representation of each bone in the total sample. It is based on the ratio between the Number Represented Bones (NRB) and Number Expected Bones (NEB) according to the Minimum Number of Individuals represented (Bello and Andrews, 2006).

The age of the individuals was estimated from the dental eruption and wear stage and long bone fusion (Campillo and Subirà, 2004; Lovejoy, 1985; Olivier, 1960). To determine the age of non-long bones such as tarsals or vertebral bones other parameters were used: bone size, density and osteometry. In this case, the reference comparative collection, including individuals of both sexes and different age ranges, was extremely helpful. The search of pathologies was performed through an ocular inspection and compared with specific atlas (Campillo, 2001) and the pathological laboratory reference samples.

Sex and stature were estimated based on the measurements taken from *tali*, *calcanei* and *patellae*, although the bone that gave more results was the *talus*. The high fragmentation rate of the long bones from El Espinoso and the poor conservation state prevented taking necessary measurements in bones such as the femur and tibia. Usually, those long bones are the most common ones used to discern the sex and stature among individuals. However, in El Espinoso the high representation of feet bones (*tali* and *calcanei*) and *patellae* bones with a better preservation allowed to determine the sex and stature. Besides, these bones have a high percentage of success (around 80%) as it is indicated in recent published studies (Introna *et al.*, 1998; Kemkes-Grottenthaler, 2005; Bidmos, 2006; Gualdi-Russo, 2007; Pablos *et al.*, 2013, 2014). These short bones have been found as an alternative to the classical measurements of long bones, in cases they are absent or highly fragmented. Nevertheless, these studies depend largely on the study population and should be used as a complement to classical analysis. Firstly, eleven measures of each *talus* was performed (T1: maximum length; T2: maximum breadth; T3: talar height; T4: trochlear length; T5: trochlear breadth; T6: trochlear height; T7: neck length; T8: length of the talus head; T9: breadth of the talus head; T10: length of the calcaneal posterior articular surface; and T11: breadth of the calcaneal posterior articular surface). Later, a Principal Components Analysis (PCA) was achieved with the data to estimate the sex of them. Moreover, two mathematical formulas (Table 3) have been made from the maximum length of *tali* to calculate the stature of individuals (Pablos *et al.*, 2013).

In addition, a taphonomic analysis was performed to analyze the different biostratinomic and diagenetic modifications identified on the skeletal remains within the deposit. These processes have been studied in El Espinoso cave, explaining its different variants and establishing different stages of affection on the bones. This allowed to extract interpretations about which processes have altered the biological remains from his death until their discovery. At the same time the weathering stages were analyzed to determine whether this was a single episode of burial or if, alternatively, El Espinoso cave was used at different phases of burial throughout the years. For this, both bioestratinomic and diagenetic agents have been analyzed. The bioestratinomic agents is composed for: carnivore activities (Binford, 1981), cut marks (Solari Giachino, 2010) burnt marks (Etxeberría, 1994) and animal trampling. And the diagenetic agents for: weathering (Behrensmeyer, 1978), dissolution, concretion, (Botella *et al.*, 1999), trampling (Olsen and Shipman, 1988) and furtive actions. Also, bone breakage has been studied in detail. Thus, the angle, profile, edge and circumference of the fractures were analyzed to ascertain whether the fractures respond to an anthropogenic activity or if they were caused by natural processes and moreover to meet the time that breakage occurred: *perimortem* or *postmortem* (Vila and Mahieu, 1991).

Sex	Formula
Males	1440.089 + 5.055 x ML
Females	1101.778 + 9.866 x ML

TABLE 3. MATHEMATICAL FORMULAS TO ESTIMATE THE STATURE OF INDIVIDUALS.

Furthermore, a spatial analysis was made with the aim of understanding the disposal of dead bodies and recognize different areas of taphonomical conservation within the site. For this, the spatial analysis consisted of squaring the plane of the cave and representing by different shades of colors the quantitative distribution of human remains and the different taphonomical stages of the dissolution and calcite concretions.

Finally, it was possible to contact with the plunderers, take a photos and take a small sample that was measured with Energy Dispersive X-ray Spectroscopy (EDS) in the Faculty of Sciences of the University of Cantabria that provided their metal composition. Unfortunately, it was impossible to return the grave goods to the museum. However, we have initiated the necessary procedures to deliver the materials in the shortest time possible.

Results

1230 human remains were identified. They belonged to a MNE of 732 and a MNI of 20 individuals (Table 4) of different ages: 2 children (0-3 years), 4 children (3-12 years), 5 subadults (12-20 years), 7 adults (20-50 years) and 2 old adults (over 50 years). The MNI was calculated based on the *tali* (MNI=17), while the teeth added three more individuals, in particular three children. To estimate the sex and stature, as it was indicated, due to the absence of long bones, short bones such as *tali*, *calcanei* and *patellae* were used for this purpose. Thus, 24 *tali* were recovered and the PCA results (Figure 3) placed in a multivariate graphic the morphological differences indicated that they might belong to 7 male individuals, 5 female, 3 children and 2 more individuals with an undetermined age and sex. Respect to the stature, *talus* gave an average height of 1.71 m for male adults and 1.60 m for females.

The age of death profile shows an attritional mortality, determining a funerary tradition and not a catastrophic phenomenon.

The taphonomical results report significant post-depositional activities within the cave although no human butchering activities, such as cut marks or anthropic breakage, were identified. Thus, 66.2% of the remains presented recent fractures, but any fresh breakage was identified (Figure 4). The high fragmentation of the bones is probably due to the concretions and water activities that affected the bone surfaces on 81.2% and 97.5% of skeletal remains, respectively. The carnivore activity was identified only in 1% of total NR (punctures: 0.3%; pits: 0.4%; and furrows: 0.3%) discarding them as cause of human bone breakage. Meanwhile, the trampling has not had great influence on the breakage of the archaeological record, as trampling marks are only present in 0.7% of the remains. However, the significant alteration of the surface of the bones due to water processes could cause loss of such traces. The exhaustive study carried out allowed to identify the different weathering stages which revealed different burial episodes. Most of remains have low weathering stages: W0 (54.4%), W1 (21.3%), W2 (19.1%), W3 (4.1%), W4 (0.9%) and W5 (0.2%). The absence of significant remains with high degrees and the presence in more than half of W0 (null weathering) shows that the cave was used for funerary practices in a relatively short

Skeletal element	NR	MNE	MNI
Skull	138	9	5
Maxillae	6	4	4
Mandible	7	6	5
Teeth	147	147	11
Hyoid	2	2	2
Cervical vt	22	22	
Thoracic vt	21	21	
Lumbar vt	8	8	
Vertebrae indet.	56		
Sacrum-coccyx	21	8	8
Os coxae	18	4	4
Ribs	42	40	
Scapula	13	13	5
Clavicle	4	4	4
Sternum	3	2	2
Humerus	37	14	13
Ulna	30	12	12
Radius	19	7	5
Carpals	37	37	8
Metacarpals	17	17	6
Hand phalanges	85	85	
Femur	39	10	10
Patella	21	21	15
Tibia	25	10	9
Fibula	10	5	4
Tarsals	42	42	11
Calcaneus	22	22	14
Talus	25	24	17
Metatarsals	42	42	11
Foot phalanges	30	29	
Phalanges indet.	65	65	
Indet.	176		
Total	1230	732	17+3

TABLE 4. SKELETAL PROFILE REPRESENTATION.

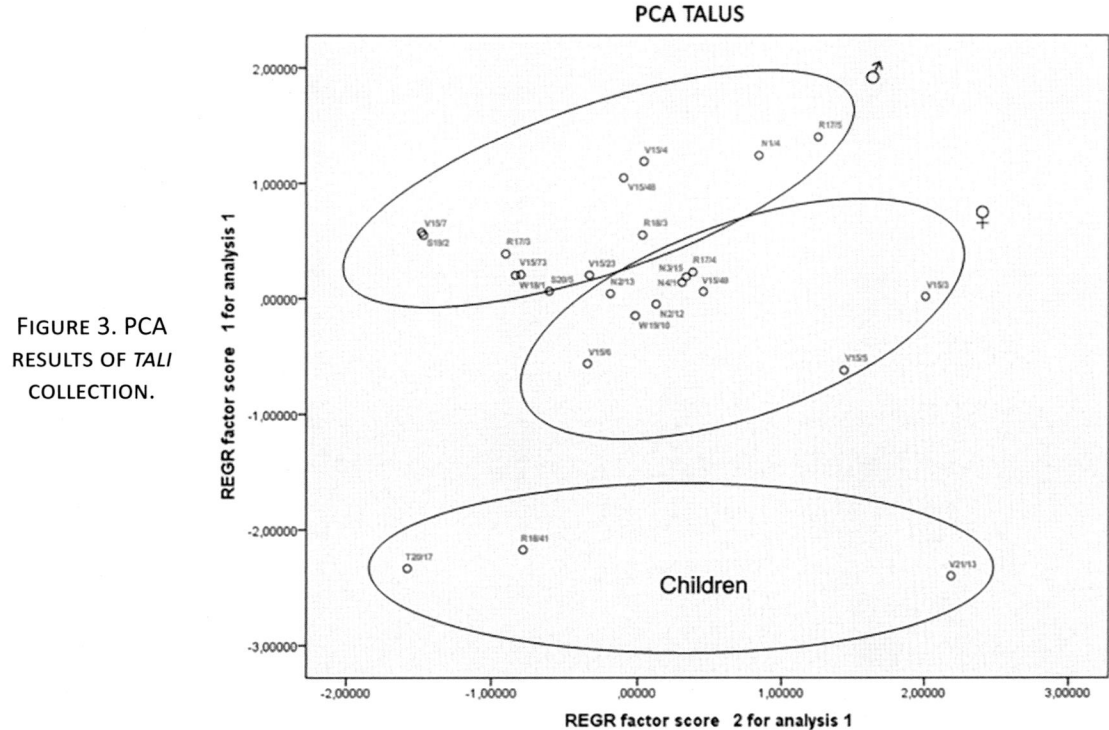

FIGURE 3. PCA RESULTS OF *TALI* COLLECTION.

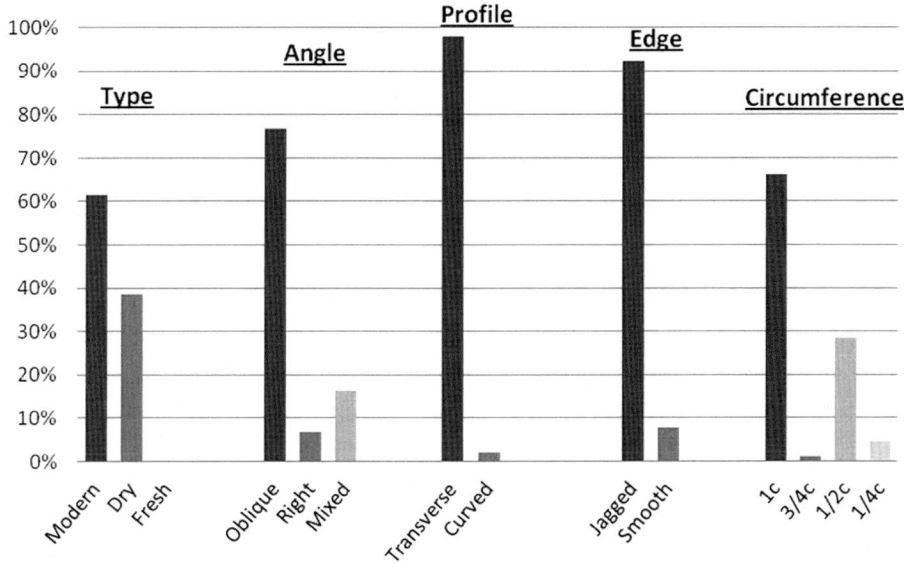

FIGURE 4. BREAKAGE OF THE LONG BONES: TYPE, ANGLE, PROFILE, EDGE AND CIRCUMFERENCE OF THE FRACTURES.

period of time (few generations at most) since there is not a sufficient heterogeneity to assert that the cave was used for a long period of time.

The IAP was 16% and the FR is 1.7. These data show the poor preservation of the assemblage and the high fragmentation of the record, respectively. In El Espinoso there is not a preponderance of bones usually found on secondary deposits (such as skull and long bones), while it is often the presence of short bones and low bone-density, such as patella, talus or calcaneum which indicates the primary character of the burials. Respect to Fragmentation Rate, skulls and long bones are the anatomical elements with higher values (3.4 for skull, 2.6 for long arm bones and 2.8 for long leg bones).

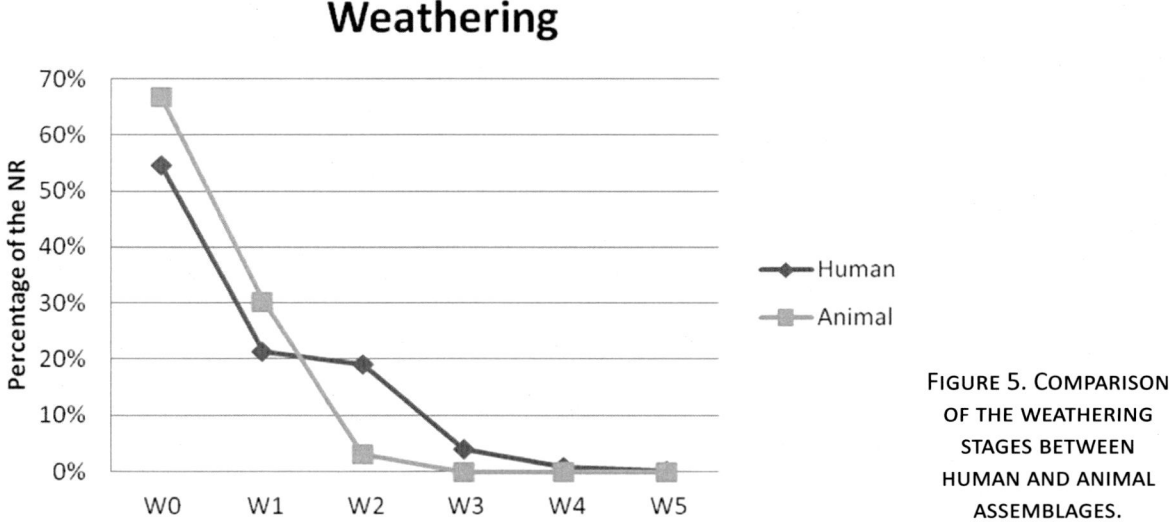

FIGURE 5. COMPARISON OF THE WEATHERING STAGES BETWEEN HUMAN AND ANIMAL ASSEMBLAGES.

Therefore, there is clearly a differential preservation within the deposit. This could be related to the extraction of the long bones and skulls outside the cave once the bodies are decomposed to carry out a secondary deposition somewhere else, leaving on the cave many of the small bones.

Burial treatment was difficult to assess. Some bones presented slight and small traces of contact with fire (2.68% of NR). However, it was difficult to assess if these alterations were contemporaneous to the burials. Moreover, within the human bone assemblages, domestic animal species were also found (NR = 33) represented by cow (NR = 13), pig (NR = 4) and ovicaprides (NR = 13), red deer were also represented with 3 bones though. Whether or not these animals could have been grave goods is unknown. Thus, 12.1% of faunal bones showed butchering activities and 15.2% of the NR had fresh fracture, possible for marrow-extracting. Nevertheless, a comparison of the taphonomic modifications between human and faunal remains was achieved. The aim was to draw parallels in terms of contemporaneity between both categories. Both assemblages show similar weathering traces (Figure 5). Both animal and human remains have a high percentage of low stages (W0 = 54.5%-66.7%; W1 = 21.3%-30.3%; and W2 = 19%-3%) and a slight presence of high stages (at around 1%). However, in the absence of further evidence and more dates, it is uncertain to relate the butchering activity and the burning traces with a specific type of burial ritual.

Some pathologies were visible on the human remains of El Espinoso. On the 147 studied teeth, eleven had caries (7.48%), five dental calculus (3.4%) and two a periodontal disease (1.4%). While on the bones, osteoarthritis was identified in five bones of two different individuals (patella, vertebral bones and metatarsal). In six bones were also identified antemortem fracture (all them belongs to long bones or phalanges). The bones suffered fractures and later soldered in life of the individual.

The spatial distribution of the human remains within Sala de los Muertos has revealed two areas with different taphonomic modifications and intensities. Dissolution and calcite concretions affected more Zone A than B. Dissolution is 20% higher in the Zone A than B and calcite concretions a 40% higher in Zone A than in Zone B. Besides, it was possible to identify that the natural niches within the cave were intentionally used to deposit the complete bodies of the dead.

Finally, it was known that three bronze bracelets, one ring and one pendant were extracted from the site by plunderers. These elements were interpreted as part of the grave goods which were deposited with the human bodies. Of the three bracelets, the biggest one measures approximately 6 cm in diameter and the other two are of small dimensions between 3-4 cm in diameter (Figure 6), which could belong to a juvenile or child individual. Bracelets have a greenish color, with a smooth surface

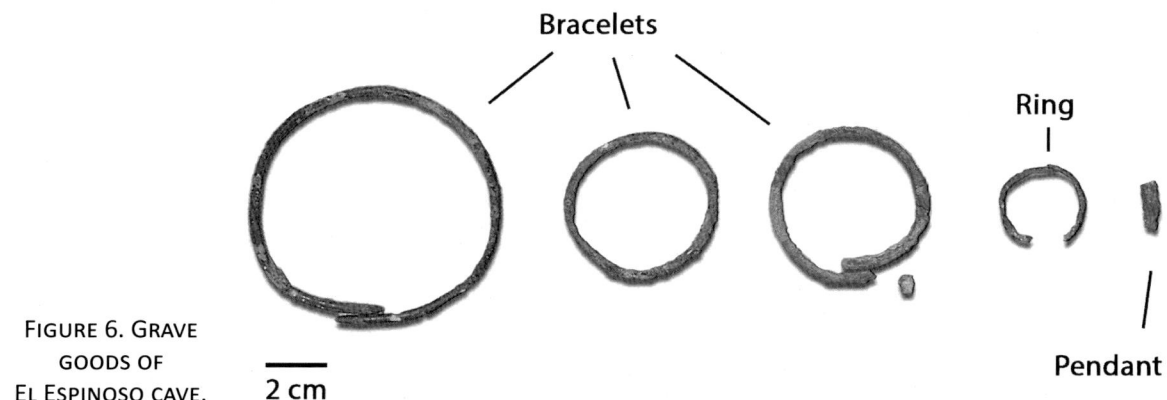

FIGURE 6. GRAVE GOODS OF EL ESPINOSO CAVE.

and no apparent decoration is visible. These characteristics resemble the ones found next to a woman in Fuentenegroso cave, located 12 km away from El Espinoso (Barroso *et al.*, 2007). The EDS results show a 87.3% percentage of copper and a 12.7% of tin which implies a pure bronze alloy, without residues of other minerals such as lead that often appears in small percentages within copper and tin. Those 'most impure" bronzes are frequent mainly during Late Bronze Age in the Cantabrian region. Therefore, the composition of El Espinoso metals are characteristic of Bronze Age (Arias Cabal and Armendáriz, 1998).

Apart from human and animal bones plus the metallic findings, no other archaeological evidences have been documented at the site.

Conclusions

In conclusion, the radiocarbon date done on a human tooth, the archaeological context where human remains were found and the specific taphonomical modifications, as well as the metallic grave goods and the EDS results confirms that El Espinoso was used as a burial cave during the Bronze Age. On the one hand, the information obtained in this study allows to confirm that this is the only collective burial known in the western Cantabrian Region during this cultural period. Moreover, in light of other findings and dates, a funerary tradition is confirmed in this region for two thousand years. Until now, in eastern Asturias only the materials from Fuentenegroso had been the subject of an anthropological study. Apart from the unpublished anthropological and taphonomical information here obtained, this study has applied several novel methodological aspects that are not commonly used in this type of context with recent chronologies. Therefore, in the future this kind of anthropological studies should be taken into account to study bone collections as this one. On the other hand, this is the first time that a taphonomic analysis has been applied to a burial cave located in the western Cantabrian Region.

Acknowledgements

We want to thank the opportunity provided by the Instituto Internacional de Investigaciones Prehistóricas de Cantabria (IIIPC) and the University of Cantabria to develop this work.

References

Arias Cabal, P. (1995) – La cronología absoluta del Neolítico y el Calcolítico de la región cantábrica: estado de la cuestión. Eusko Ikaskuntza, p. 15-39.
Arias Cabal, P.; Armendáriz, A. (1998) – Aproximación a la Edad del Bronce en la Región Cantábrica. In: Fábregas, R.; A Idade do Bronce en Galicia: novas perspectivas. Cadernos do seminario de Sargadelos, 77, p. 47-80.

Arias Cabal, P.; Martínez Villa, A.; Pérez Suárez, C. (1986) – La cueva sepulcral de Trespando (Corao, Cangas de Onís, Asturias). Boletín del Instituto de Estudios Asturianos, 120, p. 1259-1289.

Armendáriz, A.; Etxeberría, F. (1983) – Las cuevas sepulcrales de la Edad del Bronce en Guipúzcoa. Munibe, 35, p. 247-354.

Armendáriz, A. (1990) – Las cuevas sepulcrales en el País Vasco. Munibe, 42, p. 153-160.

Barroso, R.; Bueno, P.; Camino, J.; Balbín, R. de (2007) – Fuentenegroso (Asturias), un enterramiento del Bronce Final-Hierro en el marco de las comunidades atlánticas peninsulares. Pyrenae, 38, 2, p. 7-32.

Behrensmeyer, A. (1978) – Taphonomic and ecological information from bone weathering. Paleobiology, 4 (2), p. 150-162.

Bello, S.; Andrews, P. (2006) – The intrinsic pattern of preservation of human skeletal and its influence on interpretation of funerary behaviors. In Gowland, R. Knusel, C. (eds.): Social archaeology of funerary remains. Oxford: Oxbow Books, p. 1-13.

Bidmos, M. (2006) – Adult stature reconstruction from the calcaneus of South Africans of European descendent. Journal of Clinical Forensic Medicine, 13, p. 247-252.

Binford, L. (1981) – Bones, Ancient Men and Modern Myths. Studies in archaeology. Academic Press. Orlando.

Blas Cortina, M.A. de (1983) – La prehistoria reciente en Asturias. Estudios de Arqueología Asturiana, Nº1, Fundación Pública de Cuevas y Yacimientos Prehistóricos de Asturias.

Blas Cortina, M.A. de (1996) – La minería prehistórica y el caso particular de las explotaciones cupríferas de la Sierra del Aramo. Gallaecia, 14/15, p. 167-195.

Botella, M.; Alemán, I.; Jiménez, S. (1999) – Los huesos humanos: manipulación y alteraciones. Bellaterra. Barcelona.

Campillo, D, (2001) – Introducción a la paleopatología. Bellaterra. Barcelona.

Campillo, D.; Subirà, M.E. (2004) – Antropología física para arqueólogos. Ariel Prehistoria. Barcelona.

Cuenca Solana, D. (2013) – Utilización de instrumentos de concha para la realización de actividades productivas en las formaciones económico-sociales de cazadores-recolectores-pescadores y primeras sociedades tribales de la fachada atlántica europea. PuBLiCan. Santander.

Etxeberría, F. (1994) – Aspectos macroscópicos del hueso sometido al fuego. Revisión de las cremaciones descritas en el País Vasco desde la Arqueología. Munibe, 46, p. 111-116.

Gonzalez Morales, M.R. (1995) – Memoria de los trabajos de limpieza y toma de muestras en los yacimientos de las cuevas de Mazaculos y El Espinoso (La Franca, Ribadedeva) y La Llana (Andrín, Llanes) en 1993. Excavaciones Arqueológicas en Asturias 1991-94, p. 65-78.

Gualdi-Russo, E. (2007) – Sex determination from the talus and calcaneus measurements. Forensic Science International, 171, p. 151-156.

Introna Jr, F.; Di Vella, G., Campobasso, C.P. (1998) – Sex determination by discriminant analysis of patella measurements. Forensic Science International, 95, p. 39-45.

Kemkes-Grottenthaler, A. (2005) – Sex determination by discriminant analysis: an evaluation of the reliability of patella measurements. Forensic Science International, 147, p. 129-133.

Lovejoy, C.O. (1985) – Dental wear in the Libben population: Its functional pattern and role in the determination of adult skeletal age at death. American Journal of Physical Anthropology, 68, 10: 4.

Lyman, R.L. (1994) – Quantitative Units and Terminology in Zooarchaeology. American Antiquity, Vol. 59, Nº1, p. 36-71; Society for American Archaelogy.

Marín-Arroyo, A.B. (2010) – Arqueozoología en el cantábrico oriental durante la transición Pleistoceno/Holoceno. La Cueva del Mirón. PUbliCan. Santander.

Noval Fonseca, M.A. (2014) – Excavación arqueológica en la cueva de El Toral III (Andrín, Llanes). Excavaciones Arqueológicas en Asturias 2014, p. 381-384.

Olivier, G. (1960) – Pratique anthropologique. París. Vigot Frères.

Olsen, S.L.; Shipman, P. (1988) – Surface modification on Bone: Trampling versus Butchery. Journal of Archaeological Science, 15, p. 535-553.

Ontañón, R. (2003) – Caminos hacia la complejidad: El Calcolítico en la región cantábrica. Universidad de Cantabria.

Pablos, A.; Martínez, I.; Lorenzo, C.; Gracia, A.; Sala, N.; Arsuaga, J.L. (2013) – Human talus bones from the Middle Pleistocene site of Sima de los Huesos (Sierra de Atapuerca, Burgos, Spain). Journal of Human Evolution, 65, p. 79-92.

Pablos, A.; Martínez, I.; Lorenzo, C.; Sala, N.; Gracia-Téllez, A.; Arsuaga, J.L. (2014) – Human calcanei from the Middle Pleistocene site of Sima de los Huesos (Sierra de Atapuerca, Burgos, Spain). Journal of Human Evolution, (in press).

Pales, L.; Garcia, M. (1981) – Atlas ostéologique pour servir à l'indentification des Mammifères du quaternaire. Herbivores. Centre National de la Recherche Scientifique. Paris.

Scheuer, L.; Black, S. (2000) – Developmental juvenile osteology. London. Elsevier Academic Press.

Schmid, E. (1972) – Atlas of Animal Bones. Elsevier Publishing Company. London.

Solari Giachino, A. (2010) – Identificación de huellas de manipulación intencional en restos óseos humanos de origen arqueológico. Universidad de Granada.

Vila, P.; Mahieu, E. (1991) – Breakage patterns of human long bones. Journal of Human Evolution, 21: p. 27-48.

White, T.; Folkens, P. (2005) – The human bone manual. Elsevier.

Diet and ritual in the western Mediterranean Copper Age: human and animal stable isotopes from the collective burial at S. Caterina di Pittinuri (Sardinia, Italy)

Luca Lai[1,2], Ornella Fonzo[3], Elena Usai[4], Luca Medda[5], Robert Tykot[1], Ethan Goddard[6], David Hollander[6] and Giuseppa Tanda[7]

[1] Dept. of Anthropology, University of South Florida, Tampa, FL, U.S.A.
[2] Dept. of History, Cultural Resources and Territory, University of Cagliari, Italy
[3] Osteology Laboratory, Museum Genna Maria, Villanovaforru (VS), Italy
[4] Dept. of Life and Environmental Sciences, University of Cagliari, Italy
[5] Dept. of Chemical and Geological Sciences, University of Cagliari, Italy
[6] College of Marine Science, University of South Florida, Tampa, FL, U.S.A.
[7] Inter-departmental Centre for Mediterranean Prehistory and Protohistory (C.I.P.P.M.), University of Cagliari, Italy
melisenda74@yahoo.it

Abstract

C, N and O isotopic ratios, which reflect an organism's overall diet, were measured on human and animal remains from S. Caterina di Pittinuri, a Copper Age site in western Sardinia, to get a glimpse of the behavioral and ecological relations between species.

Humans, despite the coastal location, did not exploit marine resources; their diet included animal proteins, but was mainly based on crops. Swine values support previous identification as wild boars, stressing the ritual importance of wild game. The wider significance of the data is discussed, for both methodology and ritual economy.

Keywords

Copper age, funerary archaeology, diet, Mediterranean, stable isotopes

Résumé

Les rapports isotopiques de C, N et O ont été mesurés sur des restes humains et animales provenants des fouilles de S. Caterina di Pittinuri, un site de l'Age du Cuivre dans la Sardaigne occidentale, pour jeter un coup d'œil sur la diète et les liens parmi les espèces. Les habitants, malgré leur position coutière, négligeaient les ressources marines; leur diète se basait plus sur les céréales que sur les protéines animales. Les valeurs isotopiques portent à identifier les suidés comme des sangliers, ce qui souligne l'importance rituelle des animaux sauvages. Les données sont discutées, soit pour la méthodologie soit pour l'économie rituelle.

Mots-clés

Age du cuivre, archéologie funeraire, alimentation, Méditerranéen, isotopes stables

Introduction

From the first reactions to the most simplistic processualist views, it has been clear that what is represented in burial contexts does not linearly reflect social or behavioural features of the living community (Carr 1995). Burials, however, do provide a unique window into the material correlate of past lifeways in which the social organization and the belief systems were somehow reflected. Isotopic studies have grown in the last decades to become one of the main elements of the archaeological toolkit to explore the relationships between humans and the ecosystem, in the specific cultural fashions to be recognized and reconstructed for any given patio-temporal unit. In the very rare cases when faunal and human remains are found together, with stable isotopes we can have a glimpse on the ecological ties between humans and other species that were mediated by social and ritual practices.

Of course, single contexts and situations need to be carefully decoded and analysed at the proper scale, and the limits of representativeness must be clearly identified for any conclusions drawn. In the Western Mediterranean Copper Age, such ecological relationships provide indications on the complex link between the theorized subsistence patterns, and their realization in specific contexts and fields of practice, where humans, other living beings, and objects can be viewed as agents (Robb 2010; Robb 2004).

For instance, a general interpretive model for economic change in Western Europe has been that of the intensification of animal products exploitation, with an emphasis on the secondary ones (Sherratt 1983), a model that has stood the test of time (Greenfield 2010), but whose specific aspects need still need to be investigated from many theoretical and methodological perspectives, especially in the Mediterranean as opposed to the continental area, due to differential preservation of several types of investigative proxies. The rock-cut tomb of Santa Caterina di Pittinuri, an undisturbed context on the west coast of Sardinia (Figure 1.1), is an ideal case study to understand the interconnectedness of economy, ecology, and ritual in their links to funerary practices, as it offers material culture and both human and animal remains.

The corridor and room A (Figure 1.2) represent the location of ritual practices consisting of food processing and deposition; in the first two rooms the largest portion of ceramic materials and abundant animal bones were retrieved. Rooms B, C and D represent the final collective resting place for the large majority of human remains, disarticulated, commingled and accompanied, among other items, by a few silver rings and obsidian arrowheads (Cocco & Usai 1988). The liminal nature of the antechamber (room A) is also shown by the presence of only a few human skeletal remains, commingled with the majority of artefacts and animal remains. This is in line with current view that antechambers and central rooms were likely the location for primary deposition, followed by secondary, permanent deposition of the remains in peripheral rooms. Based mostly on ceramic style, with the addition of lithic and metal artefacts, the material assemblage recovered has been assigned to the local cultures named Filigosa and Abealzu (Cocco & Usai 1988), ascribed to the end of the 4th- first half of the 3rd millennium BC., which was later confirmed by radiocarbon dating.

Material, principles and methods

Twenty-one individuals (ten humans and 11 animals) were sampled for isotopic analyses. All available humans, represented by temporal, parietal and occipital bones from well-preserved cranial specimens to prevent multiple sampling of the same individuals, were from room C. Across the whole site, no bone specimen was recorded as articulated upon recovery (Cocco & Usai 1988): most showed intense carbonate concretions and a high degree of fragmentation (Buffa *et al.*, 1995), and

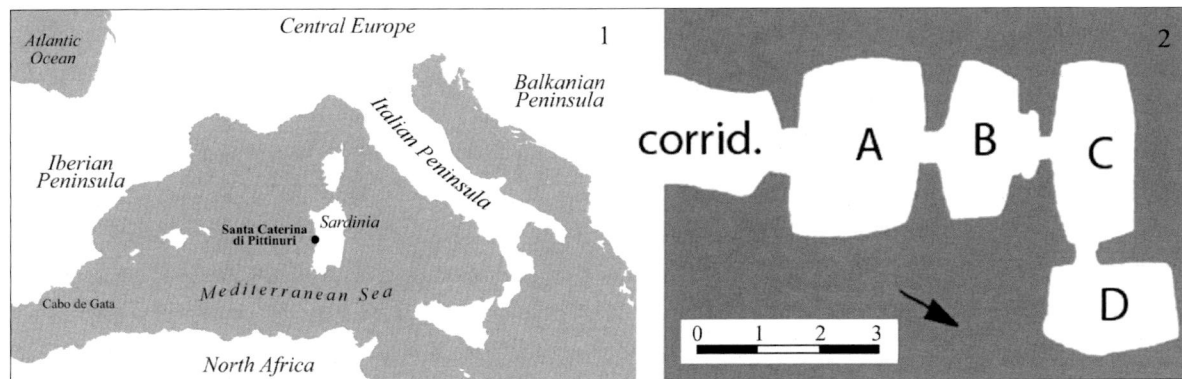

FIGURE 1. SANTA CATERINA DI PITTINURI. 1: LOCATION WITHIN THE WESTERN MEDITERRANEAN.
2: PLAN OF THE ROCK-CUT TOMB.

even after refitting and restoration, very few turned out to be complete. Besides isolated teeth, found in large quantities in all rooms but especially in room C, the most frequent skeletal districts were hands and feet. The specimens also showed differential preservation across the tomb: in room A, they were very fragmented and had thick concretions; in room B, along with one cranium were some incomplete long bones and hand and foot bones; room C yielded the majority of the skeletal remains, whereas room D yielded only small fragments.

Considering bones only, the specimens were classified also for age at death (Borgognini Tarli & Pacciani 1993; Ferembach *et al.*, 1980), and divided into adults + subadults, infants, and foetuses, keeping the rooms apart in calculating the Minimum Number of Individuals (Marini *et al.*, 1997). A cumulative, updated MNI adding up the different rooms subtotals amounts to 86 individuals. Conversely, considering the likelihood that remains from different cells may have belonged to the same individuals, the MNI would coincide with room A, which had the highest estimate for each age class (30 individuals). Considering teeth instead, Vargiu *et al.* (2009) calculated the much higher number of 339 individuals. This implies that an at least ten-fold loss of bone/individuals has occurred since the beginning of depositions: presumably, skeletal remains represent the later depositions better and rather than the earlier ones, which might date back to the Middle-to-Late Neolithic.

Sex estimation (Ferembach *et al.*, 1980) was carried out only in the rare cases which allowed it, resulting in the identification of 8 males and 7 females. This is a weak but important indication of burial without sex-based distinction. Stature was estimated based on the average length of complete long bones that showed sex-linked features (robusticity, muscular insertions etc.), according to Trotter and Gleser (1952): cm 164,0±5,1 (♂) and cm 153,5±5,6 (♀). Among the pathological conditions recorded (following Ortner & Putschar 1981) are arthrosis on vertebrae, metatarsals, metacarpals and phalanges, and frequent antemortem tooth loss. Based also on the isolated teeth, besides calculus and various degrees of tooth wear, this human group has shown the highest frequency of caries in the island's prehistory (Coppa, pers. comm. 2004).

The animal remains are composed mainly by swine/*Sus* (~40 individuals), with negligible amounts of sheep/goat. These Sus remains, largely represented by mandibles, were tentatively attributed to wild boars rather than domestic pigs, and showed no butchering cutmarks, suggesting they were not simply refuse from meals but rather offerings (Fonzo *et al.*, 2013). The majority (classified according to Barone 1982; Wilkens 2003) came from room A and arrived to the laboratory in fragmentary conditions: they mainly consist of scattered lower teeth and incomplete mandibles, with a morphology suggesting, with some caution (Albarella *et al.*, 2006), that most individuals were wild. Among the swine individuals identified, both sexes are represented; adults are prevalent, whereas subadults are a dozen or less (for age identification: Wilkens 2003).

From room A came also about ten ovine specimens (identified as in Boessneck *et al.*, 1964; Zeder & Pilaar 2010) belonging to at least one adult and one subadult, and two fragments of bovine humerus and pelvis – the only remains pertaining to this species (unfortunately not available for sampling due to concerns regarding the preservation of diagnostic morphological features). In the middle of the room, on the floor, a fragment of antler and two incomplete deer mandibles were recovered, among the oldest *Cervus* remains recognized in Sardinia.

In the inner rooms a few teeth and long bones of *Sus* were recovered, which pertain to a foetus and an infant; furthermore, roughly ten ovine specimens – teeth and metapodia (the latter pertain to at least four individuals) one of which shows some traces of intervention on the distal end. Finally, one fragment of bovine tooth was also identified.

At least twenty individuals of *Prolagus sardus* and at least two foxes pertained to the top layers of all rooms except the corridor, and could therefore be intrusive. The study of a few hundred remains of microfauna and birds is still in progress.

Two radiocarbon dates are available from the collection (table 1). One, Beta-72235, has no specific recorded provenience within the tomb, and the associated $\delta^{13}C$ overlaps better with faunal values than with humans. The main point to underline is that the two dates are non-overlapping, and together cover a 2σ range of ~1200 years. The MNI of over 300 calculated based on teeth is therefore less surprising since it can be spread over a millennium or more, accounting for roughly 30 depositions per century, or ten per generation.

Both human and animal remains were sampled for C, N and O isotopes, which reflecting to some degree the food consumed over several years before an organism's death can be used as dietary and environmental proxies. The foundation of isotopic research is based on the principle that 'you are what you eat' – that is, the various tissues in an animal's body are derived from its dietary intake and, to some degree, they preserve a quantitative trace of it. The main food categories that can be easily identified as different from terrestrial C3 diets are C4 plants and marine resources; for an overview of the principles, methods, isotopic notation system and interpretive issues many works are available (Hoefs 1997; Jim et al., 2004; Schwarcz 2000; Tykot 2004). Whereas apatite $\delta^{13}C$ is an indicator of overall diet, collagen $\delta^{13}C$ and $\delta^{15}N$ derive mostly from protein intake.

Compared to diet, collagen $\delta^{13}C$ values are higher than the diet by about +5‰, apatite 13C are about +10-14‰; so, from average plant values of -26‰ in a typical C3 ecosystem, herbivore bone collagen is about -21‰, and bone apatite around -14‰. There is a smaller change going up the food chain, so human values within C3 ecosystems are typically around -19‰ (collagen) and -12‰ (apatite), with variation related to ecosystem-wide environmental factors (Van Klinken et al., 1994), to their intake of animal tissues (Ambrose & Norr 1993; Schwarcz 2000) and to differences in the source of carbohydrates and lipids. Nitrogen isotopic values increase typically by up to +6‰ per trophic level (O'Connell et al., 2012). In terrestrial ecosystems, nitrogen is fixed or absorbed by plants, and as the plant signature ($\delta^{15}N$ 0-4‰), is passed on up the food chain, average herbivore values are about 4-8‰, and carnivores values about 8-12‰ (in temperate environments). Marine ecosystems, due to their longer food chains, have a larger range of $\delta^{13}C$ and especially $\delta^{15}N$ values (Richards & Hedges 1999; Schoeninger & Deniro 1984).

Apatite $\delta^{18}O$ is generally correlated to both local temperature and local precipitation. The correlation between biogenic $\delta^{18}O$ in phosphates and carbonates on one hand, and meteoric water $\delta^{18}O$ values on the other, holds particularly for large mammals that are obligate drinkers, so we can use the oxygen isotopic signature in bone as a proxy to the atmospheric signature. Therefore, by its being a proxy for the climatic conditions at the time and place of tissue formation, it can help pinpoint individuals who spent part of their life elsewhere relative to the majority of a given group (Koch 1998; Kohn & Cerling 2002).

Site	Specimen Lab #	Refs.	# lab (USF)	# lab	Date BP ± error and $\delta^{13}C$	Range cal BC and probability (program Oxcal 4.0)	
						1σ	2σ
S. Caterina di Pittinuri	?	Dept. Archives*		Beta-72235	4050 ± 140 -21.3‰	cal BC 2871-2801 0.169 2792-2788 0.008 2780-2463 0.824	cal BC 2916-2199 0.998 2161-2153 0.002
S. Caterina di Pittinuri	cr. 10, room C	Lai 2008, 2009	9480	AA-72148	4496 ± 43 -20.2‰	cal BC 3336-3263 0.392 3244-3209 0.193 3192-3151 0.222 3138-3102 0.193	cal BC 3355-3087 0.953 3060-3030 0.047

* Dept. of Life and Environmental Sciences, formerly Dept. of Experimental Biology, University of Cagliari

TABLE 1. THE TWO RADIOCARBON DATES FROM THE ROCK-CUT TOMB AT SANTA CATERINA DI PITTINURI (CUGLIERI, SARDINIA).

For this study, ca. 1 g of bone was selected per individual, cleaned from soil or concretions, ultrasonicated and dried. Preparation (Tykot 2004) followed a procedure somewhat different from the standard, but of comparable quality (Ambrose 1990), which does not involve powdering and gelatinization and allows visual assessment throughout the process: samples were soaked in dilute NaOH to remove acid contaminants; collagen was extracted by soaking in dilute HCl in two or more ~24-h baths and for ~24 h in a methanol-chloroform solution to remove lipids. The resulting pellets were dried, aliquots weighed into tin capsules and analysed in continuous-flow mode with a Carlo-Erba 2500 Series II CHN analyser, coupled with a ThermoFinnigan Delta+XL stable isotope ratio mass spectrometer (precision 2σ better than ±0.3‰ for $\delta^{15}N$, than ±0.2‰ for $\delta^{13}C$). To assess reliability of results, besides visual inspection through preparation, C:N ratios were also used. To isolate the apatite, ~10 mg of bone powder per sample were treated with a ~72-hour bath in 2% sodium hypochlorite to dissolve the organic portion; non-biogenic carbonate was removed by soaking it for ~24 hours in a 1.0M buffered acetic acid/sodium acetate solution (Garvie-Lok et al., 2004; Koch et al., 1997; Lee-Thorp & Sponheimer 2003). 1 mg of the resulting powder was analysed on a ThermoFinnigan Delta+XL mass spectrometer, in dual-inlet configuration, equipped with a Kiel III individual acid bath carbonate system (precision 2σ better than ±0.04‰ for $\delta^{13}C$; than ±0.06‰ for $\delta^{18}O$). Both instruments are located at the Paleolab, University of South Florida.

As indirect proxies of the integrity of samples, carbonate yields were measured after each preparation step (Nielsen-Marsh & Hedges 2000). In order to monitor diagenetic processes, the Crystallinity Index (CI) and Carbonate to Phosphate ratio (C/P) were calculated from FTIR measurements, and the calcite and fluorapatite peaks were identified. Principles and details of this method, widely used in archaeological applications, are discussed elsewhere (Shemesh 1990; Weiner 2010: 286-292; Weiner & Bar-Yosef 1990; Wright & Schwarcz 1996). The infrared spectra were measured using a FTIR (Tensor 27, Bruker Optics) equipped with a diamond-ATR accessory and a DTGS detector. A number of 128 scans at a resolution of 4 cm^{-1} were averaged from wave number 2000 to 400 cm^{-1}.

Results and Discussion

For all results, see Table 2. While collagen yield was scarce and uneven (pig collagen was almost absent), the good quality of collagen is suggested by C:N ratios between 2.9 and 3.4, within the range of isotopically reliable collagen (Ambrose 1990). Concerning apatite results, the physiology-dependent species-specific distribution of apatite $\delta^{18}O$ and $\delta^{13}C$ (Fig. 2.a) is the best indicator that the original signal has not been homogenized by isotopically consistent diagenetic contaminant. The plot of CI and C/P ratio by species (Fig. 2.c) and the association of CI values and fluorapatite peaks (Fig. 2.d) shows as expected a strong inverse correlation, indicating the direction of a diagenetic process. The sharp distinction between human and animal remains could be explained by their different location: inside the tomb the former, in the antechamber (room A) and entrance corridor the latter. It is possible that human remains were more exposed to aerobic diagenetic processes as they lay in the inner burial space with no covering material and protected by stone slabs sealing the passage ways, whereas the animal remains in the corridor were buried by larger amounts of soil, as shown by the thickness of the layer (~90 cm vs. ~20 cm in rooms B, C, D, where human bones appeared on the surface: Cocco & Usai 1988). The origin of such thick layer could include soil washed inside by rainwater; dust brought in by wind; organic matter resulting from burning and decomposition of the offerings themselves near the hearth. Alternatively, a cause for the differential diagenetic indicators could be a different pre-burial treatment: cooking or boiling (Roberts et al., 2002) is likely for animals, as part of food processing, especially considering that there were no cutmarks indicating the use of sharp tools to disarticulate the many mandibles (Fonzo et al., 2013), so tendons and flesh must have been softened beforehand. Human remains must have lost their soft tissues without the application of a high temperature, being either left to natural decomposition or possibly defleshed (systematic examination to identify cutmarks has not been carried out yet).

A basic reading of the isotopic results already shows that the human diet, despite the coastal location, did not include any detectable amount of marine resources (Fig. 2.b). Animal values are within

USF col	Lab # apa	Original site	# ind.	location	species	sex	age	% wt.	Collagen C:N	$\delta^{13}C$	$\delta^{15}N$	Apatite $\delta^{13}C$	$\delta^{18}O$	$\delta^{13}C$ col-apa	Apatite FTIR C/P	CI	fluora-patite	cal-cite
9478	9488	S. Caterina P.	Cr.7	Room C	Homo s.s.	♀	Adult	0.0				-14.6	-5.0		0.022	5.651	Strong Peak	
9479	9489	S. Caterina P.	Cr.5	Room C	Homo s.s.	♂	Adult	2.8	3.4	-19.9	9.2	-14.2	-4.1	-5.7	0.052	5.25	Peak	No
9480	9490	S. Caterina P.	Cr.10	Room C, Basal ledge	Homo s.s.	♂	Adult	5.2	3.0	-19.6	8.8	-14.2	-4.2	-5.4	0.053	5.159	Peak	No
9481	9491	S. Caterina P.	Cr.11	Room C, Basal ledge	Homo s.s.	♂	Adult	3.5				-14.9	-4.3		0.047	5.228	Peak	No
9482	9492	S. Caterina P.	Cr.14	Room C	Homo s.s.	♂	Adult					-14.6	-4.3		0.033	5.491	Peak	No
9483	9493	S. Caterina P.	Cr.20	Room C	Homo s.s.	♀	Adult	0.0				-14.6	-4.6		0.041	5.676	Peak	No
9484	9494	S. Caterina P.	Cr.6	Room C	Homo s.s.	♀	Juvenile	0.2				-14.6	-4.3		0.025	5.724	Peak	No
9485	9495	S. Caterina P.	Cr.19	Room C	Homo s.s.		Infant	2.8	3.0	-19.4	9.8	-14.5	-4.3	-4.9	0.049	5.232	Peak	No
9486	9496	S. Caterina P.	Cr.2	Room C	Homo s.s.		Infant	2.3	3.0	-18.9	10.2	-14.4	-4.0	-4.5	0.039	5.156	Peak	No
9487	9497	S. Caterina P.	Cr.12	Room C	Homo s.s.		Infant	1.0	3.0	-19.5	9.7	-15.4	-4.3	-4.1	0.026	5.81	Shoulder	No
					Averages					-19.5	9.5	-14.6	-4.3	-4.9				
					St. deviat.					±0.4	±0.5	±0.3	±0.3	±0.6				
8667	8636	S. Caterina P.	SCP A.96	Room A	Sus s.		2 yrs	1.3				-11.0	-4.4		0.307	3.431	No	No
8668	8637	S. Caterina P.	SCP A.89	Room A	Sus s.		18-24 mos	0.0				-9.2	-5.2		0.225	3.524	No	No
8669	8638	S. Caterina P.	SCP A.94	Room A	Sus s.		12-18 mos	0.0				-11.3	-3.7		0.176	3.75	No	No
8670	8639	S. Caterina P.	SCP A.174	Corridor	Sus s.		< 8 mos	3.6		-21.0	3.9	-10.7	-4.4	-10.3	0.181	3.946	No	No
8671	8640	S. Caterina P.	SCP A.112	Room A	Sus s.		> 4 yrs	0.1				-9.4	-5.3		0.654	3.635	No	Peak
8672	8641	S. Caterina P.	SCP A.164	Room A, floor	Cervus e.	♂	Adult	3.5		-21.6	4.5	-10.4	-4.4	-11.2	0.169	3.652	No	No
8673	8642	S. Caterina P.	SCP A.1	Room A	Vulpes v.		Adult	11.4		-18.8	7.0	-11.7	-2.7	-7.1	0.257	3.235	No	No
8674	8643	S. Caterina P.	SCP A.35	Room A	Prolagus s.		Adult	6.0		-21.6	5.3	-13.8	-1.1	-7.8	0.234	3.351	No	No
8675	8644	S. Caterina P.	SCP A.242	Room A	Prolagus s.		Adult	3.4		-21.8	2.7	-13.5	-1.1	-8.3	0.234	3.432	No	No
8676	8645	S. Caterina P.	SCP A.115	Room A	Ovis/Capra		< 20 mos	4.5		-20.7	7.2	-12.4	-1.1	-8.3	0.121	4.172	No	No
8677	8646	S. Caterina P.	SCP A.206	Room A	Ovis/Capra		Adult	2.1		-20.0	5.3	-11.7	-0.8	-8.3	0.291	3.405	No	No
					Averages					-20.8	5.1	-11.4	-3.1	-8.8				
					St. deviat.					±1.1	±1.6	±1.5	±1.8	±1.5				

TABLE 2. SANTA CATERINA DI PITTINURI. ALL INDIVIDUAL DATA, ISOTOPIC AND FTIR VALUES.

expected terrestrial, C3 ecosystems but their specific values deserve a closer consideration. The absence of any isotopic signal of marine resources places the economy of the group solidly within the Neolithic tradition that marginalized the sea as an important source of food (besides single studies, see Craig et al., 2006) by replacing it with a terrestrial domesticated landscape populated by animals and plants.

Interpretation of diet was cautiously carried out considering the different species represented, and must be tentative due to the modest numbers involved. As regards the origin of proteins in humans, several possibilities are to be considered, assuming a $\delta^{15}N$ interval of about 6‰ between consumed and consumer (O'Connell et al., 2012), and taking as reference points the averages of different

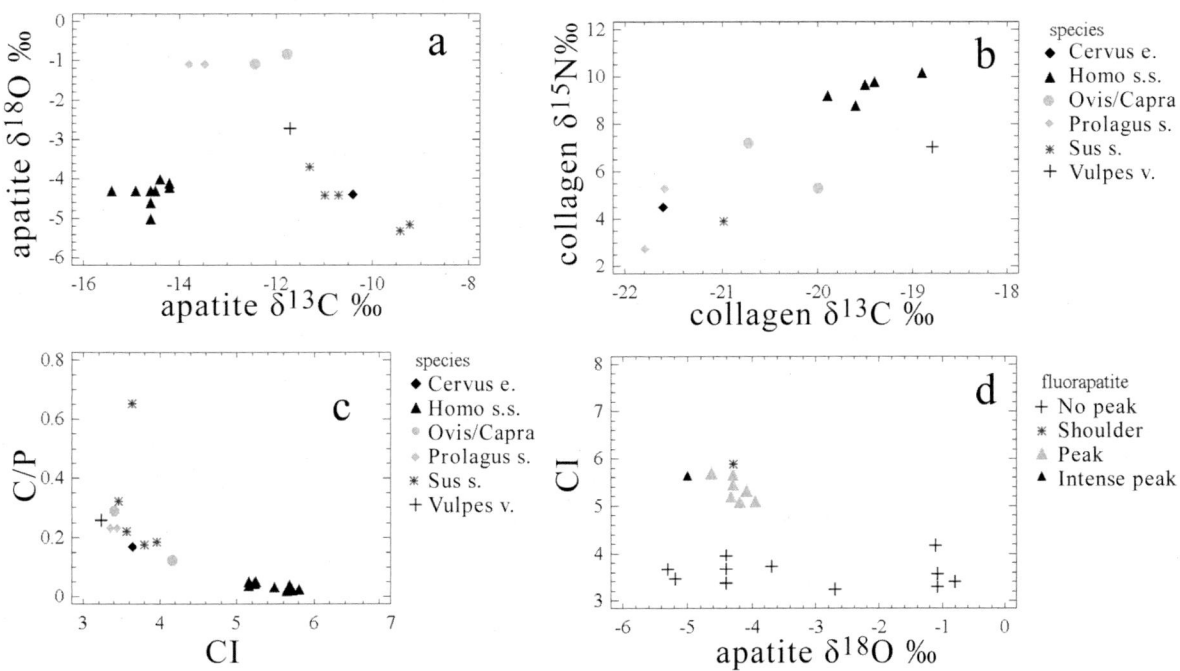

FIGURE 2. SANTA CATERINA DI PITTINURI, ROCK-CUT TOMB. ISOTOPIC AND FT-IR VALUES FOR PALEODIETARY, PALEOECOLOGICAL AND DIAGENETIC RECONSTRUCTION (SEE TEXT).

animals and values for plants (approximately around 1‰) and for legumes (likely a few permil negative). The interval between human adults on one hand and deer and pig on the other could derive from a diet where most proteins are from wild animals (with some from vegetal sources), but considering that consumption of wild game was rather occasional and linked to special events, this seems to be very unlikely. The interval with ovicaprines, a more realistic source of proteins, could reflect a fairly balanced origin of daily proteins from ovicaprines, supplemented by the non sampled bovines and by wild game, on one hand, and from vegetal sources on the other. Of course, if legumes were a substantial portion of human protein intake, the observed values would have to be considered as intermediate between extreme $\delta^{15}N$ values (up to 10‰ apart): in this case, animal sources too would have been substantial; however, a diet with a strong vegetal component without large amounts of cereal grains is also unlikely, so that in any case the quantity of animal proteins in daily diet was most probably quite small. Such scarce reliance on animal proteins can be underlined also comparatively: relative to other unpublished prehistoric Sardinian groups, and also elsewhere in the Mediterranean where the $\delta^{15}N$ human-herbivore interval is around or above 4‰ (Le Bras-Goude et al., 2006a; Le Bras-Goude et al., 2006b). The high prevalence of caries observed (Coppa, pers. comm.) possibly supports a strong reliance on starchy foods.

As concerns pigs, the protein portion of the diet, as inferred from collagen $\delta^{13}C$ and $\delta^{15}N$ on a single individual, corresponds with that of red deer and *Prolagus*, being even more depleted than sheep, supporting the identification of several individuals based on tooth morphology, as wild boars; the similarity with the value of deer and *Prolagus* suggests the forest as the most likely habitat. A similar diet for the whole group of represented pigs can only be suggested, based on the fairly consistent apatite values of the remaining four individuals (where variation can also depend on other environmental, behavioural and eco-physiological factors).

The two ovicaprine $\delta^{15}N$ values appear quite different, although within the range intermediate between humans and other herbivores; the interval can be attributed to age, with the 20 months-old sheep still carrying its enriched isotopic signal from breastfeeding. The values themselves, different from *Cervus* and *Sus*, could imply differences in the feeding areas; among many possibilities, pasture on fertilized fields, or in lowlands, or with scrubby rather than just grassy vegetation.

The greater number of apatite human samples analysed for $\delta^{13}C$ and $\delta^{18}O$ (Fig. 2.a) clusters tightly, indicating a diet and/or residence patterns less differentiated within the group compared to what is observed, for instance, at San Benedetto, Sardinia, earlier 4th millennium BC (Lai 2008: 312-316). From the few samples available, it would also seem that women were spending, or spent at some point in their life, part of the time at higher elevations or in cooler climates than men. Considering the general trend of gender roles as known for the prehistoric Western Mediterranean, it seems however unlikely that women were engaging in seasonal mobility; more likely, either men married in, which could then indicate matrilocality and/or they spent part of their lives more to the South, possibly on the Campidano plains. Alternatively, women from the mountains, North-northeast of the site, would be marrying into the area patrilocally. More focused studies on mobility involving Sr isotopes on teeth and bone could clarify these issues in the future. The infant values, difficult to interpret due to the wide age range estimated (6 year-span), are out of the scope of this paper.

Keeping in mind all these caveats on drawing inferences based on numerically very scarce data, we can cautiously suggest a possible overall scenario: since hunting, rather than barely a subsistence activity, was likely a key practice in structuring identities, maintaining gender roles and constructing social *personae*, the ritual offerings or remains of funeral feasting, consisting of defleshed body parts, apparently involved valued animals as wild game and not every-day, household-related foods.

Dairy products do not appear to leave a visible trace in the diet as would be expected with an intensification of their exploitation. Their production was already an intangible part of the Neolithic package, however their importance in daily diet had not become greater in the Copper Age group buried at Santa Caterina. Possibly this was due to the inability to digest milk, a genetic trait that became widespread only later (Leonardi *et al.*, 2012). The presence of older bovines coupled with isotopic values suggesting a mostly vegetarian diet at Scaba 'e Arriu, another Copper Age site in Sardinia (Lai 2008: 317-323) indicates that use of animal traction power may have been an innovation adopted independently from the intensification of dairy products. The frequency of caries recorded in the Santa Caterina's group may derive from lack of the protective effect of dairy products (Johansson 2002).

The onset of rituals involving drinking can be inferred by the change in vessel types and dimensions, suggesting an increase in individual consumption rather than ordinary meals from common bowls; furthermore, there is an increased relevance of wild game among the faunal remains, even though daily diet relied on plants; finally, room C, where the human remains analysed come from, is also the one with the higher number of arrowheads (eight out of 11): these are perhaps complementary symptoms of the increasing social value ascribed to hunting as part of a progressive distinction of a more masculine field of action in inter-group relationships, communication and display, opposite to a feminine domain increasingly limited to the domestic sphere (Hayden 1998). While representing the beginning of a future evolution in which maleness is more strongly associated with generalized authority tied to force and wealth, this context maintains, or even emphasizes, communal values and a horizontal social structure (Crumley 1995), which was based on the recognition of different agents with special roles and skills, and the special qualities of exotic or simply unusual items as markers of different *personae* or different social settings (Helms 1993), such as finely crafted arrowheads, wild boar and deer meat, or silver rings. A society, however, still distant from any form of hierarchical structure.

Concluding remarks

The significance of the data discussed above is multifaceted and provides methodologically useful insights, for the understanding of diagenesis in Mediterranean rock-cut burials, and more broadly for the reconstruction of cultural ecology and ritual traditions in Mediterranean Copper Age. The general methodological issues in assessing human diets based on all available animal species represented as if they were a coherent whole emerge clearly, and this study confirms the need to culturally decode the relationship between signals of different species separately.

While no statistical significance can be attributed to the data presented, the first piece of evidence is presented for Western-central Mediterranean insular Copper Age diet and ecology. This human group can be added to the extensive corpus of data showing marginalization of marine resources occurred in the Mediterranean since the Neolithic: in fact, no isotopic trace of marine foods was detected at Santa Caterina di Pittinuri, despite the coastal location of the burial. Furthermore, there are no visible clues of increased reliance on animal products, whereas considering the interval between $\delta^{15}N$ in humans and ovicaprines as a strong reliance on vegetal foodstuffs seems more likely. This is coupled with the symbolic relevance of wild boar and deer hunting: it appears that rather than displays of a generalized symbolic currency readable as parallel to authority, funerals at Santa Caterina reflected a more specific value connected to a socially structuring activity disconnected from practical relevance. In turn, this is consistent with a more heterarchical social organization, in line with collective burial and the loss of individual identity in the shared ancestral memory of the community.

Acknowledgements

Funding for the isotopic analyses was provided by the National Science Foundation, grant BCS-0612858; Sardegna Ricerche made available the spectrometer that was used for the FTIR measurements. We thank the many persons and institutions that in different ways made a significant contribution to this research.

References

Albarella, U.; Manconi, F.; Rowley-Conwy, P.; Vigne, J.-D. (2006) – Pigs of Corsica and Sardinia: a biometrical re-evaluation of their status and history. In: Tecchiati, U., and Sala, B., editors. Archaeozoological studies in honour of Alfredo Riedel. Bolzano: Province of Bolzano. p. 285-302.

Ambrose, S.H. (1990) – Preparation and characterization of bone and tooth collagen for isotopic analysis. Journal of Archaeological Science 17(4):431-451.

Ambrose, S.H.; Norr, L. (1993) – Experimental evidence for the relationship of the carbon isotope ratios of whole diet and dietary protein to those of bone collagen and carbonate. In: Lambert, J.B., and Grupe, G., editors. Prehistoric Human Bone-Archaeology at the Molecular Level. Berlin, New York: Springer. p. 1-37.

Barone, R. (1982) – Anatomia comparata dei Mammiferi domestici. Bologna: Edagricole.

Boessneck, J.; Müller, H.-H.; Theichert, M. (1964) – Osteologische Unterscheidungsmerkmale zwischen Schaf (O. aries L.) und Ziege (C. hircus L.). Khün-Archiv 78:1-129.

Borgognini Tarli, S.; Pacciani, E. (1993) – I resti umani nello scavo archeologico. Metodiche di recupero e studio. Rome: Bulzoni.

Buffa, R.; Floris, G.; Floris-Masala, R.; Lucia, G.; Marini, E.; Usai, E. (1995) – Primo resoconto sul materiale scheletrico umano proveniente dalla grotticella ipogeica di S. Caterina di Pittinuri (Oristano). Notiziario di Archeoantropologia STRAP 1:7-12.

Carr, C. (1995) – Mortuary practices: Their social, philosophical-religious, circumstantial, and physical determinants. Journal of Archaeological Methods and Theory 2(2):105-200.

Cocco, D.; Usai, L. (1988) – Un monumento preistorico nel territorio di Cornus. Ampsicora e il territorio di Cornus Atti del II Convegno sull'archeologia romana e altomedievale nell'oristanese, Cuglieri, 22 dicembre 1985. Taranto: Scorpione. p. 13-24.

Craig, O.; Biazzo, M.; Tafuri, M.A. (2006) – Palaeodietary records of coastal Mediterranean populations. Journal of Mediterranean Studies 16:63-77.

Crumley, C.L. (1995) – Heterarchy and the Analysis of Complex Societies. In: Ehrenreich, R.M.; Crumley, C.L.; and Levy, J.E., editors. Heterarchy and the Analysis of Complex Societies. Washington: American Anthropological Association. p. 1-5.

Ferembach, D.; Schwidetzky, I.; Stloukal, M. (1980) – Recommendations for age and sex diagnosis of skeletons. Journal of Human Evolution. Journal of Human Evolution 9:517-549.

Fonzo, O.; Lai, L.; O'Connell, T.C.; Goddard, E.; Hollander. D. (2013) – Offerte animali nella tomba ipogeica prenuragica di Padru Jossu presso Sanluri (VS). *Presented at the meeting* 'La Sardegna nell'età del Rame. Olbia, 25 May 2013.

Garvie-Lok, S.J.; Varney, T.L.; Katzenberg, M.A. (2004) – Preparation of bone carbonate for stable isotope analysis: the effects of treatment time and acid concentration. Journal of Archaeological Science 31:763-776.

Greenfield, H.J. (2010) – The Secondary Products Revolution: the past, the present and the future. World Archaeology 42(1):29-54.

Hayden, C. (1998) – Public and domestic: the social background to the development of gender in prehistoric Sardinia. In: Whitehouse, R.D., editor. Gender and Italian Archaeology: Institute of Archaeology, University College London.

Helms, M. (1993) – Craft and the kingly ideal. Art, trade and power. Austin: University of Texas, Austin.

Hoefs, J. (1997) – Isotope geochemistry. Berlin, New York: Springer.

Jim, S.; Ambrose, S.H.; Evershed, R.P. (2004) – Stable carbon isotopic evidence for differences in the dietary origin of bone cholesterol, collagen and apatite: Implications for their use in palaeodietary reconstruction. Geochimica et Cosmochimica Acta 68(1):61-72.

Johansson, I. (2002) – Milk and dairy products: possible effects on dental health. Scandinavian Journal of Nutrition 46(3):119-122.

Koch, P.L. (1998) – Isotopic reconstruction of past continental environments. Annual Review of Earth and Planetary Science 26:573-613.

Koch, P.L.; Tuross, N.; Fogel, M.L. (1997) – The effects of sample treatment and diagenesis on the isotopic integrity of carbonate in biogenic hydroxylapatite. Journal of Archaeological Science 24(5):417-429.

Kohn, M.J.; Cerling, T.E. (2002) – Stable isotope compositions of biological apatite. In: Kohn, M.J.; Rakovan, J., and Hughes, J.M., editors. Phosphates Geochemical, Geobiological, and Materials Importance Reviews in Mineralogy and Geochemistry. Washington, DC. p. 455-488.

Lai, L. (2008) – The interplay of economic, climatic and cultural change investigated through isotopic analyses of bone tissue: the case of Sardinia 4000-1900 BC [Ph.D. dissertation]. Tampa: University of South Florida.

Le Bras-Goude, G.; Billy, I.; Charlier, K.; Loison, G. (2006a) – Contribution des méthodes isotopiques pour l'étude de l'alimentation humaine au Néolithique moyen méridional: le cas du site Chasséen ancien du Crès (Béziers, Hérault, France). Antropo 11:167-175.

Le Bras-Goude, G.; Binder, D.; Formicola, V.; Duday, H.; Couture-Veschambre, C.; Hublin, J.-J.; Richards, M.P. (2006b) – Stratégies de subsistance et analyse culturelle de populations néolithiques de Ligurie: approche par l'étude isotopique ($\delta^{13}C$ and $\delta^{15}N$) des restes osseux. Bulletin et Mémoires de la Société d'Anthropologie de Paris 18(1-2):43-53.

Lee-Thorp, J.A.; Sponheimer, M. (2003) – Three case studies used to reassess the reliability of fossil bone and enamel isotope signals for paleodietary studies. Journal of Anthropological Archaeology 22:208-216.

Leonardi, M.; Gerbault, P.; Thomas, M.G.; Burger, J. (2012) – The evolution of lactase persistence in Europe. A synthesis of archaeological and genetic evidence. International Dairy Journal 22: 88-97.

Marini, E.; Floris, G.; Usai, E. (1997) – Nuovo materiale scheletrico umano proveniente da S. Caterina di Pittinuri (Oristano). Rendiconti del Seminario della Facoltà di Scienze dell'Università di Cagliari 67:35-36.

Nielsen-Marsh, C.M.; Hedges, R.E.M. (2000) – Patterns of diagenesis in bone II: effects of acetic acid treatment and the removal of diagenetic CO_3^{2-} Journal of Archaeological Science 27(12):1151-1159.

O'Connell, T.C.; Kneale, C.J.; Tasevska, N.; Kuhnle, G.G.C. (2012) – The diet-body offset in human nitrogen isotopic values: a controlled dietary study. American Journal of Physical Anthropology 149:426-434.

Ortner, D.J.; Putschar, W.G. (1981) – Identification of pathological conditions in human skeletal remains. Washington, DC: Smithsonian Institution Press.

Richards, M.P.; Hedges, R.E.M. (1999) – Stable isotope evidence for similarities in the types of marine foods used by late Mesolithic humans at sites along the Atlantic coast of Europe. Journal of Archaeological Science 26:717-722.

Robb, J. (2010) – Beyond agency. World Archaeology 42(4):493-520.

Robb, J.E. (2004) – The extended artefact and the monumental economy: a methodology for material agency. In: Demarrais, E., Gosden, C., and Renfrew, C., editors. Rethinking Materiality: The Engagement of Mind with the Material World. Cambridge: Oxbow Books. p. 131-139.

Roberts, S.J.; Smith, C.I.; Millard, A.; Collins, M.J. (2002) – The taphonomy of cooked bone: characterizing boiling and its physico-chemical effects. Archaeometry 44(3):485-494.

Schoeninger, M.J.; Deniro, M.J. (1984) – Nitrogen and carbon isotope composition of bone collagen from marine and terrestrial animals. Geochimica et Cosmochimica Acta 48:625-639.

Schwarcz, H.P. (2000) – Some biochemical aspects of carbon isotopic paleodiet studies. In: Ambrose S.H., and Katzenberg M.A., editors. Biogeochemical approaches to paleodietary analysis. New York: Kluwer Academic/Plenum. p. 189-209.

Shemesh, A. (1990) – Crystallinity and diagenesis of sedimentary apatites. Geochimica et Cosmochimica Acta 54:2433-2438.

Sherratt, A.G. (1983) – The secondary exploitation of animals in the Old World. World Archaeology 15:90-104.

Trotter, M.; Gleser, G.C. (1952) – Estimation of stature from long bones of American Whites and Negroes. American Journal of Physical Anthropology 10:463-514.

Tykot, R.H. (2004) – Stable isotopes and diet: you are what you eat. In: Martini, M.; Milazzo, M., and Piacentini, M., editors. Physics methods in archaeometry Proceedings of the International School of Physics 'Enrico Fermi' Course CLIV. Bologna, Italy: Società Italiana di Fisica. p. 433-444.

Van Klinken, G.J.; Van Der Plicht, H.; Hedges, R.E.M. (1994) – Bond 13C/15N ratios reflect (palaeo-) climatic variations. Geophysical Research Letters 6(21):445-448.

Vargiu, R.; Cucina, A.; Coppa, A. (2009) – Italian Populations during the Copper Age: Assessment of Biological Affinities through Morphological Dental Traits. Human Biology 81(4):479-493.

Weiner, S. (2010) – Microarchaeology. Beyond the Visible Archaeological Record. New York: Cambridge University Press.

Weiner, S.; Bar-Yosef, O. (1990) – States of preservation of bones from prehistoric sites in the Near East: a Survey. Journal of Archaeological Science 17:187-196.

Wilkens, B. (2003) – Manuale per lo studio dei resti faunistici dell'area mediterranea. CD ROM: Schio.

Wright, L.E.; Schwarcz, H.P. (1996) – Infrared and isotopic evidence for diagenesis of bone apatite at Dos Pilas, Guatemala: palaeodietary implications. Journal of Archaeological Science 23:933-944.

Zeder, M.A.; Pilaar, S.E. (2010) – Assessing the reliability of criteria used to identify mandibles and mandibular teeth in sheep, *Ovis*, and goats, *Capra*. Journal of Archaeological Science 37(2):225-242.

The artificial caves of Valencina de la Concepción (Seville)

Pedro M. López Aldana[1] and Ana Pajuelo Pando[1]

[1] Departamento de Prehistoria y Arqueología. Universidad de Sevilla
aldanaostrogodo@gmail.com

Abstract

Collective burials are one of the most common funerary practices during Late Prehistory and show a diversity of structural solutions. Nearly all contemporaneous morphological types are known to exist at the 3rd Millennium BC archaeological site Valencina de la Concepción (Seville). In typological terms, these structures discussed here fit well into the types known as 'artificial caves'. From a morphological point of view, there is significant variability concerning not only architectural aspects but grave goods and anthropological elements as well. Concerning the treatment of the bodies, the most widespread ritual is the hyperflexion of both lower and upper limbs, probably indicating the use of shrouds or bandages. Some individuals seem to share morphological features that might link them to certain family groups; DNA studies were carried out to test this observation. This type of funerary structure is definitely a novelty in the Copper Age site Valencina de la Concepción.

Keywords

Valencina de la Concepción, artificial cave, Copper Age, 3rd Millennium

Résumé

Sépultures collectives sont l'une des pratiques funéraires les plus courantes pendant plus tard Préhistoire et montrent une diversité de solutions structurelles. Presque tous les types morphologiques contemporains sont connus pour exister au 3ème millénaire avant JC site archéologique Valencina de la Concepción (Séville). En termes typologiques, ces structures intègrent bien dans les types connus comme des 'grottes artificielles'. D'un point de vue morphologique, il existe une variabilité importante concernant non seulement les aspects architecturaux, mais des objets funéraires et des éléments anthropologiques ainsi. Concernant le traitement des corps, le rituel le plus répandu est l'hyperflexion des deux membres inférieurs et supérieurs, indiquant probablement l'utilisation d'écrans ou de bandages. Certaines personnes semblent partager des caractéristiques morphologiques qui pourraient les relier à certains groupes de la famille; études d'ADN ont été effectuées pour tester cette observation. Ce type de structure funéraire est certainement une nouveauté dans le site Âge du Cuivre Valencina de la Concepción.

Mots-clés

Valencina de la Concepción, grotte artificielle, âge du cuivre, 3ème millénaire

Introduction

Valencina de la Concepción is located on the right bank of the current course of the Guadalquivir River, a few kilometres away from Seville. It seats in the north-oriental area of the ledge of the Aljarafe, basically constituted of materials of marine origin, formed by sands, silts and clays. The 3rd Millennium settlement occupies, mainly, two municipalities: Valencina de la Concepción, where the dwelling and productive area and a part of the necropolis are located, and Castilleja de Guzmán, which hosts the largest area of the necropolis. The complete site occupies an extension of around 500 hectares (Figure 1). However, without prejudice of the importance of the enormous extent of the site in the municipality of Castilleja de Guzmán, we will refer to the settlement site as Valencina, as it appears in the main historiographical works concerning the site.

Despite numerous interventions in Valencina – from 1869, year of the discovery of the Cueva de La Pastora dolmen, until 2011 there were 117 archaeological interventions, of which only 103 could

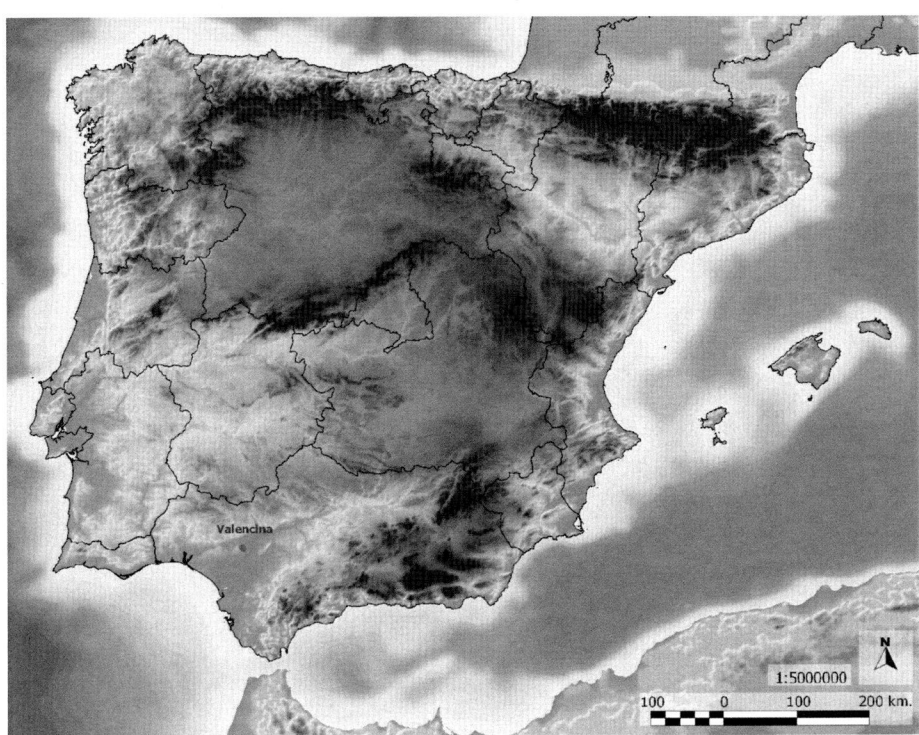

FIGURE 1. VALENCINA LOCATION ON THE IBERIAN PENINSULA.

be considered valid to document the site (Mejías, 2013) – this is a percentage of only 0.95% of true excavated surface of the site (Mejías *et al.*, in press).

The last excavations carried out in the property La Huera (Castilleja de Guzmán) in 2007 (Méndez, 2013) and in Calle Dinamarca, 3-5 (Valencina de la Concepción) in 2009 (Pajuelo, 2009; Pajuelo and López Aldana, 2013), opened new prospects in the research of the funerary structures typologically known as 'artificial caves' (Figure 2), which, until now, were absent in the necropolis of the Valencina settlement.

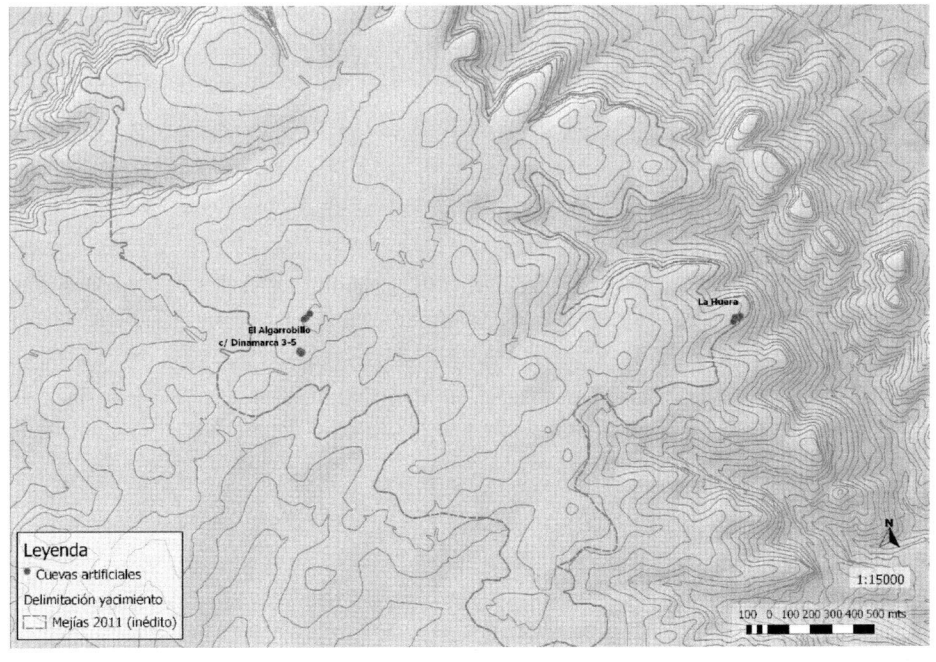

FIGURE 2. LOCATION OF ARTIFICIAL CAVES IN VALENCINA. CARTOGRAPHY DEVELOPED BY J.C. MEJIAS-GARCÍA.

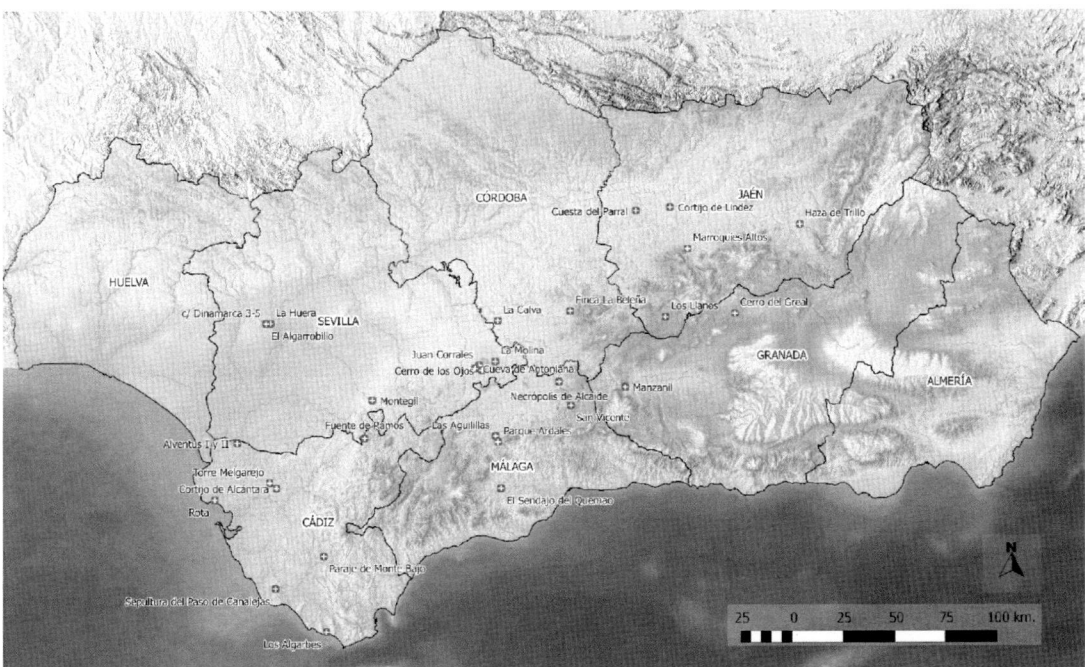

FIGURE 3. LOCATION OF ARTIFICIAL CAVES IN SOUTHERN SPAIN.

For the moment, these structures refer to the locations known as El Algarrobillo, Calle Dinamarca 3-5 and La Huera; and their location seem to correspond to very specific areas inside the mentioned necropolis.

The archaeological circumstances of these finds, such as their location and architectural features, as well as their contents, should be firstly addressed within the context of this particular settlement and then discussed within a broader geo-cultural frame, in order to approach the various issues surrounding such complex socio-economic formations.

We therefore bring up the discussion on this set of funerary structures that contribute to rate the typological variability of the funerary containers known hitherto in Valencina, and provide a novelty regarding its location and distribution in the specific geographical scope of the Guadalquivir valley.

From our point of view, an artificial cave is a structure basically composed of a chamber and a passage, fully carved underground. The chamber would be vaulted, and occasionally provided with attached niches, and also carved underground. The passage generally develops vertically towards the chamber, with different types of architectural solutions, in ramp, steps or well. When other stone elements are present, they are used to close the graves or to very specific boundaries within the structure, but never as architectural elements related to the pavement, facing or development of cover (Pajuelo *et al.*, 2013).

The distribution of artificial caves in the Andalusia region shows a double phenomenology (Figure 3). On the one hand, their location on a specific geological substrate: the vast majority of the studied caves are located on sedimentary rocks, including sandstone, calcareous sandstone, sands, shale, marl and limestone.

The second observable feature concerns its location. Excepting the three groups of artificial caves of the Valencina site (El Algarrobillo, c/ Dinamarca and La Huera), all artificial caves identified along the Guadalquivir River basin are located on the river's left bank.

Evidence of artificial caves in Valencina

The settlement of Valencina occupies an area of 514.88 hectares, with varying elevations ranging from 140 m above sea level in the north, west and south, to 115 to 135 m in the east, where the major part of the necropolis is located (Mejías, 2011).

One can clearly see a division in two areas: dwelling area and necropolis, endorsed by the location of the structures; the presence of a big separating trench.

The nearest neighbour indices and spatial autocorrelation (Moran index), that would indicate a clustered pattern to each type of structures (Mejías, 2013).

The necropolis, where the artificial caves documented in Valencina are located (El Algarrobillo, La Huera y Calle Dinamarca), has some 310 hectares and is separated from the dwelling area by a big boundary trench (Mejías, 2013).

1) El Algarrobillo (Valencina de la Concepción)

In 1991 an archaeological excavation was carried out previously to the urbanization of this zone of Valencina de la Concepción. Specifically in the so called Grid 7, a circular structure was recorded, with 4.60 m maximum diameter, containing a minimum number of 10 adult individuals who were distributed mainly near the walls. It has previously been interpreted as a 'cultic' hut (Santana, 1993).

On the other hand, in the light of the information presented in the publication, and of a re-analysis of the available data, it is concluded that another structure, the so called E.I, in Grid 3, can be categorized as an artificial cave. According to the available description, it is a structure composed by 2 circles connected by a passage (northeast-southwest) with 3.40 m length and 0.90 m width, in which three niches were opened, being one of them empty, The skeletal remains followed the general pattern of this type of burials as to its disposal, pilled up, although preserving in some cases certain anatomical connections, especially regarding the extremities. It contained 7 inhumations.

The artefact spectrum of the associated grave goods is very reduced: a lenticular cup, two fragments of a thickened almond form edge dish, a large silex sheet and two polished stones (Santana, 1993).

2) La Huera (Castilleja de Guzmán)

The artificial cave of La Huera (Figure 4) is situated in the municipality of Castilleja de Guzmán, located on top of the southern slope of a hill. This structure is carved in the geological underground, with a chamber and a small, simple passage. The chamber has a circular trend, ranging between 2 m in the northwest-southeast axis and 2.80 m in its northeast-southwest axis. A small vaulted cavity was opne in the southwest quadrant of the chamber. The passage, meanwhile, opens in the southeast area of the chamber, facing slope of the hillside (Méndez, 2013).

The skeletal remains are largely disarticulated. However, primary articulated burials and partially articulated associations have been found, with 3 burials in flexed lateral decubitus. These are placed at the contour of the chamber. A total of 22 individuals have been identified, of which, according to their age range, 14 adults, 3 pre-adults and 5 children. They generally present poorly marked sexual dimorphism, with gracile complexions and similar morphological ranges between sexes (Méndez, 2013).

The associated grave goods consist of closed shaped ceramic vessels with good surface treatment, besides, low carinated stew pots and a pot and other kinds of vases. The stone material is constituted by knapped industry (blades and arrowheads) and polished stone materials (an axe, a hand grinder and a hammer), mainly made of siliceous rock. Among the stone material, there is a significant

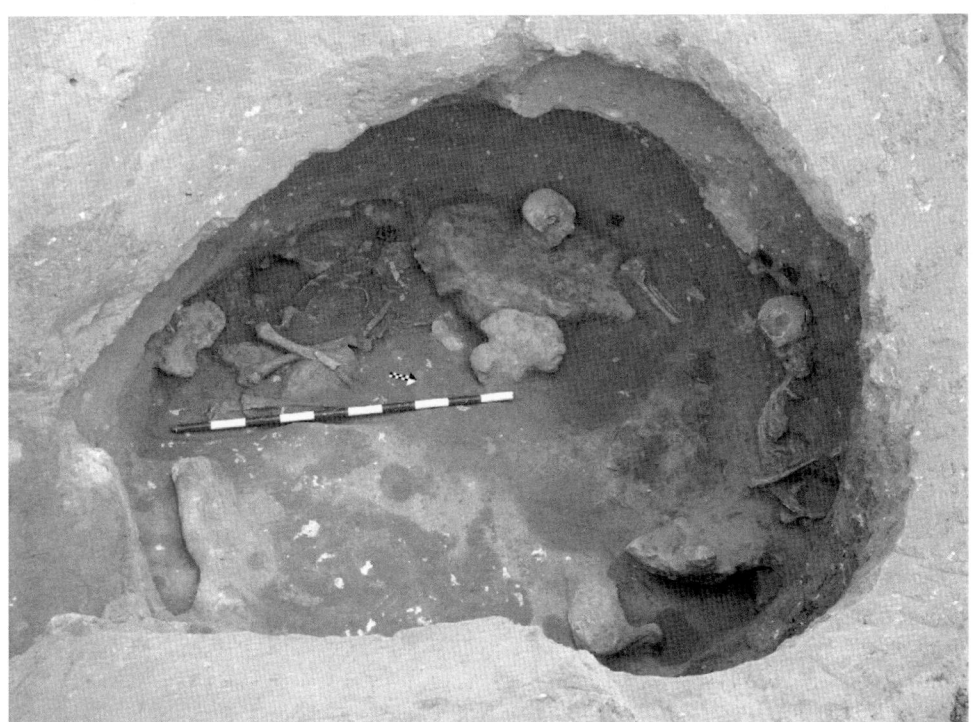

FIGURE 4. LA HUERA. PHOTO OF ELENA MÉNDEZ.

presence of prismatic and ovoid shaped pieces, in this case referred to as 'baetyloid objects' with symbolic and ritual function (Méndez, 2013).

The archeozoological remains are very scarce. Ovicaprids (goat/sheep) and *Sus* sp. (pig) are present. The same pattern is observed in what concerns the shell remains, with the few remains limited to one right leaflet of *Pecten maximus*, L. (Linnaeus, 1758). The worked bone industry includes the presence of two pin shafts, which could well belong to the group of moving head pins.

A date of 3220-3120, 2910-2860 BC (cal. 1 σ) was obtained for this artificial cave (García Sanjuán *et al.*, in press).

3) Calle Dinamarca, 3-5 (Urbanization El Algarrobillo, Valencina de la Concepción)

In the Urbanization El Algarrobillo a set of funerary structures was identified. Their morphology points out to those structures typologically known as artificial caves. A total amount of 5 structures were identified, 4 of which, with different sizes and shapes, have been partially excavated (Pajuelo and López Aldana, 2013). None of them was completely excavated, which prevented more accurate information of its architectural definition.

Structure 48

This is the simplest of all excavated structures of this set (Figure 5). As in the remaining structures, neither its limits could exactly be defined, nor was it fully excavated. The collected skeletal remains belong to c. 4 individuals. A single sample from one individual was collected for DNA analysis.

Structure 51

It is an oval-shaped structure with irregular boundaries and progressive bell-shaped walls. Here the skeletal remains of 3 individuals in anatomical connection have been recovered. One of them was in right lateral decubitus, another in left lateral decubitus and the third one in supine with his legs very

Figure 5. Estructura 48 calle Dinamarca 3-5.

Figure 6. Estructura 51 calle Dinamarca 3-5.

bent backwards and to the left (Figure 6). All had flexion and hyperflexion of lower and upper limbs. Five samples were collected for DNA analysis.

Structure 28

In this case, we have a structure of some complexity, with a trefoil plan which has three niches, two of them with an approximate northwest alignment and the third one located to the southwest (Figure 7). The human skeletal remains are located in the northwest niches, whereas the southwest niche, although having preserved layers of 0.80 m deep, had neither skeletal remains nor artefacts, with the exception of two 'baetyloid objects' located in the intersection with the other niches and similar to those discovered in La Huera. In the northern niche, the skeletal remains which could be identified correspond, according to the field records, to a total amount of 7 individuals, all articulated in right lateral decubitus, including two females and one child. 3 samples were collected for DNA analysis.

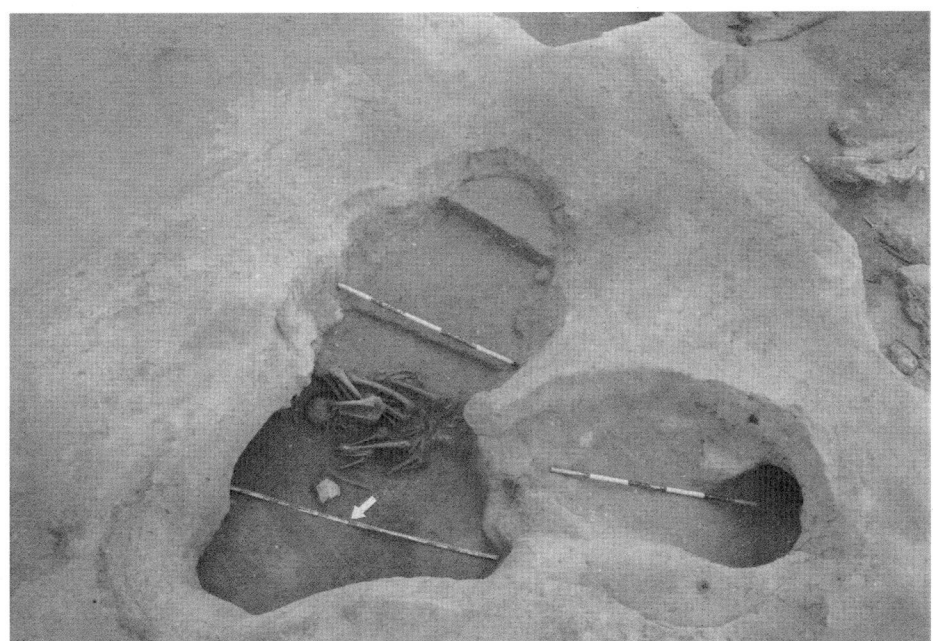

FIGURE 7. ESTRUCTURA 28 CALLE DINAMARCA 3-5.

Structure 5

This is the most complex structure, both for its architectural design as for the number of buried individuals, approximately 54. Three primary burials with articulated skeletons in flexed right lateral decubitus and the presence of partial anatomical articulations have been recorded in this structure. The continuity of funerary contexts was confirmed beyond the lowest excavated levels hence, the excavation work did not exhaust the stratigraphic sequence.

This structure has a possible passage, a first chamber (chamber 2) with a niche in its north side, a second chamber (main chamber) connected to the first one, and an independent circular niche (northwest niche) next to the main chamber and at a higher level (Figure 8). This northwest niche contained a total amount of 15 individuals.

The main chamber has a *quasi* circular section with irregular boundaries and its walls gradually acquire a bell shape. Its main axis is NNW-SSE oriented. The complete sequence of use of this funerary structure from its foundation

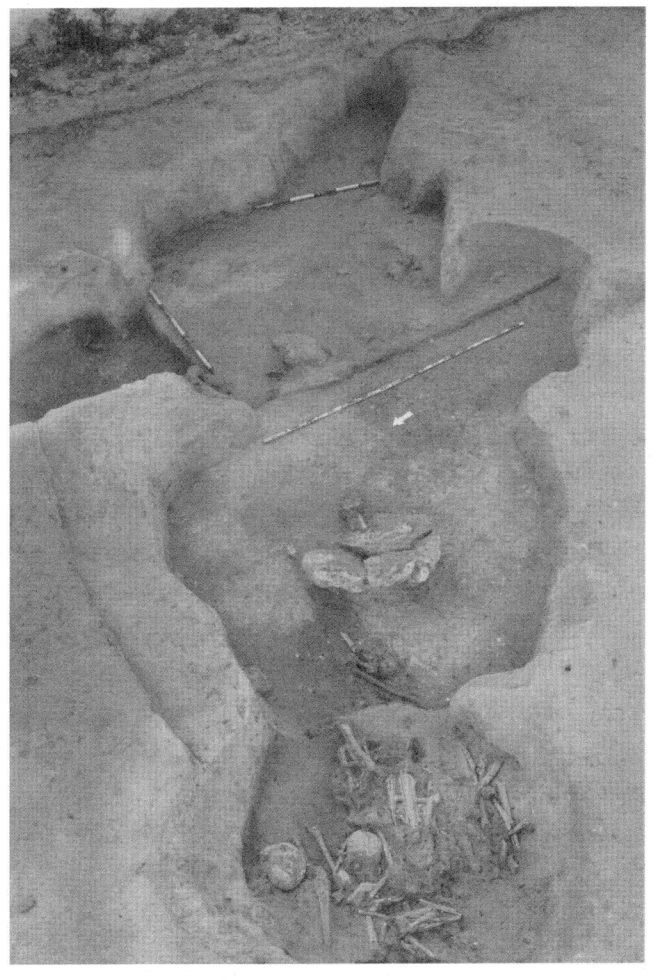

FIGURE 8. ESTRUCTURA 5 CALLE DINAMARCA 3-5.

until amortization and abandonment is unknown, but, at least, the different phases of use could be recorded, maybe from a time of full operation until its complete abandonment as a funerary space.

Five phases could be recorded, the first, and more recent in time, corresponds to the time when burials no longer occur and natural, geomorphologic processes develop with no direct anthropogenic cause. In the second phase, the structure would have been almost full but with some structural elements coming to the surface, like the cap of the possible 'skylight' roughly located in the center of the main chamber. In the third phase, the use of this space as a funerary receptacle was probably sporadic, once the structural deterioration had begun with fragmentation of the outer layer of the walls and collapsing of fragments of the covering. In a fourth phase, the collapse of the hedge can be witnessed. And finally the fifth phase is the moment of full swing, *i.e.* the funerary activity itself, with the presence of grave goods and other items.

In this context, and based on the anthropological field records, over 3,000 human remains were determined. A particular morphological feature was identified in only 3 individuals, amongst all the inhumations: a fissure on both sides of the mandible. This particular feature might indicate some kind of genetic link between the three individuals, as no other remains show similar features.

This set of bones shows various manifestations that inform us of the funerary practices. In this case we can reduce them to the crowding processes of skeletons, aiming to create space to proceed to new depositions. This is particularly evident in the individuals 1 and 2 (male and female) which were found in anatomical connexion and share space with others (Figure 9) which, although showing many anatomical connections, cannot be defined as complete skeletons.

The archaeological grave goods recovered in this set of structures seem scarce when compared with thouse obtained in other burial types. It is limited to 180 talcum necklace beads, a small pottery cup with 4 perforated hubs, 2 arrowheads (one in rock crystal), 2 limpet valves having their surfaces modified (Pajuelo and López Aldana, 2013), identified as *Patella* sp., in recent works at the PP4-Montelirio sector, some limpets with similar features were classified as *Cymbula nigra* (Liesau *et al.*, 2014), a retouched flint blade with trapezoid section, a polished stone axe and 2 shafts of bone pins like those moving head pins found in La Huera, although this identification is here also uncertain. Furthermore, what we have been calling 'ideological products' (Pajuelo and López Aldana, 2001) are

FIGURE 9. 1 AND 2 INDIVIDUALS OF THE STRUCTURE 5 CALLE DINAMARCA 3-5.

also represented by one object that, according to other criteria, is a so-called 'hopper' idol made of ivory. Twenty-six samples of human osteological tissues were collected for DNA analysis.

Dates of 3000-2930 and 2890-2860 BC (cal. 1 σ) were obtained (García Sanjuán *et al.*, in press).

Distribution of the funeral spaces

The evidences of skeletal remains in this archaeological site can be located in two distinct areas (Figure 10). On the one hand, outlining the area where the dwelling and productive structures were found, thus forming an arch on the outside of the domestic areas that connects to a priority and exclusive area of necropolis that extends to the southeast (Cruz-Auñón and Mejías, 2013: 186).

On the other hand, this zone that has been defined as a necropolis includes an inner area, which shall be referred to as a domestic space and productive activity area. Burials found herein always involve a different type of structures, not always built for funerary purposes: pits, 'silo' forms, trenches, ditches, huts, production spaces, etc. At some point in their functional life, such structures were converted into funerary containers for human remains, either with or a 'cultic' character (Cruz-Auñón and Mejías, 2013: 186).

The necropolis is alike to evidence an internal articulated organization, clustered in two huge funerary monuments. The most spectacular structures (by its architectural complexity, dimensions and grave goods) are few and far between other types, showing its selectivity within the group.

By its border spatial location and by its contents, artificial caves discussed here seem to correspond to qualitatively devalued groups within a pyramidal hierarchical structure. Under this same

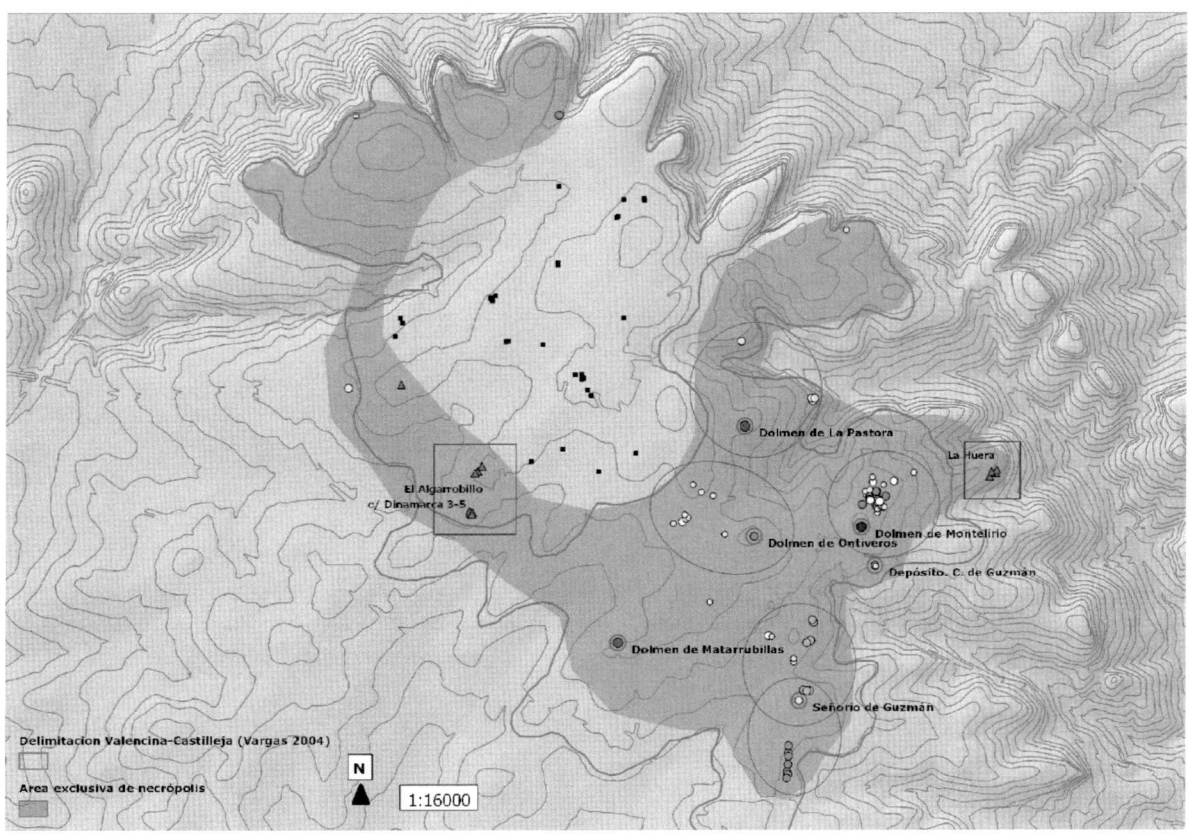

FIGURE 10. TYPES AND DISTRIBUTION OF BURIALS IN VALENCINA
(SOURCE: CRUZ-AUÑÓN & MEJÍAS 2013: FIG. 4).

premise, could be included those structures whose primitive functionality was not to accommodate burials.

In light of the great typological diversity of the burial structures, framed in chronologies obtained mostly in dwelling or productive contexts, and ranging between 3200 and 2000 BC, with most of the dating concentrating between 2700 and 2200, one might wonder about the reasons that generated this variability; not only in terms of the architecture of the funerary containers but also regarding the grave goods (rich and abundant *e.g.* in the Montelirio dolmen and scarce and austere in the artificial caves), or the own demographic composition of the burials.

Probably, this disparity observed and proven is the concrete realization of the social contradictions and inequalities inherent to strongly hierarchical socio-political models, within which different social identities and entities coexist, which, in most of the cases seem to obey nuclear or extended family groups (Cruz-Auñón and Mejías, 2013: 196-197; López Aldana *et al.*, 2015).

Conclusions

The unique spatial distribution observed in the artificial caves of Andalusia, is due to two factors that are not directly related. On the one hand, the need to locate the graves in a lithologic substrate that facilitates its excavation with the tools and media of the time. On the other hand, the influence of the settlement pattern of 3rd. millennium BC societies and their particular forms of burial. All this indicates a substantially common ritual behaviour, despite formal varieties typical of specific communities.

An interesting aspect is the forced closure of these structures, indicating that they house finite groups (Cruz-Auñón and Mejías, 2009), which basically respond to parent groups of tribal origin and character, though they endure and remain in the face of evidence of hierarchy processes (Ramos, 1997). The number of individuals and the age-sex relationship seem to corroborate the maintenance of the tribal structure, but these processes towards social complexity may not always lead to family aggregations (Cruz-Auñón and Mejías, 2013), and the structure 5 in Calle Dinamarca, 3-5 with 56 individuals and its continued use or the case of La Huera corroborating the same pattern, can be clear examples of this.

With the intention of determining kinship of these groups, a total of 35 samples were taken for DNA analytics in the individuals buried in Calle Dinamarca, 3-5, by the *Institut für Anthropologie* of the *Johannes-Gutenberg-Universität Mainz* (Germany). The Institute indicated that, of all these, 11 samples were analyzed and unfortunately proved unsuccessful. It seems that the same fate has befallen other samples from other Valencina locations. The reasons may have to do with poor conservation conditions of the samples collected, for the much warmer climate in the south, but also quite influenced by the constitution of the soil (too acidic or too wet), since the soil conditions are very important for long-term survival of DNA in bones and teeth. However these circumstances should be deeper analyzed.

At the same time, we believe that the ritual used in the burial is a noteworthy aspect, fully confirmed in Calle Dinamarca, 3-5. It consists in the use of bandages or shrouds (or similar tool) in the bodies to allow flexion-hyperflexion of both lower and upper limbs. All this indicates a substantially common ritual behaviour, characteristic of particular communities and basically framed in the Andalusia region, in areas that have been terming as peripheral areas (López Aldana and Pajuelo, 2001; Ramos *et al.*, 2004). And even though there are obvious relationships between settlements, the integration materializes only very occasionally at the necropolis level, which in itself reflects a genuine political territory where different patterns are related to social coercion (Arteaga, 1992; Nocete, 1994; López Aldana and Pajuelo, 2001; Ramos *et al.*, 2004). So it is not surprising that within the necropolis of Valencina there is evidence for coercive situations, where besides, and based not only in production-consumption, the convergence of the related those related to productive forces, which maintain certain behavioural normalization that materialize in certain formal aspects of the tombs.

In this sense, the burials could be determined either by a spatial hierarchy based on large settlements from which smaller ones depend on (López Aldana and Pajuelo, 2001), that would impose standards and rules when it comes to burying the dead; or by an incipient resistance that opposes certain burial forms against the 'standard' forms prevailing over the 'system'.

References

Arteaga, O (1992) – Tribalización, jerarquización y estado en el territorio de El Argar. *Spal* 1, p. 179-208. Sevilla.

Cruz-Auñón, R.; Mejías, J.C. (2009) – Sistemas de información geográfica y análisis espacial aplicados al estudio de la dispersión del registro arqueológico en la necrópolis del III milenio a.n.e. del 'El Negrón' (Gilena, Sevilla). Estudios de Prehistoria y Arqueología en homenaje a Pilar Acosta Martínez, p. 207-232. Sevilla.

Cruz-Auñón, R.; Mejías, J.C. (2013) – Diversidad de identidades en el asentamiento de Valencina de la Concepción (Sevilla). *In* García Sanjuán, L.; Vargas Jiménez, J.M.; Hurtado Pérez, V.; Ruiz Moreno, T. and Cruz-Auñón Briones, R. (eds.): *El Asentamiento Prehistórico de Valencina de la Concepción (Sevilla): Investigación y Tutela en el 150 aniversario de Descubrimiento de La Pastora,* p. 175-200. Universidad de Sevilla. Sevilla.

García Sanjuán, L.; Beavan, N.; Díazguadarmino-Uribe, M.; Díaz-Zorita Bonilla, M.; Fernández Flores, A.; Hamilton, D.; López Aldana, P.M.; Méndez Izquierdo, E.; Pajuelo Pando, A.; Vargas Jiménez, J.M.; Wheatley, D.; Whittle, A. (in press) – Cronología radiocarbónica y modelado bayesiano del asentamiento de Valencina de la Concepción (Sevilla, España): hacia una cronología de alta resolución de la Edad del Cobre en el Sur de la Península Ibérica. Congreso Internacional Nuevas Tecnológias Aplicadas a la Investigación Arqueológica, 'ARQUEOWORLD'. Valencina de la Concepción (Sevilla). 6-8 Noviembre 2014.

Liesau Von Lettow-Vorbeck, C.; Aparicio Alonso, M.T.; Araujo Armero, R.; Llorente Rodríguez, L.; Morales Muñiz, A. (2014) – La fauna del sector PP4-Montelirio del yacimiento prehistórico de Valencina de la Concepción (Sevilla). Economía y simbolismo de los animales en una comunidad del III milenio. Menga. Revista de Prehistoria de Andalucía nº 05. 2014. p. 69-97. Antequera.

López Aldana, P.M.; Pajuelo, A. (2001) – 'Estrategias político-territoriales de un poder central: el Bajo Guadalquivir en el III milenio a.n.e.'. *Revista atlántica-mediterránea de prehistoria y arqueología social* 4, p. 207-227. Cádiz.

López Aldana, P.M.; Pajuelo Pando, A.; Mejías-García, J.C.; Cruz-Auñón, M.R. (2015) – 'Variabilidad funeraria en las sociedades del III milenio en el sector Señorío de Guzmán de Valencina-Castilleja (Sevilla)'. *In* Rocha, L.; Bueno-Ramirez, P. and Branco, G. (eds.): *Death as Archaeology of Transition: Thoughts and Materials,* p. 257-274. BAR International Series 2708. Oxford.

Mejías-García, J.C. (2011) – *El asentamiento de Valencina en el III milenio a.n.e. Sistema de Información Geográfica y Análisis Espacial de un recinto de fosos* (Memoria D.E.A. inédita, Universidad de Sevilla). Sevilla.

Mejías-García, J.C. (2013) – Análisis espacial en el asentamiento y necrópolis de Valencina: patrones de distribución y sectorización. *VI Encuentro de Arqueología del Suroeste Peninsular,* p. 463-500. Villafranca de los Barros.

Mejías-García, J.C.; Cruz-Auñón, M.R.; Pajuelo Pando, A.; López Aldana, P.M. (2015) – Análisis del modelo de organización espacial de la necrópolis de Valencina. La complejidad social a debate. *In* Branco, G.; Rocha, L.; Duarte, C.; Oliveira, J. and Bueno Ramirez, P. (eds.) – *Arqueologia de Transicão: O Mundo Funerário. Actas II International Congress of Transition Archaeology,* p. 52-70. CHAIA. Unviersidad de Évora. Évora.

Méndez Izquierdo, E. (2013) – 'La cueva artificial de la Huera (Castilleja de Guzmán, Sevilla)'. *In* García Sanjuán, L.; Vargas Jiménez, J.M.; Hurtado Pérez, V.; Ruiz Moreno, T. and Cruz-

Auñón Briones, R. (eds.): *El Asentamiento Prehistórico de Valencina de la Concepción (Sevilla): Investigación y Tutela en el 150 aniversario de Descubrimiento de La Pastora*, p. 247-263. Universidad de Sevilla. Sevilla.

Nocete, F. (1994) – La formación del estado en las campiñas del Alto Guadalquivir. Monográfica Arte y Arqueología. Granada.

Pajuelo, A.; López Aldana, P.M. (2001) – Ideología y control político durante el III milenio a.n.e. en el Bajo Guadalquivir. *Revista atlántica-mediterránea de prehistoria y arqueología social* 4, p. 229-255. Cádiz.

Pajuelo, A. (2009) – Excavación Arqueológica Preventiva en C/ Dinamarca 3-5. Urb. El Algarrobillo (Valencina de la Concepción). Sevilla. (Memoria inédita – Delegación Provincial de la Consejería de Cultura de la Junta de Andalucía. Sevilla).

Pajuelo, A.; López Aldana, P.M. (2013) – 'La necrópolis de cuevas artificiales y fosas de C/ Dinamarca 3 y 5 (Valencina de la Concepción, Sevilla)'. *In* García Sanjuán, L.; Vargas Jiménez, J.M.; Hurtado Pérez, V.; Ruiz Moreno, T. and Cruz-Auñón Briones, R. (eds.): *El Asentamiento Prehistórico de Valencina de la Concepción (Sevilla): Investigación y Tutela en el 150 aniversario de Descubrimiento de La Pastora*, p. 281-292.Universidad de Sevilla. Sevilla.

Pajuelo Pando, A.; López Aldana, P.M.; Cruz-Auñón Briones, R.; Mejías García, J.C. (2013) – Las cuevas artificiales de Valencina. Análisis y propuestas de la distribución espacial a escala regional. *Actas VI Encuentro de Arqueología del Sudoeste Peninsular,* p. 225-318. Villafranca de los Barros.

Ramos, J., Espejo, M.M.; Cantalejo, P. (2004) – La formación social clasista inicial (milenio III y II a.n.e.) en los entornos de Ardales (Málaga). *Simposios de Prehistoria Cueva de Nerja*, p. 309-320. Málaga.

Santana, I. (1993) – Excavación arqueológica de urgencia en El Algarrobillo, Valencina de la Concepción (Sevilla). *Anuario Arqueológico de Andalucía/1991*, p. 548-553. Sevilla.

Multiple burials in pit graves from Recent Prehistory at Southwest of Iberia: The cases of Monte do Vale do Ouro 2 (Ferreira do Alentejo), Ribeira de S. Domingos 1 and Alto de Brinches 3 (Serpa)

Tânia Pereira[1], Ana Maria Silva[2,5], António Valera[3], Eduardo Porfírio[4]

[1] Department of Life Sciences, University of Coimbra, Portugal
[2] Laboratory of Prehistory, CIAS- Research Center for Anthropology and Health, University of Coimbra, Portugal
[3] NIA – ERA Arqueologia SA
[4] Palimpsesto – Estudo e Preservação do Património Cultural Lda., Coimbra, Portugal
[5] UNIARQ – WAPS – University of Lisbon
taniafepereira@gmail.com

Abstract

The recent work of rescue archaeology in Portugal has shown an increasing number of pit graves from different time periods, dated from the Late Neolithic until the Final Bronze Age.

The aim of the present work is to present some preliminary results of a study on pit funerary contexts of Alto de Brinches 3 (Serpa), Ribeira de S. Domingos 1 (Serpa) and Monte do Vale do Ouro 2 (Ferreira do Alentejo).

These pits were used as multiple burials (minimum number of individuals between 3 and 5) in several positions and orientations. Adult and non-adult individuals of both sexes are present. Among the more relevant data was the evidence of non-masticatory use of two teeth recovered from pit 102 of Monte do Vale do Ouro 2 and evidences of exposure to fire on individuals from pit 97 from the same site.

Keywords

pit graves, Southwest Iberia; Late Neolithic/Bronze Age; non-masticatory use of teeth; evidence of fire

Résumé

Les travaux récents de l'archéologie de sauvetage au Portugal a permis la détection d'un nombre croissant de tombes à fosse des périodes différentes, datées du Néolithique jusqu'à Age du Bronze Final.

Le but de ce travail est de montrer quelques résultats préliminaires sur des contextes funéraires dans la fosse de Alto de Brinches 3 (Serpa), Ribeira de S. Domingos 1 (Serpa) et Monte do Vale do Ouro 2 (Ferreira do Alentejo).

Ces fosses ont été utilisées comme sépultures multiples (nombre minimum d'individus entre 3 et 5) dans plusieurs positions et orientations. Individus des deux sexes, les adultes et non adultes sont représentés. À la fosse 97 de Monte do Vale do Ouro, deux individus ont montré traces de l'action du feu. La preuve de l'utilisation non-masticatoire des dents dans l'échantillon de Monte do Vale do Ouro (fosse 102) est aussi pertinente.

Mots-clés

Sud-Ouest Ibérique; Néolithique/Bronze Final; utilisation non-masticatoire des dents; preuves de feu

Introduction

The consecutive works of rescue Archaeology have revealed new data about the funerary practices of Late Prehistoric communities of Southwest Portugal (Alentejo). In the district of Beja few funerary structures dated from Late Prehistory were known. For that reason, the discourse on funerary archaeology for the region of Alentejo was based on Megalithism. However, with the increasing rescue archaeology, the discovery of burials in pits, ditches and *hypogea* increased in the last decade (Valera 2012).

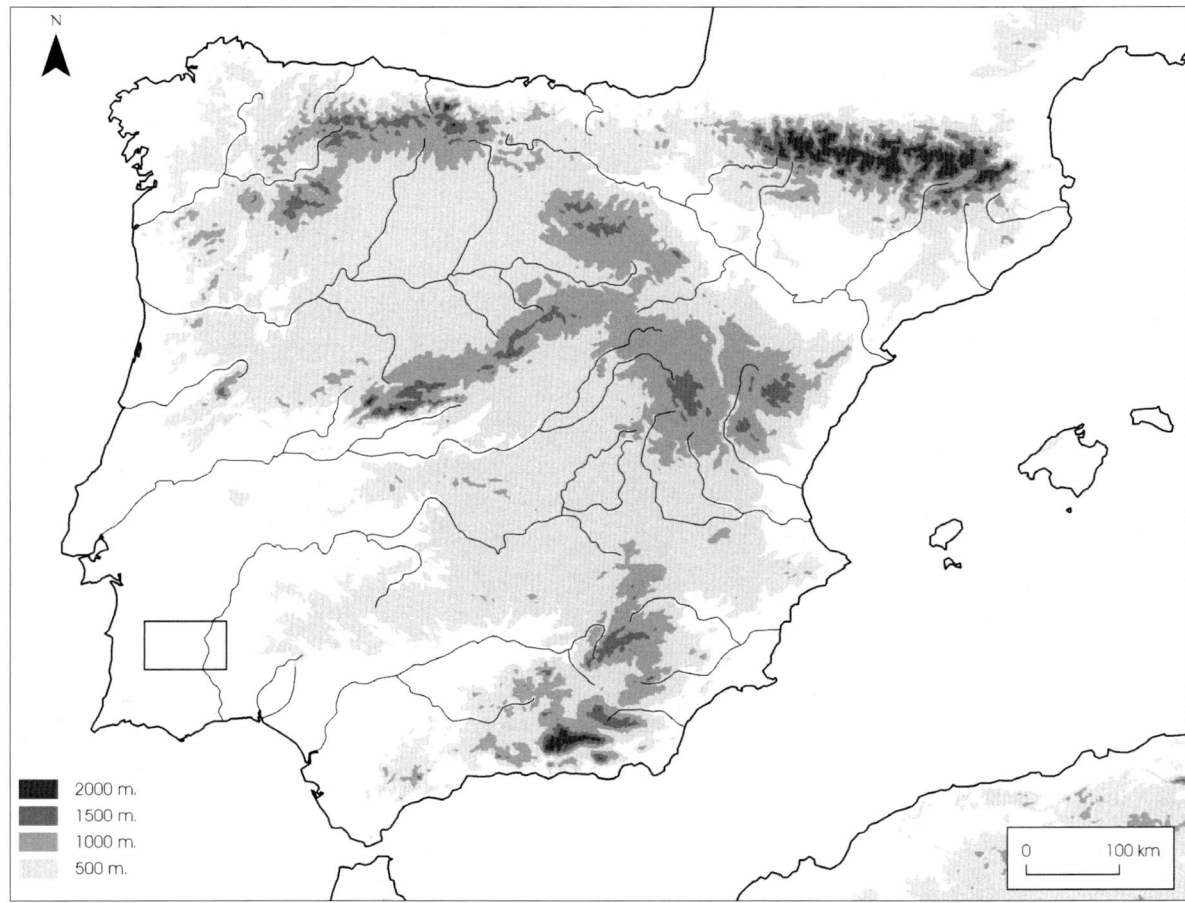

FIGURE 1. GEOGRAPHIC LOCALIZATION IN THE IBERIAN PENINSULA OF THE STUDIED AREA.

In this work three archaeological sites from the district of Beja excavated by private archaeological companies (Omniknos, ERA Arqueologia SA and Palimpsesto) were analyzed. These correspond to multiple burials in pits from Monte do Vale do Ouro 2 at Ferreira do Alentejo (dated from the Chalcolithic and Bronze Age), Ribeira de S. Domingos 1 at Brinches (dated from the Late Neolithic/Chalcolithic) and Alto de Brinches 3 at São Salvador (dated from Chalcolithic) (Figure 1).

The aim of this work is to contribute to the comprehension of funerary practices of the Late Prehistoric communities of Southwest of the Peninsula. Through observation of burial positions and orientations, presence/absence of artefacts and type of structures, attempts were made to better understand the funerary rituals of these populations and possible burial patterns. Furthermore, the osteological study included the estimation of the Minimal Number of Individuals (MNI) *per* context, the age at death assessment and sexual diagnosis of the individuals in order to get insights of their biological aspects.

Materials and Methods

Two pits from Monte do Vale do Ouro 2 were studied. Pit 97 contained three burials (9701, 9702 and 9703) and a few deciduous teeth. Burials 10202, 10205 and 10207, and a few scattered bones (unit 10200) were identified in the pit 102. Anatomical connections 805, 807, 808 and 809; burials 812, 813 and 814, and some scattered bones (unit 806) were exhumed from Ribeira de S. Domingos 1. At Alto de Brinches 3 only one pit was analyzed, which included burials 661 and 656, the anatomical connections 639 and 668, and the ossuaries 453, 469, 637 and 659. In general, the human remains were very fragmented. Moreover, in some cases the cortical surface displayed severe surface alterations. For those reasons, the methods were adjusted.

Age at death estimation for the non-adult sample was carried out following the methods proposed by Smith (1991) and AlQahtani *et al.*, (2010) using dental remains. For the adult sample age at death was assessed according to methods detailed by MacLaughlin (1990) and Schaefer and co-workers (2009). Sexual diagnosis was based on cranial features (Ferembach *et al.*, 1980; Buikstra and Ubelaker 1994) and long bones (Wasterlain 2000) were performed according to standard methods. The preliminary field data were also taken into account. Some human remains display traces of exposure of fire. In order to confirm this, they were submitted to the analysis of *Fourier Transform Infrared Spectroscopy* (FTIR) a methodology that is based on the measuring of Crystallinity Index (CI) and carbonate to phosphate ratio (C/P) (Thompson *et al.* 2009) in the bones. The CI values slowly increases in the dead bone once its composition becomes more ordered, although some diagenetic changes can raise the values of CI (Thompson *et al.*, 2009). However, the highest peaks of this index generally indicate the burning of the bones. The measuring of the CI is combined with the C/P ratio that should decrease as a result of burning (Thompson *et al.*, 2009).

Results

Monte do Vale do Ouro 2

Monte do Vale do Ouro 2 is located in Ferreira do Alentejo, in the district of Beja, Southwest of Portugal. Although during the excavations 112 structures have been intervened, only two presented funerary contexts. These are pits 97 (dated from Chalcolithic) and pit 102 (dated from Bronze Age) (Moro Berraquero and Figueiredo 2013). Both pits had circular contour and convergent walls containing multiple human burials. Pit 97, located on Southeast sector, had a diameter of 1.65 m and was 0.71 m deep. The burials were deposited on the bottom of the pit and covered by a single stratigraphic unit (Moro Berraquero and Figueiredo 2013). Located on Northeast sector, pit 102, had 1.22 m of diameter and was 1.16 m deep. In this pit three distinct phases of inhumation were identified (Figure 2) (Moro Berraquero and Figueiredo 2013).

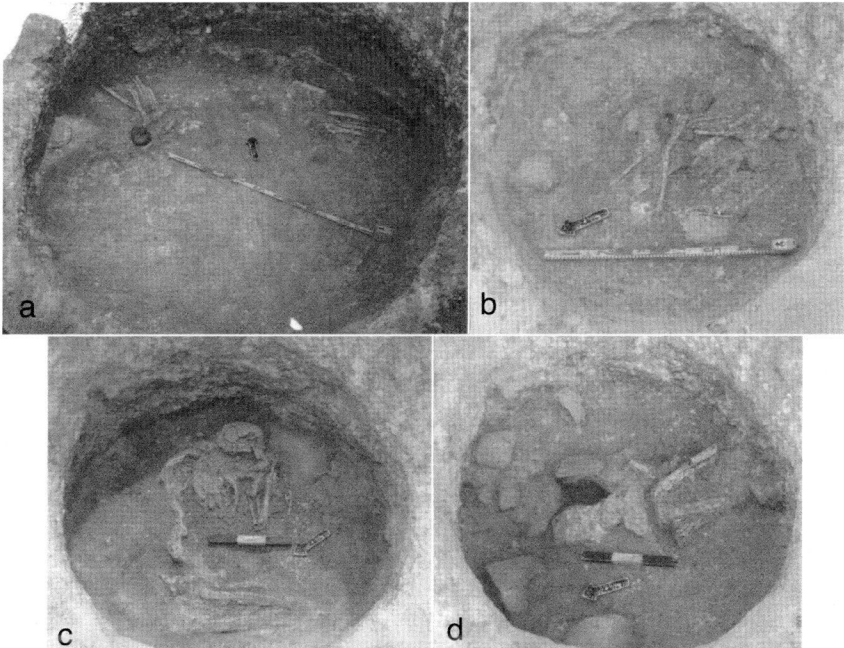

FIGURE 2. PIT 97 AND 102 OF MONTE DO VALE DO OURO 2 (A – BURIALS 9701, 9702 AND 9703; B – BURIAL 10202; C – BURIAL 10205; D – BURIAL 10207) (MORO BERRAQUERO & FIGUEIREDO 2013).

Individual	Bones	Age at death	Sexual diagnosis
Individual 9701	Third molar	Adult	F
Individual 9702	Third inferior molar	15.6-16.2 years old	-
Individual 9703	Permanent teeth	8-11 years old	-
Scattered teeth	Deciduous teeth	1.5-3.8 years old	-

FIGURE 3. DEMOGRAPHIC PROFILE OF THE INDIVIDUALS EXHUMED FROM PIT 97 OF MONTE DO VALE DO OURO 2.

Pit 97

During the excavation of pit 97 three burials (9701, 9702 and 9703) were identified. Posteriorly, some deciduous teeth along with some fragments of a skull and a mandibular condyle were also found in stratigraphic unit 9703. These discoveries changed the final MNI from pit 97 to 4 (Figure 3).

Sex diagnosis was only possible for the adult individual 9701. The gracile aspect of the occipital condyle and the long bones diaphysis suggests they belong to a female individual. The apex of the inferior and superior third molars was closed but the low dental wear observed on its occlusal surfaces indicates that it probably belonged to a young adult. The remaining individuals are non-adults. The individual 9702 displayed half formed roots in the third inferior molars, thus aged between 15.6-16.2 and 16.5-17.5 years old according to Smith (1991) and AlQahtani et al., (2010), respectively. The inferior permanent teeth of the burial 9703 were still developing revealing that the skeleton belonged to an 8-12 to 9.5-13.5 years old individual, according to Smith (1991) and AlQahtani et al., (2010). The deciduous teeth of the fourth individual showed an age at death estimation of around 2.5 years according to AlQahtani et al., (2010).

The individual 9701 deposited in dorsal *decubitus*, with orientation W-E was poorly preserved (Moro Berraquero and Figueiredo 2013), specially the axial skeleton and only the diaphysis of the long bones were better preserved. Traces of fire were found on this individual but these do not seem to be uniform along the skeleton. The most affected areas were the axial and appendicular skeleton (clavicle and right humerus, distal part of the right femur and both tibia and fibula). The colours of the bones ranged from black, blue and white. In some cases different colours were present in the same bone. Individual 9702, deposited below 9701, was inhumed in right lateral *decubitus*, with its skull pointing to NW (Moro Berraquero and Figueiredo 2013). Traces of fire were also found on this individual, as both femurs displayed black colour (Figure 4). The individual in burial 9703 was found in right lateral *decubitus*, and very fragmented (Moro Berraquero and Figueiredo 2013). There were not visible traces of fire on this skeleton.

At the beginning, the different colours observed among bones from these skeletons raised doubts about their origin: signs of fire or the result of other taphonomic agents? So, an analysis of FTIR (*Fourier Transform Infrared Spectroscopy*) (Thompson et al., 2009) was performed on bones of both skeletons (9701 and 9702) to confirm the exposition to fire. For the analysis, two bone samples (one black and one beige) from each skeleton were selected. A sample of the tibia of the individual 9703 was also sent to analysis. The results showed that the bones with beige colour revealed higher crystallinity indexes (CI) and lower carbonate to phosphate ratios (C/P), a result not expected on unburnt bones. The black samples showed levels of CI and C/P that are compatible with an inhumation that has not been in contact with fire. When analysing the results it is possible to infer that the three individuals had been exposed to fire of low to medium temperatures, and not in an uniform way along the skeleton. The unexpected beige colour in burnt bones may have occurred by some process of discoloration caused by other taphonomic agents.

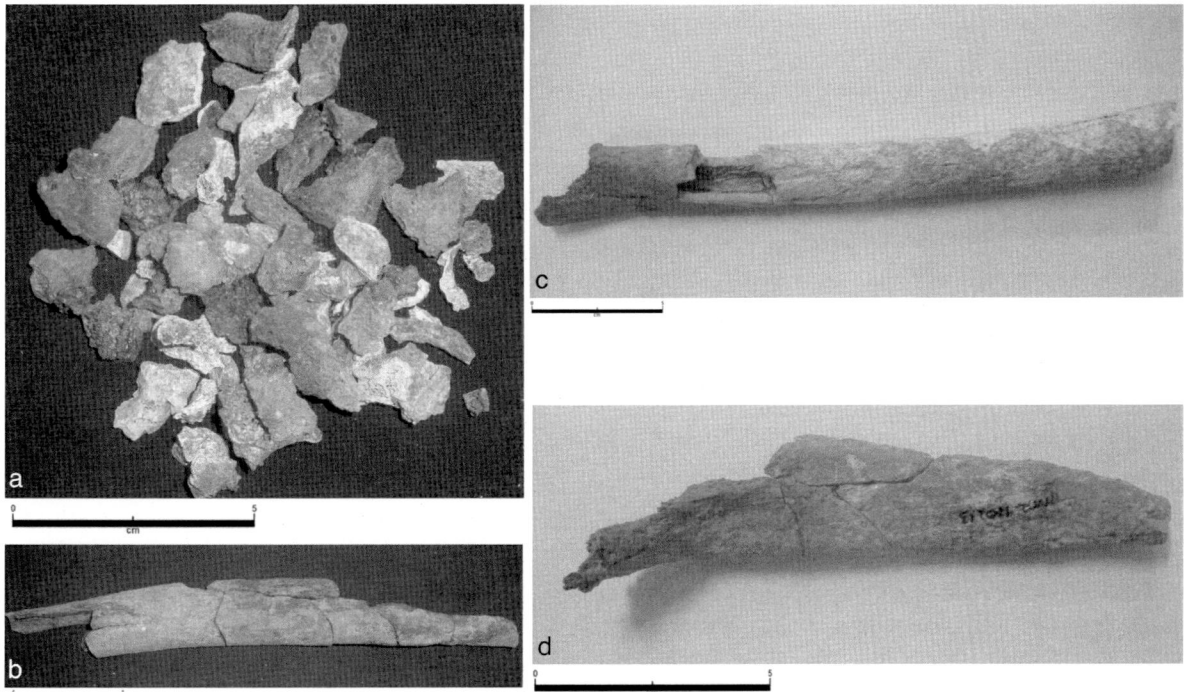

FIGURE 4. TRACES OF FIRE ON INDIVIDUALS 9701 AND 9702 FROM PIT 97 OF MONTE DO VALE DO OURO 2
(A – FRAGMENTS OF SKULL FROM INDIVIDUAL 9701; B – FRAGMENT OF TIBIA FROM INDIVIDUAL 9701;
C AND D – LEFT AND RIGHT FEMURS FROM INDIVIDUAL 9702).

Pit 102

Three burials (10202, 10205 and 10207) were identified during fieldwork of pit 102. A few scattered bones in stratigraphic unit 10200 (fragments of femur and ulna) seem to indicate that at least one more individual was present. These fragments do not seem to be related to none of the previous burials: individual 10202 was a non-adult; the thickness of the cortical bone of individual 10205 did not match; and individual 10207 had all the long bones diaphysis almost complete. Furthermore, there was a premolar that could not be related with none of the above individuals but could belong to the same individual of stratigraphic unit 10200. Thus the MNI of this pit is 3 adults and 1 non-adult (Figure 5).

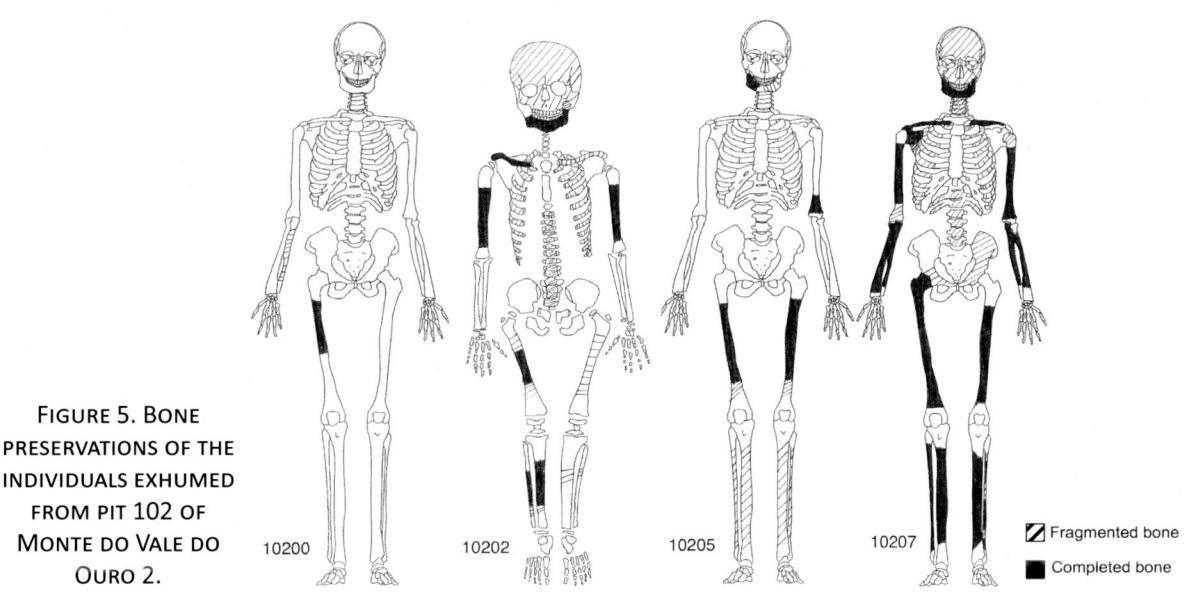

FIGURE 5. BONE PRESERVATIONS OF THE INDIVIDUALS EXHUMED FROM PIT 102 OF MONTE DO VALE DO OURO 2.

It was not possible to observe the position or orientation of the burial 10200. The osteological material was very fragmented and few bones were preserved. The burial 10202 was found in right lateral *decubitus*, with the skull orientated to SE, the individual 10205 was deposited in right lateral *decubitus* with flexed limbs and the burial 10207 was found in left lateral *decubitus* with flexed limbs and skull to SE (Moro Berraquero and Figueiredo 2013). This last skeleton represents the best preserved one in this pit with complete long bones diaphysis.

The robustness of bones from skeleton 10200 suggests a male individual and the gracile aspect of bones belonging to 10205 suggests a female skeleton. *Antemortem* tooth loss and the reduced thickness of cortical bone suggest the later was an older individual. Some cranial features (mastoid process and mental eminence) and the vertical diameter of femur's head (39 mm) of the individual 10207 revealed a female individual. The open apex of the lower right third molar and the not fused sternal epiphysis of the clavicle suggest an age at death around 19 to 22.5 years old.

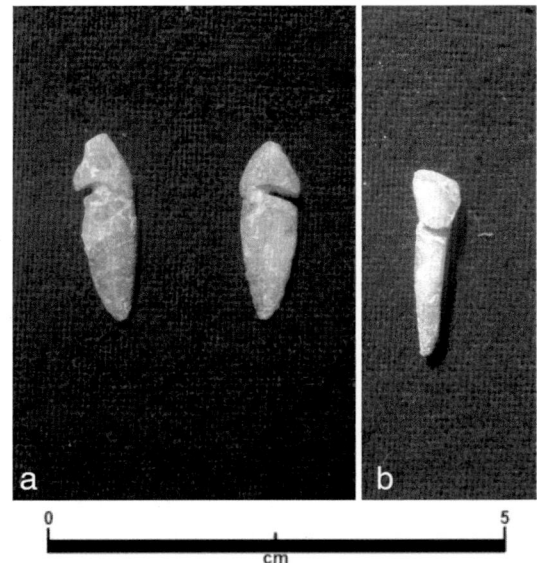

FIGURE 6. DENTAL WEAR ON OCCLUSAL AND LINGUAL SURFACE OF THE TWO SUPERIOR LATERAL INCISORS AND A SULCUS ON THE CEMENT-ENAMEL JUNCTION: A – LATERAL MESIAL VIEW; B – ANTERIOR LINGUAL VIEW (LEFT SUPERIOR INCISOR).

The individual 10202 was the only non-adult in this pit with an age at death estimation ranging from 5-7 to 6.5-7.5 years old, according to Smith (1991) and AlQahtani *et al.*, (2010), respectively.

Two antimeres superior lateral incisors were found in the stratigraphic unit 10200 of this pit and could not be associated with any of the others burials. These display unusual tooth wear on the lingual and occlusal area of the teeth and a sulcus on the cement-enamel junction (Figure 6). It is possible that these teeth belonged to individual 10205 considering its wear.

Ribeira de S. Domingos 1 – Pit 1

The archaeological site of Ribeira S. Domingos 1 is located in Brinches (Serpa; district of Beja). Pit 1 revealed human remains along with evidences of Late Neolithic/Chalcolithic archaeological materials (Valera 2012).

This pit has a circular plan and concave walls with 1.60 m of diameter and 1.55 m depth (Fig. 7). Six individuals were deposited in the bottom of the pit. However, only five were available for study. Some disturbances of the anatomical connections may be explained by the reuse of the structure (Miguel and Godinho 2009). In association with the burials a skeleton of a little animal (maybe a rabbit) was found. In a second phase, the Southwest part of the pit collapsed covering half of the structure. On the uncovered half, two bowls and a dormant were deposited, followed by two different stratigraphic units with fragments of ceramic. After that the structure was closed (Miguel and Godinho 2009).

In addition to the burials found in this pit (808, 809, 812, 813 and 814), some anatomical connections (805, 807) and scattered bones (806) were also discovered. The laboratory work has allowed the detection of the correlation between some of these anatomical connections.

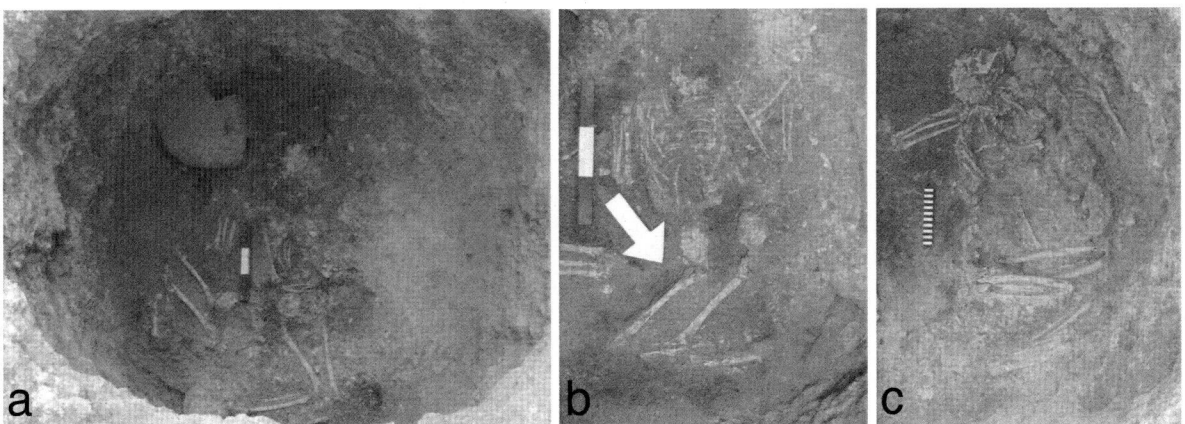

FIGURE 7. INDIVIDUALS ON PIT 1 FROM RIBEIRA DE S. DOMINGOS 1
(A – BURIAL 808; B – BURIAL 809; C – BURIALS 812 AND 813)
(MIGUEL & GODINHO 2009).

Burial 808 belongs to an individual that passed away between 8 and 12 years old. This skeleton had present the maxillae and mandible, left humerus, radio, ulna, tibia and fibula, both scapulas, clavicles, hip bones and femurs and also some inferior and superior permanent teeth. Fragments of skull, right humerus and 6 permanent upper teeth in development were found in the stratigraphic unit 806. These bones are compatible, in terms of skeletal and dental maturity, with incomplete individuals labelled as 808 and 805. Therefore they were studied together (805+806+808), and from now on designate as individual 808. This individual was probably deposited in ventral *decubitus*, with orientation SE-NO (Miguel and Godinho 2009).

The burial 809 belongs to an individual around 11 years old (according to dental calcification, Smith 1991). Anatomical connection 807 includes several lower and upper permanent teeth in development besides some deciduous teeth. The ages at death assessment of these teeth matched with the age of the individual 809, and thus, were considered to represent the same individual (807+809). The composite individual 809 (807+809) was deposited in dorsal *decubitus*, orientated SW-NE (Miguel and Godinho 2009).

The individual in burial 812 was deposited in lateral flexed *decubitus*, with its hand next to the mandible. The orientation of the body was E-W (Miguel and Godinho 2009). The skeleton was very fragmented including the diaphyses of the long bones.

The burial 813 was deposited in flexed ventral *decubitus*, with the hand next to the right humerus. It was oriented E-W (Miguel and Godinho 2009). The long bones diaphyses were preserved but the ends were destroyed.

It was not possible to register the position and the orientation of individual 814 due to its high level of fragmentation (Miguel and Godinho 2009).

In sum, the MNI of this pit is 5, 3 non-adults and 2 adults (excluding the remains not available for study). Sex diagnosis revealed that individual 812 is probably a male due to the mental prominence and robustness of his bones. Individual 813 displays some cranial features (mastoid process and zygomatic process) that indicate a female individual.

The age at death estimation revealed that individuals 812 and 813 were adults, due to the complete calcification of the third molar. All other individuals were non-adults. The age at death estimation was carried out based on dental calcification: individual 808 died between 7.5-12.6 and 10.5-12.5

years old; individual 809 died between 7.5-11.5 and 8.5-13.5 years old; individual 814 died between 4.8-6.8 and 5.5-6.5 years old according to Smith (1991) and AlQathani *et al.* (2010), respectively.

Alto de Brinches 3

Alto de Brinches 3 is located in São Salvador (Serpa, district of Beja). The site has occupations from distinct chronological periods. In the present study, only the contexts dated to the Chalcolithic period are included, pit 691. This structure has a circular contour with 2.37 m of diameter and it was 1.03 m deep (Fig. 8). A slightly depression (0.40 m wide, 1 m in length and 0.22 m deep) was excavated in the filling of the pit containing a burial (661) (Fig. 8). This depression was interpreted as a flat grave by Inocêncio (2013).

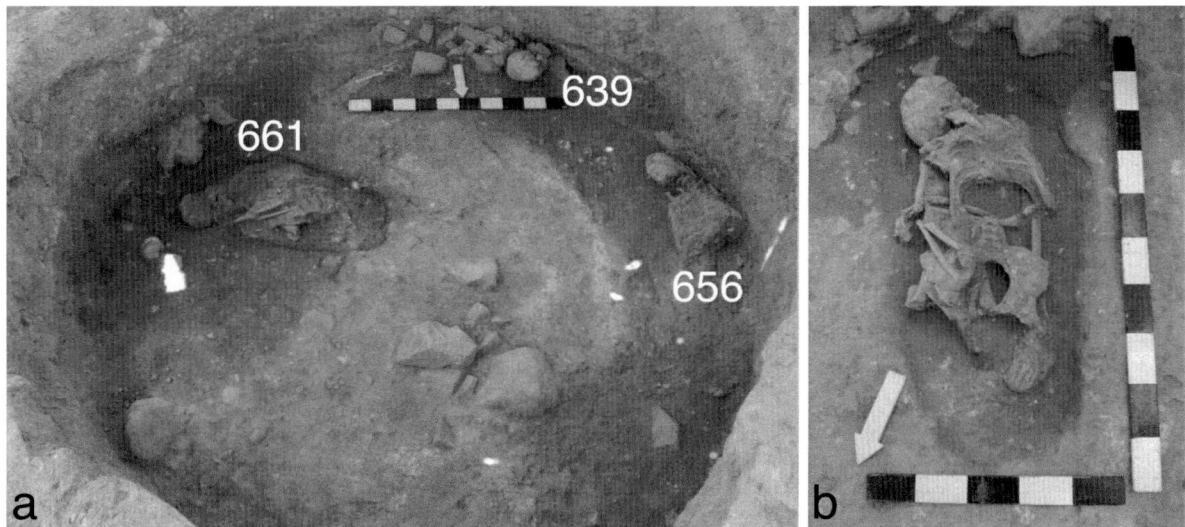

FIGURE 8. PIT 691 OF ALTO DE BRINCHES 3 (RODRIGUES *ET AL.* 2012): A – ANATOMICAL CONNECTION 639 AND BURIALS 656 AND 661; B – BURIAL 661 DEPOSITED ON THE FLAT GRAVE.

The MNI exhumed from **pit 691** was obtained from long bones, which revealed the presence of at least 2 adults since it was possible to match bones from different anatomical connections and ossuaries (Fig. 9).

The bones from anatomical connection 639, the scattered bones 668, and the ossuaries 659 and 453 belonged to individual 1. Only the right humerus from the ossuary 469 belonged to this individual. The anatomical connection of the skull with the vertebrae suggested that the individual was deposited in lateral right *decubitus* with the orientation W-E (Alves *et al.*, 2010). The epicondyle width measured during fieldwork indicated a female individual. Moreover, the open apex of the third superior molars indicates a young adult.

The bones from burial 656, the ossuary 637 and the left tibia and fibula from ossuary 469 belong to individual 2. The skeleton was deposited in lateral left *decubitus* with the orientation S-N (Alves *et al.*, 2010). Cranial and hip bone features of this skeleton suggest a male individual. The third molar of individual 2 was completely formed, confirming an adult individual.

In **flat grave 689,** individual 661 was deposited in ventral *decubitus*, with the orientation SE-NW. The left superior limb was flexed with the humerus over the right forearm and the ulna and radio over the left hipbone. The right superior limb was flexed under the chest. The flexed inferior limbs were

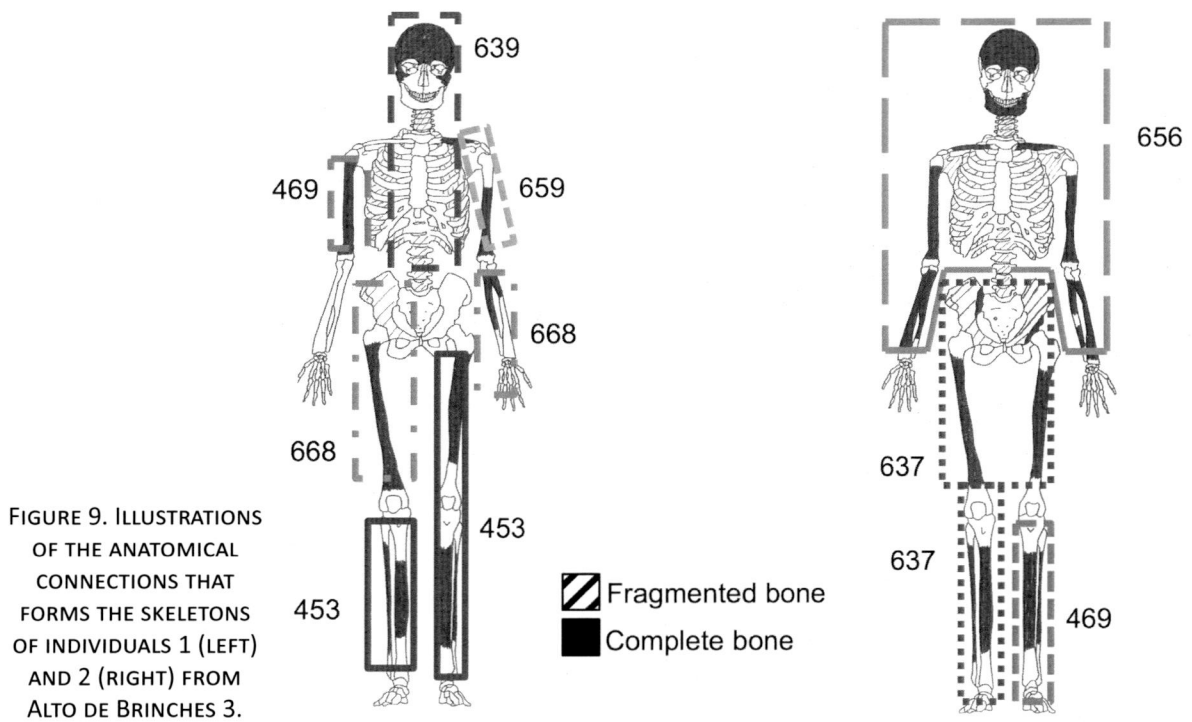

FIGURE 9. ILLUSTRATIONS OF THE ANATOMICAL CONNECTIONS THAT FORMS THE SKELETONS OF INDIVIDUALS 1 (LEFT) AND 2 (RIGHT) FROM ALTO DE BRINCHES 3.

under the pelvis and chest (Alves *et al.*, 2010). The sexual diagnosis is based on the observations during the fieldwork: the morphology of the hipbone, the *inion* and the epicondyle width (45.5 mm) suggest a female individual (Alves *et al.*, 2010). Regarding age at death estimation, cranial sutures were in advanced stage of obliteration.

Discussion

All pits analysed in this work had multiple burials. Human remains were recovered *in situ*, in anatomical connections and commingled. However, in at least in one of the sites (Alto de Brinches 3) there is a structure of the same chronology with a single burial.

The MNI of these burial pits ranged from 3 (Alto de Brinches 3), 4 (on both pits of Monte do Vale do Ouro 2) to 6 (Ribeira de S. Domingos 1). The positions of inhumation observed are very diverse, including dorsal, lateral (right and left) and ventral *decubitus*. Although no clear trend is visible the majority of burials were deposited in lateral *decubitus*. Several orientations were also registered: W-E, E-W, NW-SE, SE-NW and S-N (Pereira 2014).

Traces of fire in several bones from the three skeletons exhumed from pit 97 of Monte do Vale de Ouro 2 was among the unexpected finds. These observations prompted an FTIR analysis to confirm if the alterations were indeed due to exposition to fire or due to another taphonomic agent. The results confirmed inconsistent exposure to low intensity fire. Such evidences cannot be interpreted as a practice of cremation. The origin of the fire is not known. Some traces of fire found on Late Prehistoric contexts of the Peninsula have been interpreted as a consequence of cleaning fires that occurred on the surface (Armendariz 1990). Some authors refer that the fire could be a consequence of the illumination during the inhumation (Rojo Guerra *et al.*, 2002) but this would not be expected in this kind of structure. The possibility of the fire being symbolic is also proposed (Matutano 2013). Regarding to the bones from Monte do Vale do Ouro 2 we do not know if the fire was intentional or accidental, for practical or ritual reasons (Pereira 2014). It is important to mention that no signs of fire were observed in the environment involving the human bones.

At Alto de Brinches 3 some data suggest that the bones were rearrange, in some cases still with soft tissues holding skeletal elements in articulation. This rearrangement may have occurred for several reasons: ritual manipulation, space requirement or taphonomic agents (Rodrigues *et al.,* 2012). In the same site, on the flat grave excavated inside de pit 691, there was a skeleton in ventral *decubitus*, possibly inhumed in some type of covering of perishable material that allowed the preservation of its position. Next to the skull of this burial there was a polished bone artefact.

The Ribeira de São Domingos pit contained several individuals, despite its small size, including 4 complete and 2 incomplete skeletons. The rearrangement of the bones probably results from the funerary reutilization of the pit (Miguel and Godinho 2009).

In sum, the pit burials analysed here display the growing evidence of heterogeneity and complexity of the funerary practices in Late Prehistory as proposed by Valera (2012). Demographic profile of the exhumed human remains includes individuals of both sexes, adults and non-adults. Moreover, in Monte do Vale do Ouro 2 and Ribeira de S. Domingos 1, non-adults individuals prevail (Pereira 2014).

One of the most curious aspects found in this study was the evidence of non-masticatory use of teeth: two superior lateral incisors recovered from pit 102 of Monte do Vale do Ouro 2 display a lingual sulcus, on the cement-enamel junction. This lesion may have resulted from the continuous friction of some kind of thread or wire in the area. The tenuous wear seen on the distal part of the lingual surface of these teeth supports this hypothesis. Dental alterations similar to these have been interpreted as a consequence of activities such as: weaving, basketry, production of nets, ropes and fibers, being the teeth used as a third hand (Lorkiewicz 2011).

Final considerations

The emergence of new data on burials in pits, hypogeum and ditches reveals the complexity and heterogeneity of the funerary world of Alentejo's Late Prehistory. Although small and limited by taphonomic conditions, the sample studied in this work contributes to a better understanding of the funerary contexts in this territory. Nevertheless, it is important to continue this research in order to understand the diversity of funerary solutions and practices of these human populations besides their biological and social characterization.

References

AlQahtani, S.J.; Hector, M.P.; Liversidge, H.M. (2010) – Brief communication: the London atlas of human tooth development and eruption. American Journal of Physical Anthropology. 142: 3, p. 481-490.
Alves, C; Porfírio, E.; Serra, M; Estrela, S.; Rodrigues, Z. (2010) – Minimização de Impactes sobre o Património Cultural decorrentes da Construção do Reservatório de Serpa Norte (Serpa). Relatório final da escavação arqueológica de Alto de Brinches 3. Excavation report. Coimbra: Palimpsesto, Estudo e Preservação do Património Cultural, Lda.
Armenadariz, A. (1990) – Las Cuevas Sepulcrales en el País Vasco. Munibe (Antropologia-Arkeologia). San Sebastian. 42, p. 153-160.
Buikstra, J.; Ubelaker, D. (1994) – Standards for data collection from human skeletal remains. Proceedings of a Seminar at the Filed Museum of Natural History. Fayetteville, Arkansas: Arkansas Archaeological Survey Research Series 44.
Ferembach, D.; Schwidetzky, I.; Stloukal, M. (1980) – Recommendations for age and sex diagnoses of skeletons. Journal of Human Evolution. 9, p. 517-549.
Inocêncio, J.P. (2013) – Contextos e Práticas Funerárias Calcolíticas no Baixo Alentejo Interior (Sudeste Alentejano). Master's thesis in Archaeology presented to University of Minho. Braga.
Lorkiewicz, W. (2011) – Nonalimentary Tooth Use in the Neolithic Population of the Lengyel Culture in Central Poland (4600-4000 BC). American Journal of Physical Anthropolgy. 144, p. 538-551.

Maclaughlin, S.M. (1990) – Epiphyseal fusion at the sterna end of the clavicle in a modern Portuguese skeletal sample. Antropologia Portuguesa. Coimbra. 8, p. 59-68.

Matutano, P.V. (2013) – Cueva Maturras (Ciudad Real, España): el papel del fuego en un contexto funerario del III Milenio a.C. *Saguntum. Papeles del Laboratorio de Arqueología de Valencia.* 45, p. 39-47.

Moro Berraquero, J.; Figueiredo, A. (2013) – Subconcessão da Auto-estrada do Baixo Alentejo. Lanço C. Relatório final dos trabalhos arqueológicos de Monte de Vale do Ouro 2. Excavation report. Porto: Omniknos.

Miguel, L.; Godinho, R. (2009) – Minimização de Impactes sobre o Património Cultural decorrentes da execução do Bloco de Rega de Brinches (Fase de Obra). Relatório preliminar dos trabalhos arqueológicos de Ribeira de S. Domingos 1. Excavation report. Lisboa: Era-Arqueologia SA.

Pereira, T. (2014) – Enterramentos em fossa no distrito de Beja. Práticas funerárias e estudo dos vestígios osteológicos da Pré-história recente. Master's thesis presented to University of Coimbra. Coimbra.

Rodrigues, Z; Estrela, S.; Alves, C.; Porfírio, E.; Serra, M. (2012) – Os contextos funerários do sítio Alto de Brinches 3 (Serpa): dados antropológicos preliminares. In Actas do V Encontro de Arqueologia do Sudoeste Peninsular. Almodôvar: Município de Almodôvar. p. 73-83.

Rojo Guerra, M.A.; Kunst, M.; Palomino, L. (2002) – El fuego como procedimiento de clausura en tres tumbas monumentales de la Submeseta Norte. In Rojo Guerra, M.A.; Kunst, M., eds. – Sobre el significado del fuego en los rituales funerarios del Neolítico. Valladolid, p. 21-38.

Schaefer, M.; Black, S.; Scheuer, L. (2009) – Juvenile Osteology: a laboratory and field manual. London: Academic Press.

Silva, A.M.; Leandro, I.; Pereira, D.; Valera, A.C. (2014) – Collective secondary cremation in a Pit Grave: a unique funerary context in Portuguese Chalcolithic burial practices. Journal of Comparative Human Biology. 66: 1, p. 1-14.

Smith, B.H. (1991) – Standards of human tooth formation and dental age assessment. In Kelley, M.; Larsen, C.S., eds. – Advances in Dental Anthropology. New York: Wiley- Liss, p. 143-168.

Stiner, M.; Kuhn, S.L.; Weiner, S.; Bar-Yosef, O. (1995) – Differential Burning, Recrystallization, and Fragmentation of Archaeological Bone. Journal of Archaeological Science. 22, p. 223-237.

Thompson, T.J.; Gauthier, M.; Islam, M. (2009) – The application of a new method of Fourier Transform Infrared Spectroscopy to the analysis of burned bone. Journal of Archaeological Science. 36, p. 910–914.

Valera, A. (2012) – Ditches, pits and hypogea: new data and new problems in South Portugal Late Neolithic and Chalcolithic funerary practices. In Gibaja, J; Carvalho, A.; Chambon, P., eds. – Funerary Practices in the Iberian Peninsula from the Mesolithic to the Chalcolithic. Oxford: Archeopress, p. 103-112.

Wasterlain, S. (2000) – Morphé: análise das proporções entre os membros, dimorfismo sexual e estatura de uma amostra da Colecção de Esqueletos Identificados do Museu Antropológico da Universidade de Coimbra. Master's thesis in Human Evolution presented to University of Coimbra. Coimbra.

Bioarchaeological analysis at the Copper Age site of Valencina de la Concepción (Seville, Spain): The PP4-Montelirio sector

Sonia Robles Carrasco[1], Marta Díaz-Zorita Bonilla[2], Virginia Fuentes Mateo[1] and Leonardo García Sanjuán[1]

[1] Department of Prehistory and Archaeology, University of Seville
[2] Institut für Ur- und Frühgeschichte und Archäologie des Mittelalters, Tübingen
marta.diaz-zorita-bonilla@ifg.uni-tuebingen.de

Abstract

In this paper a broad overview of the burial practices at the Copper Age mega-site of Valencina de la Concepción is offered. New bioarchaeological data from 20 funerary structures show that collective and individual in primary and secondary positions were the common practices at the PP4-Montelirio sector. Although the bone remains are quite fragmented and the preservation is not optimal, they reflect the entire population from young subadults to mature adults. Most of the pathological conditions refer to oral pathologies likely related to diet.

This is opening new interpretations of the social organisation, cultural practices and subsistence patterns of these communities during the 3rd millennium BC in the Lower Guadalquivir valley.

Key words
Bioarchaeology, Copper Age, Paleopathology, Burial patterns

Résumé

Cette étude présente une vue d'ensemble des pratiques funéraires des communautés qui vivaient à le mega-site Chalcolitique de Valencina de la Concepción. Les nouvelles données bioarchéologiques issues de 20 structures funéraires du secteur PP4-Montelirio révèlent que les sépultures sont collectives et individuelles et que les individus sont aussi bien en position primaire que secondaire. Bien que les restes osseux soient très fragmentés et que leur état de conservation ne soit pas optimal, ces restes reflètent l'intégralité d'une population, de jeunes subadultes jusqu'à des adultes d'âge avancé. L'essentiel des pathologies se réfère à des pathologies orales potentiellement liées à l'alimentation.

Ces données permettent une nouvelle interprétation de l'organisation sociale, des pratiques culturelles et des modes de subsistance de ces communautés qui ont vécu dans la vallée du Bas Guadalquivir au cours du troisième millénaire avant J.-C.

Mots-clés
Bioarchéologie, Âge du cuivre, Paléopathologie, Mode d'inhumation

Introduction

The Partial Plan 4 Montelirio (henceforth PP4-Montelirio) sector is part of the Valencina de la Concepción – Castilleja de Guzmán site (henceforth Valencina), which located near modern-day Seville, is one of the most important settlements of the Iberian Copper Age (Figure 1). A total of 134 structures with Chalcolithic materials were excavated at the PP4-Montelirio sector between 2007 and 2008 (Figure 2). Of these 134 structures, 61 presented evidence of the formal deposition of human remains, and were thus considered burial deposits. Of them, 5 are megalithic structures, 20 are negative structures with stone elements, 35 are negative structures without stone elements and 1 is doubtful because of the ambiguous quality of the finds (Mora Molina *et al.*, 2013).

This paper presents unpublished bioarchaeological data corresponding to 17 burial structures of the PP4-Montelirio sector. According to the field records made by the excavator, José Peinado Cucarella,

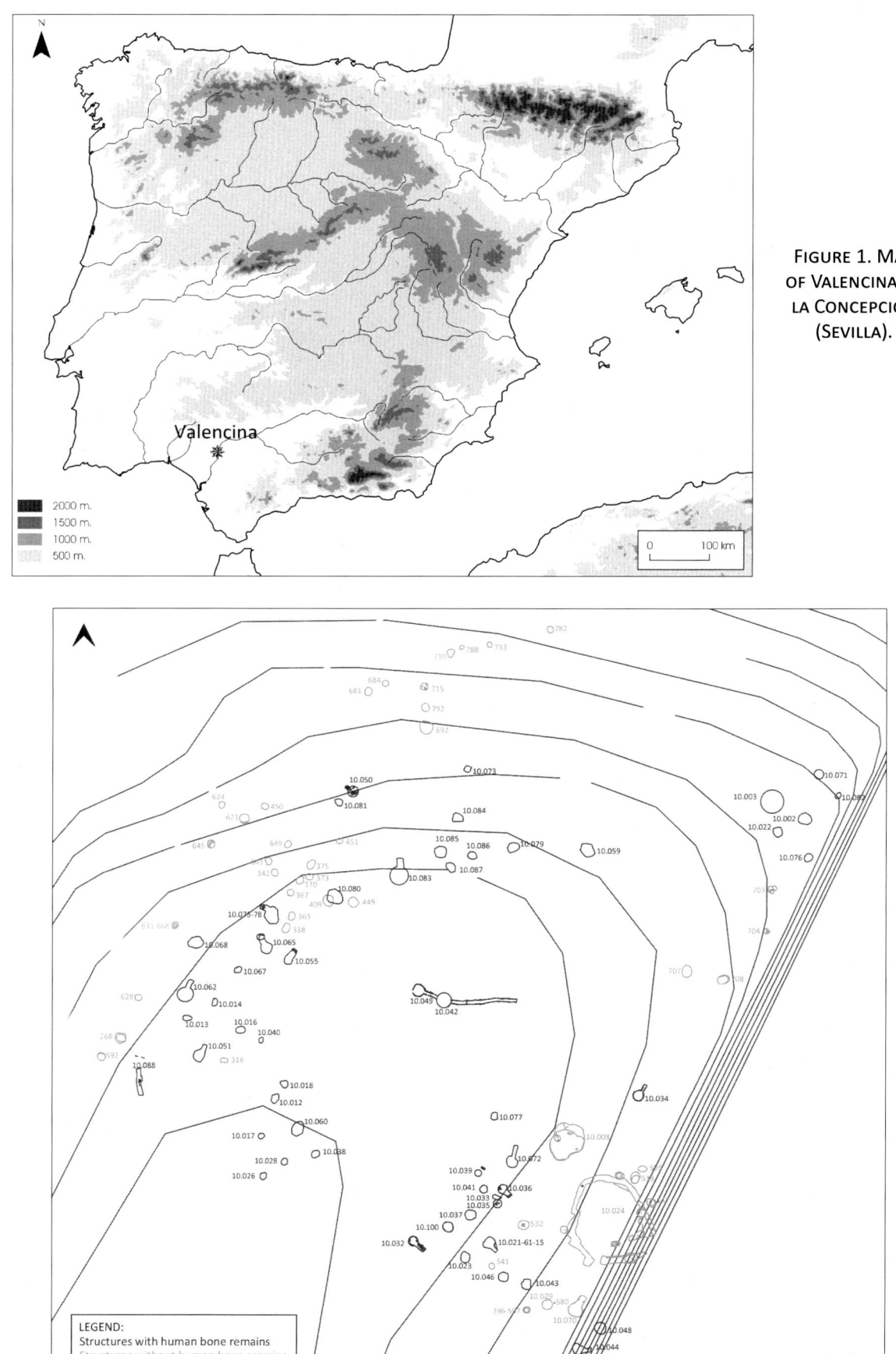

FIGURE 1. MAP OF VALENCINA DE LA CONCEPCIÓN (SEVILLA).

FIGURE 2. MAP WITH STRUCTURES WITH AND WITHOUT HUMAN BONE REMAINS AT THE PP4-MONTELIRIO SECTOR.

the estimated MNI (Minimum Number of Individuals) in these 17 structures was 1 in each case (Peinado Cucarella, 2008). The purpose of this study has been to carry out a bioarchaeological and demographic characterisation of this assemblage of human remains as well as to confirm whether these structures presented in fact individual inhumations, as the predominant burial pattern in Valencina is collective. Additionally, this paper includes unpublished anthropological data from three other burial structures from the PP4-Montelirio sector (Fuentes Mateo, 2013). Altogether, therefore, this study presents the results from the bioarchaeological analysis of 20 of the 61 burial structures found at PP4-Montelirio, with different MNI and degrees of preservation. The fresh data presented here provides a broader perspective of the burial practices, demography and living conditions of the communities that inhabited and/or frequented the settlement of Valencina during the 3rd millennium BCE. This study adds to previous research on the bioarchaeological evidence found at this sector, both from an anthropological (Díaz-Zorita Bonilla, 2017; Díaz-Zorita Bonilla, 2013; Robles Carrasco and Díaz-Zorita Bonilla, 2013) and a faunal point of view (Liesau, 2014).

Materials and Methods

The general state of preservation of the sample studied here is deficient as the bone material is highly fragmented, with some taphonomic effects that have severely damaged the preservation of the bone tissue.

It is important to mention the fact that there are a number of problems with the bone records from the PP4-Montelirio sector. For example, despite some individuals having been observed as having a clearly articulated anatomical position (suggesting they were intentionally deposited in a specific position) during the excavation (as is recorded in the field plans and photographs), the incorrect labelling of bone remains in the majority of the cases has prevented us from distinguishing between each one of the individuals in the laboratory. Additionally, some bone remains that can be seen in fieldwork photographs do not always appear in the boxes kept in the Archaeological Museum of Seville (Table 1).

After cleaning the remains they were classified, recorded, photographed, packaged and labelled with their bone and sedimentological record. The MNI has been estimated according to the anatomical classification for bones and teeth, degree of development and laterality.

Prior to beginning the study, the different taphonomic processes that affect both the bones remains and teeth were evaluated in addition to being recorded and described in detail according to Johnson (1985). The age of the individuals has been estimated using Ubelaker's (1979) dental eruption and development chart, a dental wear chart (Brothwell (1987) and Lovejoy (1985) and the observation of epiphyseal unions (Scheuer and Black, 2000). In one case in which there is a conserved fragment of the pubic symphysis, the pubic symphysis aging method has been utilised separately for both sexes in relation to age according to Brooks and Suchey (1990). In another unique case, the age of a fragment of the auricular surface of the ilium has been estimated (Lovejoy *et al.*, 1985). The age groups established in this study are as follows: Infant I (from birth to six years old), Infant II (7-12), Juvenile (13-17), Young adult (18-25), Middle-aged (26-40), Mature adult (41-60) and Older adult (>60). In addition we use on the one hand, an Adult group without a precise age category but used to differentiate from those individuals who are considered sub-adults and whose age estimation is < 17 years, without greater accuracy due to the lack of or the characteristics of the remains observed.

Sex determination has been carried out by observing the classic morphological features of the skull and the mandible (Buikstra and Ubelaker, 1994). The categories utilised are male and female, probably male or female and ambiguous individuals when the features on which we base the assessment are not well-defined, as with indeterminate sex when we do not have the specific bones for the assessment (Campillo and Subirá, 2004).

Structure	Type	MNI	Sex	Age
10.002	C	2	U	U
10.003	A	1	F?	YA (18-25 years)
10.005	C	2	U	INDV-1: MID (> 25 years)
				INDIV-2: I2 (8 years ± 24 months)
10.012	C	5	U	INDIV-1: YA (18-25 years)
				INDIV-2: YA (18-25 years)
				INDIV-3: AO (12 years ± 30 months)
				INDIV-4: I1 (4 years ± 12 months)
				INDIV-5: YA (18-20 years)
10.013	B	1	F?	A (18-30 years)
10.035	C	2	U	INDIV-1: A (20-35 years)
				INDIV-2: I2 (7-10 years)
10.044	B	3	U	INDV-1: MID (26-40 years)
			M	INDV-2: MA (41-60 years)
			U	INDV-3: MID (26-40 years)
10.055	B	1	U	A (20-30 years)
10.059	B	1	M?	MID (26-40 years)
10.073	B	3	F?	INDV-1: MID (26-40 yeas)
			F?	INDV-2: MID (26-40 years)
			U	INDV-3: A (20-30 years)
10.074	C	1	U	AD (18-35 years)
10.075-78	B	4	U	INDV-1: MID (26-40 years)
			F?	INDV-2: MID (26-40 years)
			U	INDV-3: YA (18-25 years)
			U	INDV-4: MID (26-40 years)
10.077	C	1	U	A (33-55 years)
10.080	B	2	F?	INDV-1: A (33-55 years)
			U	INDV-2: S (< 16 years)
10.084	B	1	F?	A (18-35 years)
10.100	A	1	U	U

Key to table= A= megalithic; B= negative with stone element; C= negative without stone element; U= undetermined, F?= probably female; M?= porbably male; M= male; YA= young adult; MID= middle adult; AO= adolescent; I1= infant I; I2= Infant II; S= subadult; A= adult; MA= mature adult

TABLE 1. LIST OF STRUCTURES WITH BIOARCHAEOLOGICAL ANALYSIS.

The World Dental Federation (FDI) chart has been followed for the study of the dental pieces. In order to represent the dental pieces preserved in each structure, an odontogram which numbers the dental pieces following the dental formula of the World Dental Federation (FDI) has been used.

For an exhaustive study of the dental caries, on the other hand, the location of a lesion and its condition have been recorded according to the scoring system of Buikstra and Ubelaker (1994) which has also been used to describe the expression of dental calculus. With regard to linear enamel hypoplasia (LEH), the degree of severity classification proposed by Trancho Gayo and Robledo Sanz (2001) was used, just as the age of onset of the episode of hypoplasia is calculated using the equations elaborated by Walker et al. (1991) (Table 2).

The pertinent measu-rements were taken using a 150 mm digital caliper and a measuring tape to record both the bone and dental material. All of the teeth have been measured and different measurements have been taken (AC: Height of the Crown, MD: Mesiodistal Diameter, BL: Buccolingual Diameter). The crown module, the robustness index of the crown and the index have been calculated. Furthermore, for those teeth where an anomaly in the enamel has been observed (Table 4), the following measurements have been made: the maximum width of the groove, the distance between the cervical margin of the defect and the neck of the tooth, and the cervical-incisal extension of the groove as the distance between the cervical margin of the defect and the incisal end, along the axis of the tooth (Dori and Moggi-Cecchi, 2014). The ASUDAS method was followed for identifying and recording the distinct morphological features that define the form of the crown or of the root (Turner *et al.*, 1991).

Once the MNI was estimated and everything was recorded both graphically and on data sheets, tooth and bone samples were extracted for a mobility analysis using stable isotopes $^{87}Sr/^{86}Sr$ and $\delta^{18}O$, a palaeodiet analysis using $\delta^{13}C$ and $\delta^{15}N$ and radiocarbon dating, all of which is currently under way.

Results

From a taphonomic point of view, important effects from weathering and bio-disturbance are generally observed on the bones in the form of reddish or blackish stains, small, linear grooves and both transverse and longitudinal fractures and cracks. The use of glue during fieldwork and fractures caused during the excavation process have been noted on dental elements. A reddish colour was identified on a few bone fragments from Structure 10.074 that, according to the excavator's notes (Peinado Cucarella, 2008), may possibly be due to the use of pigments; meanwhile, a deep blue-blackish colour was identified on other remains, also from Structure 10.074, that is possibly from the sediment or from rubefaction.

1) The 17 burial structures

The results from the bioarchaeological study (Table 1) confirm the MNI of 1 for 8 of the 17 structures, including structures numbered 10.003, 10.013, 10.055, 10.059, 10.074, 10.077, 10.084 and 10.100. In 4 other cases, the MNI estimated after the laboratory study is 2 (10.002, 10.005, 10.035 and 10.080), while in one case the final Minimum Number of Individuals is 5 (10.012). That being said, the estimation of a MNI of 1 for these eight structures does not necessarily imply that we consider them to be individual inhumations, as each of them presents their own problems and characteristics.

Sex was estimated for five of the structures (10.003, 10.013, 10.059, 10.080 and 10.084) (Table 1), with the identification of individuals who are probably male (4.76%), probably female (19.09%) or indeterminate (76.19%). Age, on the other hand, has been estimated for individuals in all of the structures except for 10.002 and 10.100, with two individuals with an indeterminate age (9.52%). Almost all of the age groups are present in the individuals with estimated ages, ranging from Infant I (from birth to 6 years old) to Mature adult (41-60 years old) (Table 1).

In terms of pathologies, the conditions observed include osteoarthritis in a third left metatarsal bone (Structure 10.002) and in a medial phalanx of a left foot (10.005), exostosis on a fragment of metatarsal bone (10.002), osteitis in a fragment of an ulna from an indeterminate side (10.035) and periostitis on five tibia fragments < 6 cm (10.002).

With regard to oral pathologies, periodontitis is observed in three mandibles (individual 1 from Structure 10.059, individual 1 from Structure 10.080 and individual 1 from Structure 10.080), dental calculus (83 dental pieces; 28.32%) and dental wear (238 dental pieces; 81.22%). Two central incisors from Structure 10.013 show anomalous dental wear on the entire lingual side, leaving the dentine exposed along the entire lingual and incisal surfaces. Other dental pathologies include caries (7 decayed pieces; 2.38%, of which 6 belong to individual 1 from Structure 10.080), root hypercementosis (2 teeth from individual 1 from Structure 10.080; 0.68%) and LEH (2 teeth from individual 2 from Structure 10.035; 0.68%) (Table 2, Figure 3) where the measurement of the episodes observed indicates their appearance around the first two years of life.

Physical activity markers are observed, understood as enthesopathies in a fragment of fibula probably from the right side (Structure 10.002) at the distal end of the diaphysis, as well as along the rough line of two left femurs (Structures 10.059 and 10.084). Morphological anomalies have also been observed, such as the bayonet-shaped dental root in one single case (piece 14) from Structure 10.003 and the dilaceration of the dental root (bending) at the apex of two teeth from Structure 10.003 (teeth 13, 22) (Figure 4).

Dental Hypoplasia				
Structure	Individual	Tooth	Measurements (Mm)	Age
10.035	2	21	3,67	2,83
			5,50	2,00
	2	42	2,48	2,96
			4,38	2,17
			5,82	1,57

TABLE 2. LIST OF TEETH WITH LEH.

The cranial epigenetic features recorded include the mastoid foramen in a temporal bone from Structure 10.003 and a wormian bone from Structure 10.080. Likewise, dental epigenetic features appear such as: shovel-shaped incisors (15/65 incisors, between lateral and central incisors or 23.07%), interruption of the dental cingulum (4/65 incisors, between lateral and central incisors or 6.15%), the foramen caecum or P point of the protostylid (1/96 molars, 1.04%), labial convexity (10/65 incisors, between lateral and central incisors or 15.38%), as well as a dental tubercle on a left maxillary canine from Structure 10.084.

Regarding epigenetic features, a particular morphological characteristic is observed on at least 6 teeth (6/65 incisors, between lateral and central incisors or 9.23% from four individuals of Structures 10.003, 10.044, 10.055 and 10.084), only maxillary central and lateral incisors (Table 3), which is 'a variation of the internal configuration of the incisors, consisting of the intussusception or folding of the enamel epithelium' (Gerson Reyes *et al.* 2013: 174). This internal morphological variation

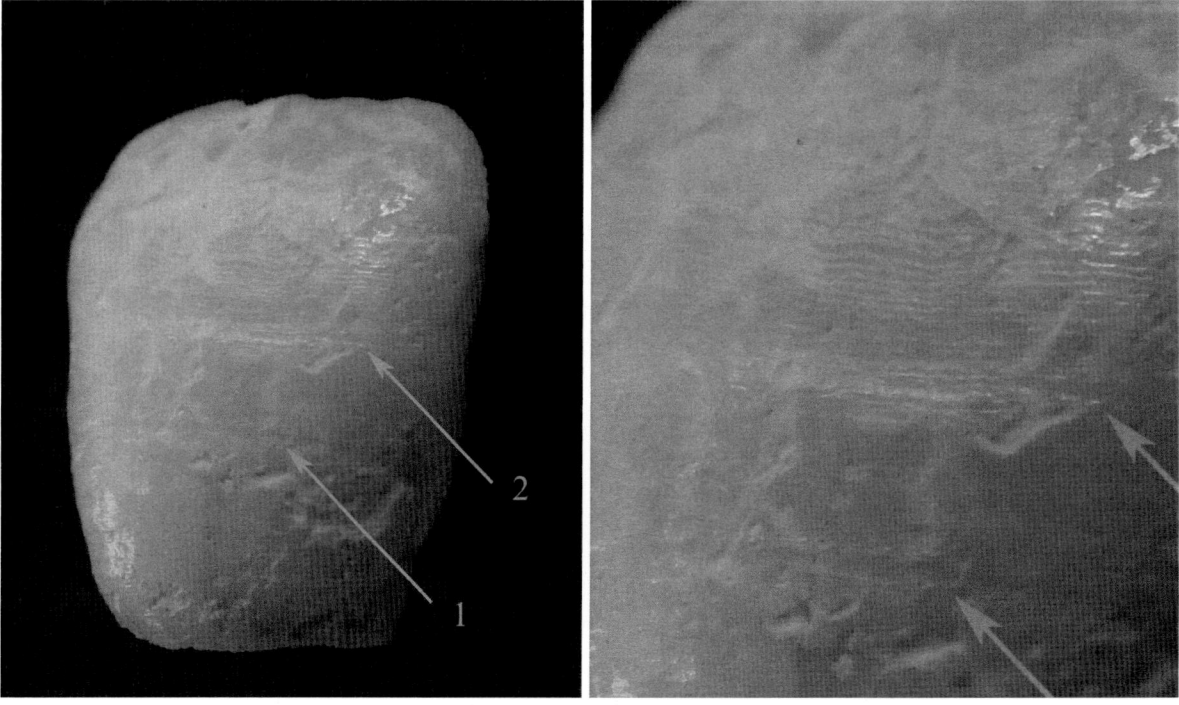

FIGURE 3. LEH AT 21, INDIVIDUAL 2 FROM STRUCTURE 10.035.

'Dens Invaginatus'		
Structure	Individual	Tooth
10.003	1	12
10.044	1	22
10.055	1	12
		21
		22
10.084	1	21
		11

TABLE 3. LIST OF TEETH WITH POSSIBLE 'DENS INVAGINATUS'.

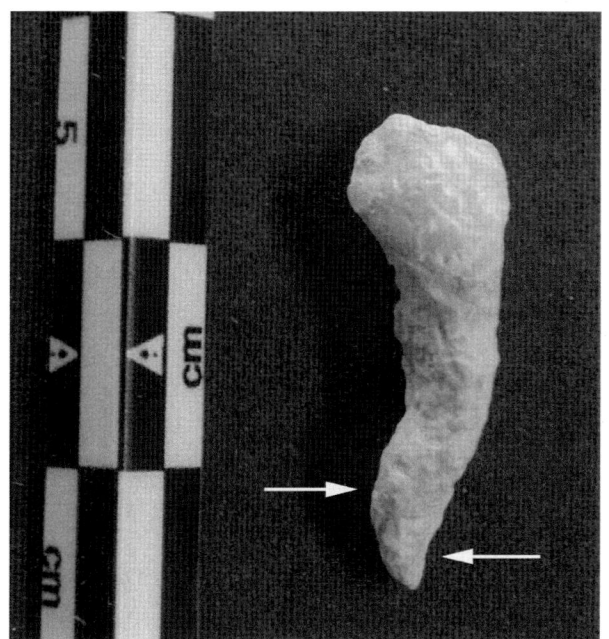

FIGURE 4. DILACERATION OF THE ROOT (TEETH 13) FROM STRUCTURE 10.003.

still needs to be diagnosed with certainty by means of a radiographic study, but the external morphology of the cases from PP4-Montelirio, consistent with those from the literature consulted (Gerson Reyes et al., 2013), is already visible at the macroscopic level. The literature indicates the possible genetic relationship with the feature of shovel-shaped incisors (Gerson Reyes et al., 2013).

In 7 anterior maxillary dental pieces (10.76%), once again in maxillary lateral and central incisors, of permanent dentition, an unusual alteration has been observed on the enamel in the form of a groove that crosses the lingual surface of an interproximal side to another, at the supragingival level. These 7 teeth correspond to three of the burial structures analysed (Structures 10.003 –individual 1-, 10.012 –individual 1- and 10.055 – individual 1), wherein four of these elements (57.14%) belong to the same individual (Table 4). The aetiology of this groove is still unknown, although there are some analogous cases (see discussion below) whose pieces are currently being studied (Figure 5).

With regard to the morphometric results, dental measurements have been taken for a total of 249 teeth, of which 213 pieces are Hypermicrodontic (85.5%), 11 Microdontic (4.41%), 18 Mesodontic (7.22%) and 7 Macrodontic (2.81%). As with the dental pieces, the long bones have also been measured for descriptive purposes. Nonetheless, the state of fragmentation of the sample has prevented the appropriate measurements from being taken concerning the height estimation of the individuals.

Enamel Alteration							
Structure	UE	Nº Tooth	Tooth	Measurements groove			Observations
				Br.Gr	D.C.	Ic.Ext.	
10.003	48-B	2.22	22	1.87	0.83	8.35	Same individual (individual 1)
		2.23	21	6.01	0.34	8.22	
		2.24	11	5.17	0.57	8.03	
		2.25	12	2.26	1.14	8.30	
10.012	246	1.1.6	21	4.57	2.01	8.13	individual 1
10.055	719	1.7	21	4.92	1.06	6.78	Same individual (individual 1)
		1.6	12	1.17	1.60	6.20	

Key to table: Br.Gr= Breadth of the groove, D.C.= distance from the cervix, Ic.Ext.= inciso-cervical lenght of the groove.

TABLE 4. LIST OF TEETH SHOWING ENAMEL ALTERATION.

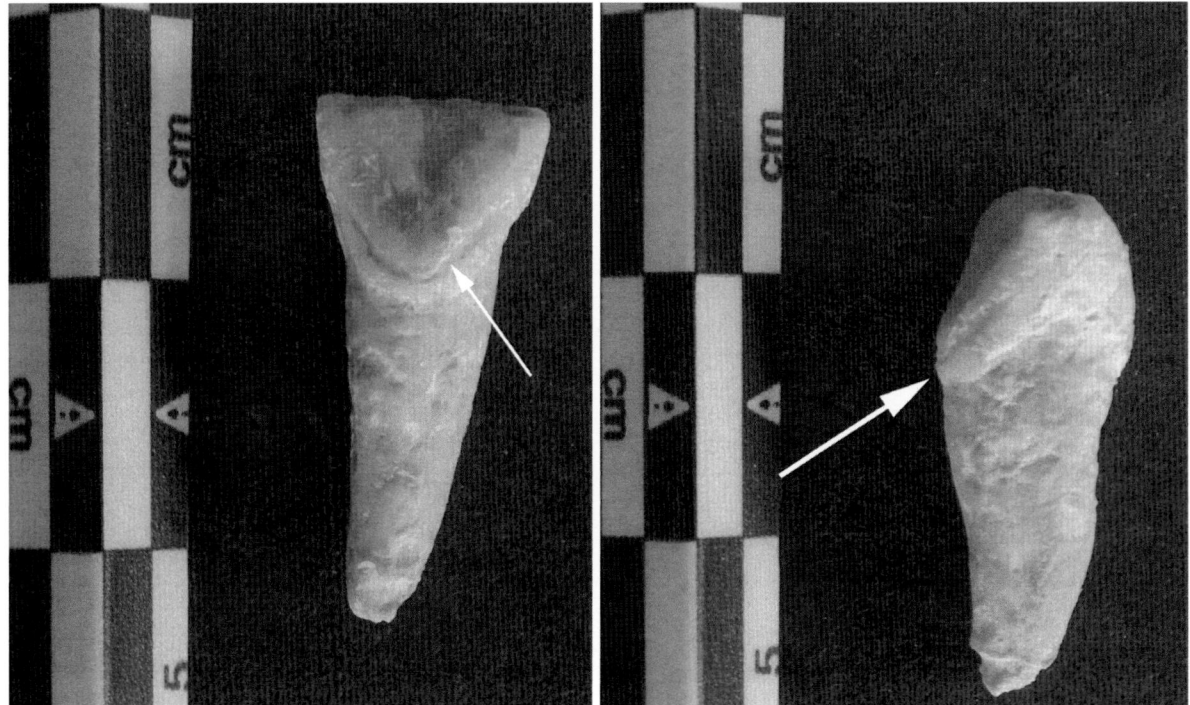

FIGURE 5. UNUSUAL ALTERATION IN ENAMEL (TOOTH 21) AT STRUCTURE 10.055.

2) Negative structures with stone elements (Structures 10.044, 10.073 and 10.075-78)

Structures 10.044, 10.073 and 10.075-78 are collective inhumations in negative structures with stone elements, with an estimated MNI of 10 among the three structures, of which 3 individuals are from Structure 10.044, 3 from Structure 10.073 and 4 from Structure 10.075-78. The burial ritual observed is that of inhumations lying in a left or right lateral decubitus position with the upper and lower extremities bent.

With regard to the sex and age of these individuals (Table 1), 6 of them are of indeterminate sex, 3 are probably female and 1 is a male.

In all cases age has been estimated based on dental wear, presenting ages ranging from young adult to mature adult (between 18 and 60 years of age), in which 7 indicate middle-aged individuals, one indicates a young adult, one indicates a mature adult and one indicates an individual that is probably an adult (Table 1).

Regarding the state of health of the individuals buried in these three structures, the majority present mild to moderate dental calculus and some caries (8/187 dental pieces representing 4.27%), none of which affect the pulp chamber; all appear in posterior dentition (premolars and molars). The dental calculus is present on 83/187 of the teeth studied (44.38%). Moreover, diverse stress marks in the form of enthesopathies on two left radii have been detected, specifically on the radial tuberosity (individual 1 from Structure 10.073 and individual 2 from Structure 10.075-78), in addition to a left femur over the anterior surface of the diaphysis and a right clavicle over the muscular insertion of the deltoids, both cases in individual 2 from Structure 10.044.

As with the rest of the structures at PP4-Montelirio, non-metric dental features are observed such as: 12 shovel-shaped superior incisors (11, 21 and 22 from individual 1 from Structure 10.073, the four incisors from individual 2 from Structure 10.073, 11, 21 and 22 from individual 2 from Structure 10.044

and 11 and 21 from individual 2 from Structure 10.078), interruption of the cingulum (left maxillary lateral incisor from individual 2 from Structure 10.078), a right mandibular canine with two roots from individual 1 from Structure 10.044, the buccal foramen caecum on four molars (46 and 47 from individual 1 from Structure 10.073 and 37 and 47 from individuals 1 and 3 from Structure 10.075-78). A supernumerary tooth that appears outside of its alveoli in individual 1 of Structure 10.075-78, although it is unknown whether it corresponds to the maxillary or the mandibular, formed by a barrel-shaped crown with three small cusps, and an incomplete root (Shah et al., 2008). A possible case of 'dens invaginatus' (Table 3) is also documented on tooth 22 of individual 1 from Structure 10.044 (Figure 6). Furthermore, at bone level, the presence of wormian bones is recorded in the lambdoid suture of individual 1 from Structure 10.075.

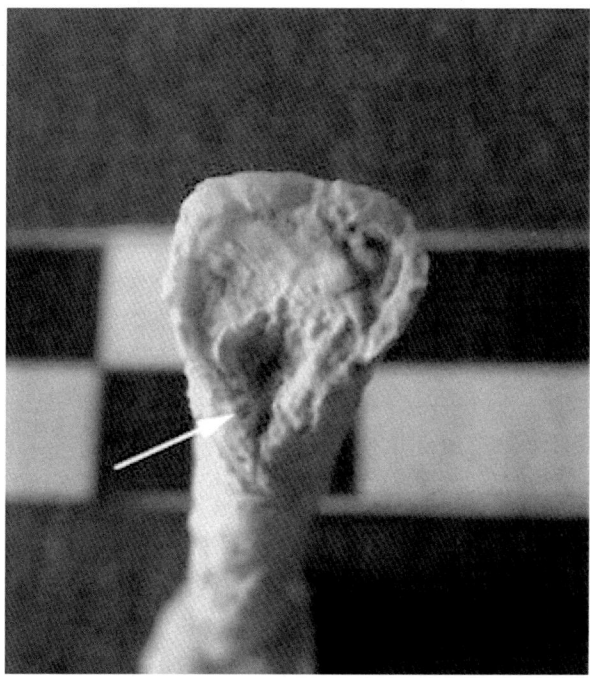

FIGURE 6. POSSIBLE CASE OF 'DENS INVAGINATUS' ON TOOTH 22 FROM INDIVIDUAL 1 AT STRUCTURE 10.044.

Discussion

As stated at the beginning, the main objective of this study is to make progress in the bioarchaeological and demographic characterisation of the population buried at the PP4-Montelirio sector and, by extension, of the populations that frequented or inhabited Valencina during the 3rd millennium BCE. This information is of crucial importance to understand the living conditions, social and demographic structure and the general cultural framework of said populations, especially given the important deficit in bioarchaeological studies that this site has traditionally suffered from in spite of the fact that human remains are practically omnipresent. Secondly, the study of the structures included in this report has the added interest of making it possible to explain whether, as was observed during the excavation, cases of individual inhumation did indeed exist at the PP4-Montelirio sector. Since the predominant burial pattern in Valencina is the collective inhumation, the presence of individual inhumations would provide important data for understanding the burial practices and the social organisation of these prehistoric communities.

1) Bone and dental morphological variation

The main purpose of the study for the estimation of the biological distance is to determine the genetic relationship of the so-called epigenetic features, although it is known that none of the morphological features of the human skeleton, not even the dental features, are free from non-genetic influences such as nutritional, pathological or other environmental factors (Ubelaker, 1979). Nonetheless, this data is not lacking in interest, since the study of these morphological traits and variants, specifically of PP4-Montelirio, attempts to determine the features, especially dental ones, which are characteristic of this population, not only as a way of characterising it, but also as a method to analyse the biological distance with regard to populations identified in other sectors and structures of the site of Valencina itself, such as Calle Dinamarca, Calle Trabajadores, La Divina Pastora, La Cima, etc. (Díaz-Zorita Bonilla, 2017) as well as other sites in the Iberian south-west such as Perdigões (Reguengos de

Monsaraz, Portugal) (Lago Miguel *et al.*, 1998 and Valera *et al.*, 2014). That being said, one of the epigenetic features that is most commonly recorded to date at PP4-Montelirio is the shovel-shaped incisor.

The possible relationship between the shovel-shaped incisor and the 'dens in dente' or 'dens invaginatus' is currently being studied; it may be an internal dental characteristic or feature associated with genetic factors that are involved in the histomorphogenetic development of teeth in the shape of a shovel (Gerson Reyes *et al.*, 2013). This anomaly is recorded at PP4-Montelirio, although subject to conducting the radiographic study. Another recently recorded feature at PP4-Montelirio is the canine with two roots (Fuentes Mateo, 2013). According to Pacelli and Márquez-Grant (2010), canines with two roots are difficult to find in human groups, but when they appear it is uncommon to find them outside of Europe.

Another recorded feature (Fuentes Mateo, 2013) is a supernumerary tooth, known as 'tuberculates'. Supernumerary teeth are additional or extra teeth that are uncommon in the primary dentition and have a frequency of 0.1-3.8% in the secondary dentition. At the same time, they are more frequent in men than in women and can occur in both the mandible and the maxilla, the latter being more common (Shah *et al.*, 2008; Menardía-Pejuan *et al.*, 2000; Scheiner and Sampson, 1997). They are often associated with Gardner syndrome, but they also occur in individuals without any apparent pathology (Ferrés-Padró *et al.*, 2009).

Furthermore, in the study of these dental epigenetic traits we similarly recorded the already mentioned morphological anomalies in dental roots which provide relevant data concerning the health and life style of these populations. It is not uncommon to find curving of the dental roots; in fact, curving in the distal direction is a general characteristic of all teeth. This is referred to as root dilaceration in the field of odontology when the curve is excessive, but it is not a pure root anomaly since the curve is located in the crown-root interface, while those that are considered root angulations occur along the root at any level (Roig and Morelló, 2006). Moreover, the bayonet shaped root is a special type of angulation that is characterised for presenting a double curving in opposite directions and is more common, precisely, in superior premolars. The cause of these root angulations tends to be traumatic, due to a mechanical obstacle owing to the presence of the maxillary sinus, which can interfere with the correct development of the root (Roig and Morelló, 2006). The curve can occur at any place along the tooth depending on the amount of root that has formed when the traumatic lesion occurs.

With regard to bone epigenetic traits, one single case is recorded (thus far) of a foramen or mastoid orifice in a cranial fragment (temporal), corresponding to Structure 10.003. This feature is generally located in the temporal bone, behind the mastoid process, although it can also appear in the occipitomastoid suture or in the region adjacent to the occipital bone. Likewise, two cases of wormian bones have been recorded.

2) Alteration in the dental enamel

The previously mentioned groove in the dental enamel on the lingual surface (Table 4) is an unusual alteration for which there is only one other similar case, corresponding to a Bronze Age population from the site of Arano di CelloresiIllasi (15 km from the city of Verona, northern Italy) (Dori and Moggi-Cecchi, 2014). Although their appearance is not related to the sex of the affected individuals (although men have more affected teeth than women), their degree of expression does seem to be related to age at death (more common in adults between 20-45 years of age), and there is no relationship between the dental calculus or plaque and the presence of the groove.

Given the absence in the literature of other similar cases in another type of archaeological population, the conclusions of this study, it seems possible to suggest that perhaps their presence at the PP4-Montelirio sector can be explained by an activity or consumption of food with chemical factors typical of these prehistoric populations. Hence, we also believe that it is a non-carious lesion of the enamel, more specifically a case of dental erosion or corrosion caused by some type of food or activity that involves that type of chemical agent, wherein the dental erosion or corrosion is understood as the irreversible, superficial loss of hard dental tissues as a result of a chemical action of acids and/or chelating substances in which bacteria do not intervene (Grippo *et al.*, 2004; Gandara and Truelove, 1999).

3) Palaeopathology

The oral pathologies do not only provide information about health, but they also supply nutritional, social and cultural information that enable us to reconstruct the living conditions of the populations from the 3rd millennium at Valencina and its surroundings. Thus, the individual from Structure 10.080 is interesting as it presents 6 decayed teeth in the superior maxilla, two teeth with hypercementosis, plaque and periodontal disease. Perhaps these oral conditions are related to a special lack of or inadequate hygiene in this individual, or maybe they are an indication of a diet that differs from that of the rest of the individuals who do not present such a high number of decayed pieces. In reference to the latter, a high frequency of caries is associated with diets that are soft and basically vegetarian, as different authors have observed (Borgognini and Repeito, 1985). The increase in the frequency of caries with the changes in the type of subsistence economy has also been observed; thus, the number of caries increases in farming populations (Turner, 1979). Additionally, root hypercementosis. This is not only connected to an intrinsic biological process, but also, according to bioanthropological studies, to malocclusion and dental stress events due to an increase in the masticatory function and excessive dental wear, and according to clinical studies to the periapical pathology, trauma and chronic periodontal inflammation, and even to Paget's disease (Hildebolt and Olnar, 1991; Hillson, 1996; Larsen *et al.*, 1991).

The degree of root hypercementosis is rarely considered, perhaps since it is a poorly understood, idiopathic dental condition. The cementum of the dental root is continuously regenerated and reabsorbed throughout life. As with other dental and even bone conditions, hypercementosis is the body's response to an imbalance, as a kind of adjustment and functionality. It is a defensive response or reaction of the dental periapical tissues by means of thickening of the root to compensate for the severe dental wear caused by an intense masticatory process, and to maintain dental contact in the occlusal plane (Kohli *et al.*, 2011).

The bone conditions recorded at the PP4-Montelirio structures studied here are enthesopathy, osteoarthrosis and periostitis, represented on bone fragments, while osteitis and exostosis are occasionally observed as conditions corresponding to pathologies that are impossible to discern as they are on isolated fragments that are not individualised.

With reference to the individuals studied in this paper, we found enthesopathies in three left femurs (Individual 1 Structure 10.059, Individual 1 Structure 10.084, Individual 2 Structure 10.044), a fibula probably from the right side (Undetermined Individual, Structure 10.002), two left radii (Individual 1, Structure 10.073 and Individual 2, Structure 10.075-78) and a right clavicle (Individual 2, Structure 10.044). It is important to highlight the presence of this left-sided bone response of femurs and radii, but the absence of bones associated with the same individual in some cases prevents us from assessing the question of symmetry for the moment. These bone alterations or changes are related to repeated and prolonged movements, postures and/or exertions, without there being any clear link with a specific job.

4) Individual or collective burials? Primary or secondary?

As indicated at the beginning of this paper, one of the objectives of this study was to verify the extent to which the 17 selected burial structures really correspond, as noted by the excavator, to individual inhumations, a crucial point for the correct interpretation of the social reality present in Chalcolithic

Valencina. This verification is not easy on account of the amount and difficulty of the factors that intervene in the characteristics these burials present.

The absence of *in-situ* observations of the bone remains from the PP4-Montelirio burial structures, has been compensated by the use of field photographs in which anatomical connections and/or relationships are clearly visible; intentional body positions interpreted as well as groups of long bones arranged in parallel with each other, sometimes to one side of the cranium, can also be observed. This arrangement of the bone remains is probably due to the dragging of the long bones in the direction of the cranium in an attempt to group together all of the bones, perhaps as a result of space reductions.

That being said, it is worth noting the diversity and complexity of the human skeletal material found at the PP4-Montelirio. As mentioned above, the results of our bioarchaeological study indicate a MNI of 1 for 8 of the 17 structures described as 'individual structures' by the excavator: they are the ones numbered 10.003, 10.013, 10.055, 10.059, 10.074, 10.077, 10.084 and 10.100. In four other cases, the MNI estimated following the laboratory study is 2 (10.002, 10.005, 10.035 and 10.080), while in one case there is a MNI of 5 (Structure 10.012). Potentially, therefore, there may have been a total of 8 individual inhumations at the PP4-Montelirio sector. This is not entirely inconsistent with other information obtained at the site of Valencina. During the excavations carried out in 2011 in the sector of Parcela Municipal (Vargas Jiménez *et al.* 2012), a simple pit was identified (Structure 435) with a single adult individual of indeterminate sex buried in the right lateral decubitus position, accompanied by half of a cattle mandible which had been placed next to its head. A recently obtained radiocarbon date of this individual gave a result of 3967±30 cal BC (CNA-1499) or 2574-2349 cal BC (2σ) (García Sanjuán *et al.*, forthcoming) which makes it one of the latest burials currently known at this site, already corresponding to a phase in which the site's occupation seems to have declined sharply. In fact, from c. 2300 cal BC onwards the practice of collective inhumations characteristic of the Copper Age in the region gives way to the individual inhumations in pits or cists characteristic of the first phase of the Bronze Age (c. 2200-1500 cal BC), as has been documented in the neighbouring necropolises of Jardín de Alá (Salteras), SE-K and SE-B (Gerena) (Hunt Ortíz *et al.*, 2008) and in Carmona (Belén Deamos *et al.*, 2015), all of them within the province of Sevilla and no more than 30 km away from Valencina. Nevertheless, given that there are no radiocarbon chronologies at the present time, it is impossible to know whether the 8 possible individual inhumations present at PP4-Montelirio would also correspond to a late phase of activity at this sector, or whether they correspond to the period of use of the dated collective burials, probably between the 30th and 28th centuries cal BC (García Sanjuán *et al.*, forthcoming).

Conclusions

Despite the important limitations of the available data, the PP4-Montelirio sector stands out for providing a broad view of the burial practices of the communities that occupied and/or frequented Valencina. We must highlight the presence of structures of both collective and individual use, which opens up new possibilities for interpreting the social organisation of said communities, especially when the absolute chronology becomes more precise. With regard to the implicit temporality in these burials, they seem to be both primary and secondary in nature. Nonetheless, the lack of in situ observations of the bone records and the complexity of burial practices observed in this context hinder interpretations for the time being, with the hope that future studies will be able to provide more data on this.

Due to a great extent to the generally poor state of preservation of the remains, sex could not be estimated for the majority of the cases (70%), while the age that appears represented in the sample reflects an ample age range, reflecting the entire population, from Infant I, specifically from 4 years ± 12 months onwards, to Mature Adult, at around 60 years of age approximately. In addition, the pathologies observed indicate oral conditions attributed to factors such as poor dental hygiene, the type of diet or nutritional deficiencies whereas the bone remains indicate conditions generally related to factors such as age, episodes of infection or trauma.

All of these bioarchaeological data along with the data provided by ongoing analytical studies will make it possible to take a step forward to attempt to answer basic questions about the biology, demography, social organisation and cultural practices of the communities of the living in the lower Guadalquivir during the 3rd millennium BC, especially with regard to patterns of subsistence, state of health and differences in behaviour and status based on variables such as age, sex or social position.

Acknowledgements

This study has been funded by the ATLAS Research Group (HUM-694) within the Second Phase (2014-2018) of the Project 'Study of Materials from the PP4-Montelirio Sector of the Valencina de la Concepción-Castilleja de Guzmán (Seville) Archaeological Area' and by the project 'Bioarchaeology of the Societies of the Copper and Bronze Ages in the Southern Iberian Peninsula', of the International Campus of Excellence of the University of Jaén (Spain), developed jointly by the Universities of Granada, Malaga and Seville. We wish to express our appreciation to the staff of the Archaeological Museum of Seville for their collaboration, and to all of the students from the University of Seville who participated in this study.

References

Armentano, N.; Malgosa, A. (2003) – Enterramientos primarios versus enterramientos secundarios. In: Aluja M.P., Malgosa, A. and Nogués R. (Eds.): Antropología y Biodiversidad. Barcelona, Bellaterra, p. 39-49.

Belén Deamos, M.; Román Rodríguez, J.M.; Vázquez Paz, J. (2015) – Ad aeternum. Enterramiento de la Edad del Bronce en Carmona (Sevilla). ARPI. Arqueología y Prehistoria del Interior peninsular, p. 164-79.

Berry, C.J.; Berry, R.J. (1967) – 'Epigenetic variation in the human cranium'.Journal of Anatomy 101:2, p. 361-379.

Brooks, S.; Suchey, J.M. (1990) – Skeletal age determination based on the os pubis: a comparison of the Acsádi-Nemeskéri and Suchey-Brooks methods, Human Evolution 3, p. 227-238.

Brothwell, D.R. (1987) – Desenterrando Huesos. vLa Excavación,Tratamiento y Estudio de Restos del Esqueleto Humano. Fondo de Cultura Económica. México.

Buikstra, J.E.; Ubelaker, D.H. (1994) – Standards for Data Collection from Human Skeletal Remains: Proceedings of a Seminar at the Field Museum of Natural History. Arkansas Archaeological Survey Research Series Nº 44.

Campillo, D.; Subirá, M.E. (2004) – Antropología Física para Arqueólogos. Barcelona, Ariel.

Carrasco, T.; Malgosa, A. (1990) – Paleopatología oral y dieta. Interpretación de la patología dental de 112 individuos procedentes de una necrópolis talayótica mallorquina (siglo VI al II a.C.). Acta Hispanica ad Medicinae Scientiarumque Historiam Illustrandam 10, p. 17-37.

Costa Caramé, M.E.; Díaz-Zorita Bonilla, M.; García Sanjuán, L.; Wheatley, D.W. (2010) – The Copper Age settlement of Valencina de la Concepción (Seville, Spain): demography, metallurgy and spatial organization. Trabajos de Prehistoria 67: 1, p. 85-117.

Costa, R.L. (1980) – Incidence of caries and abscesses in archaeological Eskimo skeletal samples from Point Hope and Kodiak Island, Alaska. American Journal of Physical Anthropology. 52, p. 501-514.

Díaz-Zorita Bonilla, M. (2013) – Bioarqueología de las prácticas funerarias del yacimiento de la Edad del Cobre de Valencina de la Concepción-Castilleja de Guzmán: revisión de las investigaciones. En García Sanjuán, L.; Hurtado Pérez, V.; Vargas Jiménez, J.M.; Ruiz Moreno, T. and Cruz-Auñón Briones, R. (Editores): *Valencina Prehistórica. Actas del Congreso Conmemorativo del Descubrimiento de La Pastora (1860-2010)*. Sevilla, Universidad de Sevilla. p. 359-368.

Díaz-Zorita Bonilla, M. (2017) – The Copper Age in south-west Spain: a bioarchaeological approach to prehistoric social organisation. BAR International Series S2840. Oxford: BAR Publishing.

Dori, I.; Moggi-Cecchi, J. (2014) – Brief Communication: An Enigmatic Enamel Alteration on the Anterior Maxillary Teeth in a Prehistoric North Italian Population. American Journal of Physical Anthropology. 154, p. 609-614.

Ferrés-Padró, E.; Prats-Armengol, J.; Ferrés-Amat, E. (2009) – A descriptive study of 113 unerupted supernumerary teeth in 79 pediatric patients in Barcelona. Medicina Oral Patología Oral Cirugía Bucal, 1;14 (3):E 146-152.

Fuentes Mateo, V. (2013) – Estudio Bioarqueológico de Tres Estructuras Calcolíticas de Sector PP4 Montelirio del Yacimiento de Valencina de la Concepción-Castilleja de Guzmán (Sevilla). Sevilla. Universidad de Sevilla. Unpublished Masters Dissertation.

Gandara, B. and Truelove, E. (1999) – Diagnosis and Management of Dental Erosion. The Journal of Contemporary Dental Practice. 1:1, p. 16-23.

García Sanjuán, L.; Cáceres Puro, L.; Costa Caramé, M.E.; Díaz-Guardamino-Uribe, M.; Díaz-Zorita Bonilla, M.; Fernández Flores, Á.; Hurtado Pérez, V.; López Aldana, P.M.; Méndez Izquierdo, E.; Pajuelo Pando, A.; Rodríguez Vidal, J.; Vargas Jiménez, J.M.; Wheatley, D.; Dunbar, E.; Bronk Ramsey, C.; Bayliss, A.; Beavan, N.; Hamilton, D.; Whittle, A. – Assembling the dead, gathering the living: radiocarbon dating and Bayesian modeling for Copper Age Valencina de la Concepción (Sevilla, Spain). Journal of World Prehistory (forthcoming).

Guijo Mauri, J.M.; Lacalle Rodríguez, R. (2013) – Una reflexión metodológica acerca de los registros antropológicos de las inhumaciones del Tercer Milenio A.C. en el Aljarafe (Sevilla). In García Sanjuán, L.; Hurtado Pérez, V.; Vargas Jiménez, J.M.; Ruiz Moreno, T. y Cruz-Auñón Briones, R. (Eds.), El Asentamiento Prehistórico de Valencina de la Concepción (Sevilla): Investigación y Tutela en el 150 Aniversario del Descubrimiento de La Pastora. Sevilla. Universidad de Sevilla, p. 333-357.

Grippo, J.O.; Simring, M.; Schreiner, S. (2004) – Attrition, abrasion, corrosion and abfraction revisited: A new perspective on tooth surface lesions. The Journal of the American Dental Association 135:8, p. 1109-18.

Hillson S. (2002) Dental Anthropology. Cambridge University Press, Cambridge.

Hunt Ortiz, M.A.; Vázquez Paz, J.; García Rivero, D.; Pecero Espín, J.C. (2008) – Dataciones radiocarbónicas de las necrópolis de la Edad de Bronce, SE-K, SE-B y Jardín de Alá (Salteras y Gerena, Sevilla). In: S. Rovira Llorens, M. García-Heras, M. Gener Moret and I. Montero Ruiz (Eds.): Actas del VII Congreso Ibérico de Arqueometría (Madrid, 8-10 de Octubre de 2007). Madrid: CSIC. p. 226-235.

Johnson, E. (1985) – Current developments in bone technology. In: Schiffer M.B. (Ed.): Advances in Archaeological Method and Theory, New York: Academic Press. Vol. 8, p. 157-235.

Lago, M.; Duarte, C.;Valera, A.; Albergaria, J.; Almeida, F.; Faustino Carvalho, A. (1998) – Provoado dos Perdigões (Reguengos de Monsaraz): dados preliminares dos trabalhos arqueológicos realizados em 1997. Revista Portuguesa de Arqueología 1:1, p. 45-152.

Liesau, C.; Aparicio Alonso, M.T.; Araujo Armero, R.; Llorente Rodríguez, L.; Morales Muñiz, A. (2014) – La fauna del sector PP4-Montelirio del yacimiento prehistórico de Valencina de la Concepción (Sevilla). Economía y simbolismo de los animales en una comunidad del III milenio. Menga: Journal of Andalusian Prehistory 5, p. 69-97.

Lopez-Bueis, I. (1999) – Marcadores de estrés musculoesquelético en los huesos largos de una población española (Wamba, Valladolid). Biomecánica VII: 13, p. 94-102.

Lovejoy C.O. (1985) – Dental Wear in the Libben Population: Its Functional Pattern and Role in the Determination of Adult Skeletal Age at death. American Journal of Physical Anthropology 68, p. 47-56.

Lovejoy, C.O.; Meindl, R.S.; Pryzbeck, T.R.; Mensforth, R.P. (1985) – Chronological metamorphosis of the auricular surface of the ilium: A new method for the determination of adult skeletal age at death. American Journal of Physical Anthropology. 68, p. 15-28.

Meindl, R.S.; Lovejoy, C.O. (1985) – Ectocranial Suture Closure: A Revised Method for the Determination of Skeletal Age at Death Based on the Lateral-Anterior Sutures. American Journal of Physical Anthropology. 68, p. 57-66.

Menardía-Pejuan, V.; Berini-Aytés, L.; Gay-Escoda, C. (2000) – Supernumerary molars. A review of 53 cases. Bull. Group. Int. Rech. Sci. Stomatol. Odontol 42, p. 101-105.

Mora Molina, C.; García Sanjuán, L.; Peinado Cucarella, J.; Wheatley; D.W. (2013) – Las estructuras de la Edad del Cobre del sector PP4-Montelirio del sitio arqueológico de Valencina de la Concepción – Castilleja de Guzmán (Sevilla). In: García Sanjuán, L.; Hurtado Pérez, V.; Vargas Jiménez, J.M.; Ruiz Moreno, T. and Cruz-Auñón Briones, R. (Eds.): El Asentamiento Prehistórico de Valencina de la Concepción (Sevilla): Investigación y Tutela en el 150 Aniversario del Descubrimiento de La Pastora. Sevilla. Universidad de Sevilla, p. 511-519.

Ortner, D.J. (2003) – Identification of Pathological Conditions in Human Skeletal Remains. Academic Press, Amsterdam.

Peinado Cucarella, J. (2008) – Memoria Arqueológica del Plan Parcial Sector PP4 'Dolmen de Montelirio' en el término municipal de Castilleja de Guzmán (Sevilla). Sevilla. Unpublished Report.

Polo Cerdá, M.; Miquel Feucht, M.; Villalaín Blanco, J.D. (2001) – Periostitis y marcadores ocupacionales en soldados franceses fallecidos durante la guerra de la independencia en Valencia. VI Congreso Nacional de Paleopatología, p. 420-429.

Reyes, G.; Rodríguez-Flórez, C.D.; Bonomie, J.; Palacios, M.; Guevara, Z. E.; Marín, A.H.; García-Sívoli, C. (2013) – Posible relación genética entre el dens in dente o densinvaginatus y el rasgo incisivos en forma de pala: estudio exploratorio. Boletín Antropológico. Año 31, nº86, Julio-Diciembre. Universidad de Los Andes. p. 173-193.

Rihuete Herrada, C. (2000) – Dimensiones Bio-Arqueológicas de los Contextos Funerarios. Estudio de los Restos Humanos de la Necrópolis Prehistórica de la Cova des Cárritx (Ciutadella, Menorca). Tesis doctoral. Universidad Autónoma de Barcelona.

Robledo Acinas, M.M.; Sánchez Sánchez, J.M. (2013) – Determinación de la edad por el estudio de la sínfisis púbica, carilla auricular y acetábulo en el coxal. Gaceta Internacional de Ciencias Forenses 6, p. 39-46.

Robles Carrasco, S.; Díaz-Zorita Bonilla, M. (2013) – Análisis bioarqueológico de tres contextos-estructuras funerarias del sector PP4-Montelirio del yacimiento deValencina de la Concepción-Castilleja de Guzmán (Sevilla). In: García Sanjuán, L.; Hurtado Pérez, V.; Vargas Jiménez, J.M.; Ruiz Moreno, T. and Cruz-Auñón Briones, R. (Eds.): El Asentamiento Prehistórico de Valencina de la Concepción (Sevilla): Investigación y Tutela en el 150 Aniversario del Descubrimiento de La Pastora. Sevilla. Universidad de Sevilla, p. 369-86.

Roig, M.; Morelló, S. (2006) – Introducción a la patología dentaria. Parte 1. Anomalías dentarias. Rev Ope Dent Endod; 5, p. 51.

Shah, A.; Gill, D.S., Tredwin, C.; Naini, F.B. (2008) – Diagnosis and Management of Supernumerary teeth. nGeneral Dentistry 35, p. 510-520.

Scheiner, M.A.; Sampson, W.J. (1997) – Supernumerary teeth: a review of the literature and four case reports. Australian Dental Journal 42: 3, p. 160-165.

Trancho Gayo, G.J.; Robledo Sanz, B. (2001) – Patología oral: hipoplasia del esmalte dentario en Sistematización metodológica en paleopatología. Jaén. p. 268-277.

Turner, C.G.; Nichol, C.R.; Scott, G.R. (1991) – 'Scoring Procedures for Key Morphological Traits of the Permanent Dentition: The Arizona State University Dental Anthropology System'. In: Kelley, M.A. and Spencer Larsen, C. (Eds.): Advances in Dental Anthropology, New York: Wiley-Liss. p. 13-31.

Ubelaker, DH. (1979) – Human Skeletal Remains: Excavation,Analysis and Interpretation. Washington, DC: Smithsonian Institute Press.

Valera, A.C.; Silva, A.M.; Márquez Romero, J.E. (2014) – La temporalidad del recinto de fosos de Perdigões: cronología absoluta de estructuras y prácticas sociales. SPAL 23, p. 11-26.

Vargas Jiménez, J.M.; Meyer, C.; Ortega Gordillo, M. (2012) – El tholos de La Pastora y su entorno:el sector oriental del yacimiento de Valencina de la Concepción (Sevilla) a través de la geofísica. Menga. Journal of Andalusian Prehistory. 3, p. 121-40.

Walker, P.L.; Dean, G.; Shapiro, P. (1991) – Estimating age from tooth wear in archaeological populations. In: Delley, M.A. and Larsen, C.S. (Eds.): Advances in Dental Anthropology, Wiley-Liss, Chichester, p. 13-31.

Assessing spatial dispersion of human remains in collective burials: A GIS approach to the burial-caves of the Nabão Valley (North Ribatejo, Portugal)

Tiago Tomé[1,2,3], Claudia Cunha[4,2], Ana Maria Silva[2],
Luiz Oosterbeek[3] and Ana Cruz[3,4]

[1] Instituto de Filosofia e Ciências Humanas – Universidade Federal do Pará, Brasil
[2] Laboratório de Pré-História, CIAS – Departamento Ciências da Vida, Universidade de Coimbra, Portugal
[3] GQP-CG, Grupo Quaternário e Pré-História, Centro de Geociências (I&D 73 – FCT)/ Instituto Terra e Memória, Portugal
[4] Programa de Capacitação Institucional MCTI/MPEG, Coordenação de Ciências Humanas, Museu Paraense Emílio Goeldi, Belém, Pará, Brasil
[5] Centro de Pré-História/Instituto Politécnico de Tomar, Portugal
tiagotome@gmail.com

Abstract

Two burial-caves of the Nabão Valley, Gruta do Cadaval and Gruta dos Ossos, each containing the remains of circa 30 individuals, were the subject of a GIS assessment, aiming at the definition of spatial dispersion patterns for the human skeletal remains. Results indicate that, although there are some general similarities in these burials, differing spatial patterns exist among both caves, particularly regarding concentrations of adult versus non-adult remains, as well as on the spatial distribution of specific skeletal parts.

Keywords

Collective burials, Geographic Information Systems, North Ribatejo

Resumé

Deux grottes de la Vallée du Nabão, Gruta do Cadaval et Gruta dos Ossos, contenant chacune les restes osseux d'environ 30 personnes, ont été soumises à une évaluation par des SIG, visant à la définition de modèles de dispersion spatiale des restes humains. Les résultats indiquent que, qu'il y ait certaines similitudes générales entre ces sépulcres, différentes configurations spatiales sont visibles entre les deux grottes, en particulier sur les concentrations des restes squelettiques d'adultes versus les restes de non-adultes, ainsi que sur la distribution spatiale des sections spécifiques du squelette.

Mots-clés

Tombes collectives, Systèmes d'Information Géographique, Haut Ribatejo

Introduction

Geographic Information Systems (GIS) applications in Archaeology represent a dynamic field, rooted in the late 1970's (Wheatley and Gillings, 2002; Chapman, 2006). The use of GIS as a toolkit for the storage, visualization, manipulation and analysis of archaeological data became more common up until the early 1990's, especially in Anglo-Saxon countries. Nevertheless, archaeological projects in Continental Europe would also take up on the use of GIS, making it a common tool in current-days European Archaeology. Nowadays, archaeological GIS covers all sorts of sub-fields and applications, being used for such different purposes as the mapping of finds or sites in a Cultural Resource Management perspective, the reconstruction and analysis of landscapes and sites (through the use, for instance, of visibility assessments, cost-path or site catchment analysis), or the development of predictive models for site locations. (Gaffney and Stancic, 1991; Lock and Stancic, 1995; Moscati, 1998; Djindjian, 1998; Lock, 2000; Wheatley and Gillings, 2002; Katsianis and Tsipidis, 2005; García Sanjuan *et al.*, 2009). In a more theoretical point of view, GIS can also be seen as 'a place to think', virtual environments in which to test hypothesis of a spatial nature (Gillings and Goodrick, 1996, *in* Chapman, 2006).

Similarly, Anthropology has also gradually adopted GIS as part of its toolkit, applying it to such diverse fields of inquiry as Social Anthropology, Paleoanthropology, Biological Anthropology or Forensic Anthropology (Aldenderfer and Maschner, 1996; Herrmann, 2002; Field *et al.*, 2007; Agosto *et al.*, 2008; Herrmann and Devlin, 2008; Dirkmaat *et al.*, 2008; Anemone *et al.*, 2011). Diversity of possible applications led to the development of approaches using GIS such as an aid to the determination of the Minimum Number of Individuals in North American collective burials (Herrmann and Devlin, 2008); in the analysis of spatial dispersion of human remains inside Honduran burial-caves (Herrmann, 2002); for the evaluation of potential migratory routes taken by the early *Homo sapiens* in the spread across Southern Asia (Field *et al.*, 2007); in creating and managing an inventory of paleoanthropological finds in Ethiopia (Anemone *et al.*, 2011).

Late Prehistory collective burials of Europe are a type of context where we believe GIS may prove to be a very important analytical tool. Such contexts often present taphonomical challenges to interpretation, due to the disarticulation and fragmentation processes human skeletal remains usually undergo. In Portugal, many of these burials were excavated throughout the 19th and 20th centuries. Many older excavations displayed little care for a detailed recording of human remains, with many bones being discarded, their study deemed useless (Silva, 2002; 2003; Boaventura *et al.*, 2014). Indeed, for a long time, it was quite common that only some of the human skeletal remains were recovered during excavation of this type of burials, namely cranial remains and larger bones, such as the *os coxae* or long bones, if they were in a good state of preservation. Also, the fact that these deposits were usually highly fragmented and disarticulated led, in many cases, to their definition as secondary burials. Regardless of these contingencies, recent assessments of Portuguese prehistoric collective burial skeletal samples have been able to shed some light on funerary aspects of these societies; for instance, several collective burials formerly considered as secondary are currently defined as primary burial sites (Silva, 2002; 2003; Tomé, 2011; Boaventura *et al.*, 2014), due to the application of methods aimed at assessing the representativeness of skeletal elements in samples composed of commingled remains, such as skeletal weight or tooth proportion (Silva, 2002; Silva *et al.*, 2009).

Materials and Methods

Two burial-caves were considered for GIS assessment, Gruta do Cadaval (CDV) and Gruta dos Ossos (GRO), both belonging to the Canteirões Late Prehistoric burial-caves complex located in the North Ribatejo, Portugal (Figure 1). Sample choice was determined by several factors: both caves share a similar morphology; they were excavated in the 1980's, with care being taken regarding tridimensional coordination of the remains; the samples have a partially overlapping, sequential, chronology – thus allowing for a comparative approach.

CDV contained a highly disturbed collective burial deposit – no organization patterning was identifiable during excavation, suggesting either that depositions were performed quite close to the surface (facilitating the dispersion of the remains due to posterior animal activity, for instance) or the presence of a more complex funerary gestures sequence, leading to a complete disarticulation of human remains. Radiocarbon dating from this context indicates a chronology spanning from the end of the 5th millennium BC to the mid-4th millennium BC, corresponding to the Middle Neolithic (Oosterbeek, 1994; 2003; Cruz, 1997).

GRO, on the other hand, contained a less fragmented skeletal sample, also forming a collective burial deposit. Fieldwork suggested that this collective burial was more structured, in terms of the reorganization of different types of bones. Radiocarbon dating indicates that this cave was used from the mid-4th millennium BC to, at least, the early 3rd millennium BC, placing it in the Late Neolithic (Oosterbeek, 1993; Cruz 1997; Tomé, 2006).

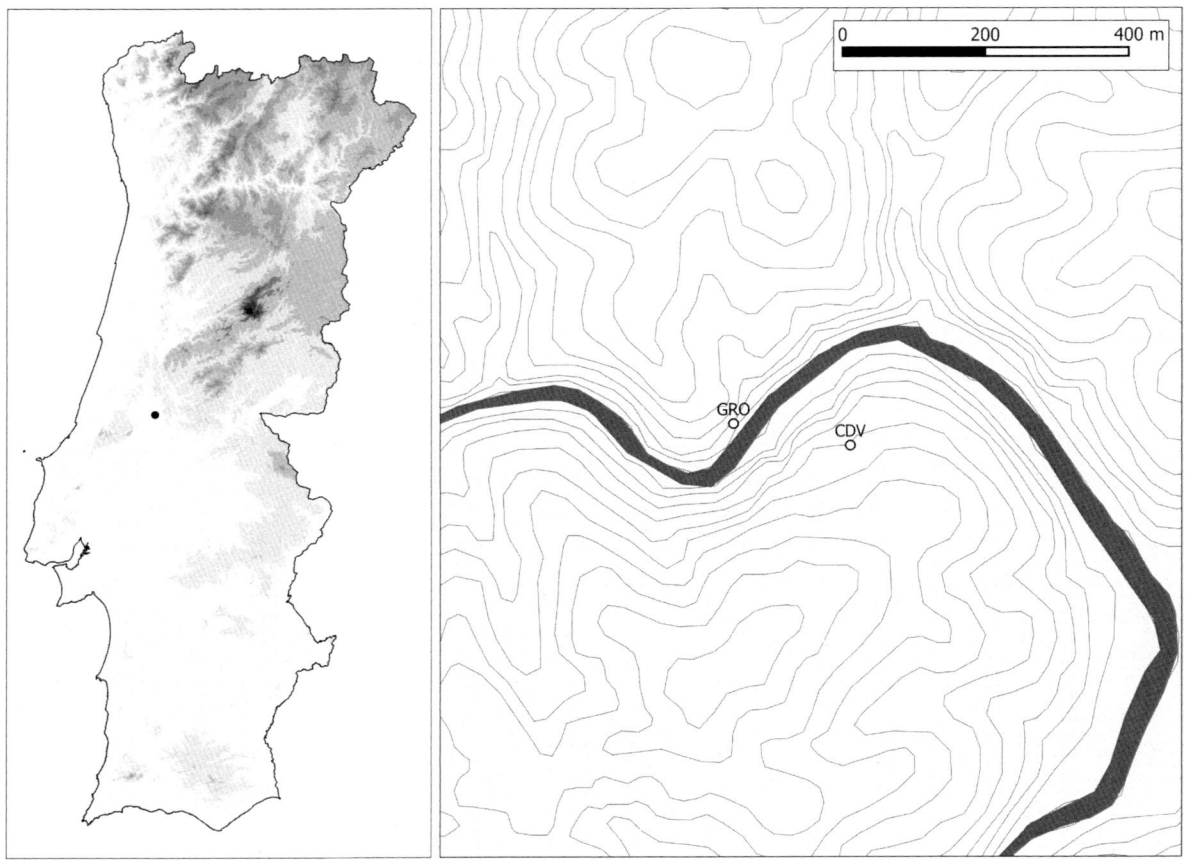

FIGURE 1. LOCATION OF CDV AND GRO.

Both CDV and GRO held the commingled remains of circa 30 individuals, including both sexes and all age categories (Tomé, 2011; Tomé and Silva, 2013).

A database combining information resulting from the osteological assessment and the original field records was assembled. While the osteological assessment represented the majority of the information, allowing us to accurately categorize and/or filter the records according to the desired analysis, field records were fundamental in providing the spatial information needed for a GIS assessment to be performed. The vast majority of human remains exhumed from both these caves were spatially referenced, allowing for several approaches to the spatial patterns. In this study we decided to develop a strategy that focused specifically on the density of human remains inside each burial deposit.

Kernel Density Estimation, when applied to geostatistics and spatial analysis in general, is a method used to create a surface from a data plot, allowing for the representation of the density of events in a given area (Larmarange, 2013). It is an appropriate technique for point data (Silverman, 1986). Density (or intensity) analysis provides a way of estimating the change of frequency of distributions for point data over the study area (Sayer and Wienhold, 2013).

This technique is used in many different fields of spatial analysis and has, in recent years, been applied to several aspects of archaeological research (see, for instance, Baxter *et al.*, 1997; Keeler, 2007; Grove, 2011; Cascalheira and Gonçalves, 2012; Sayer and Wienhold, 2013).

The point data files created from this combined dataset were used to analyze spatial dispersion of the human remains, attempting to correlate biological parameters determined in the osteological assessment. Kernel Density Estimation was performed on the point data files, generating plots representing the spatial dispersion of human remains inside each cave. A first assessment was executed using bone count (*i.e.*, the presence of a certain number of bones in each area) as the variable for plot generation. After global kernel density maps were available, representing the areas of each cave containing human remains concentrations, separate plots were generated for adult and non-adult remains, in order to determine whether there were any discernible patterns in the deposition of different age-class individuals. Finally, anatomically filtered plots were created, defining the deposition areas of cranial remains, vertebrae, long bones, hand and foot bones.

A second analytical run was performed, using the same approach, this time using bone weight as the variable for plot generation, based upon the following reasoning: if we consider a single hand, it contains 27 bones. When creating a kernel density map using the number of bones as the variable, this will produce a strong concentration in the area where that hand is deposited. On the opposite end, we would need for all of the long bones of several individuals to be tightly packed together in order to get a similar concentration depicted in that same plot. Additionally, a small fragment of a femur would be given the same influence in the density map generation as a complete femur. Thus, bone count introduces important deviations in the representation of bone density inside the burial deposit, which must be accounted for.

Bone weight, on the other hand, takes into consideration the dimensions of different anatomical elements or bone fragments thus seeming more reliable for our assessment. In order to take into consideration the smaller, lighter elements and fragments, both bone count and bone weight density maps were averaged in a third set of plots, which were then used in the analysis.

All of the data treatment and assessment was performed with Open Source GIS software (QGIS 2.2 Valmiera).

Results

Our results suggest some general similarities among CDV and GRO regarding spatial dispersion of human remains. Both caves exhibit a main depositional cluster in the central part of the room closer to the entrance. In both cases there is also a secondary cluster, located in smaller, deeper rooms (Figure 2). Thus, easily accessible funerary deposits were formed, allowing for the post-depositional manipulation of human remains. Areas of more difficult access inside both caves were, nevertheless, used for funerary purposes, although human remains concentration on such regions was clearly less intense.

Besides the overall resemblances, our results reveal that each burial context displays its particular features regarding the spatial dispersion of human remains. When comparing adult versus non-adult

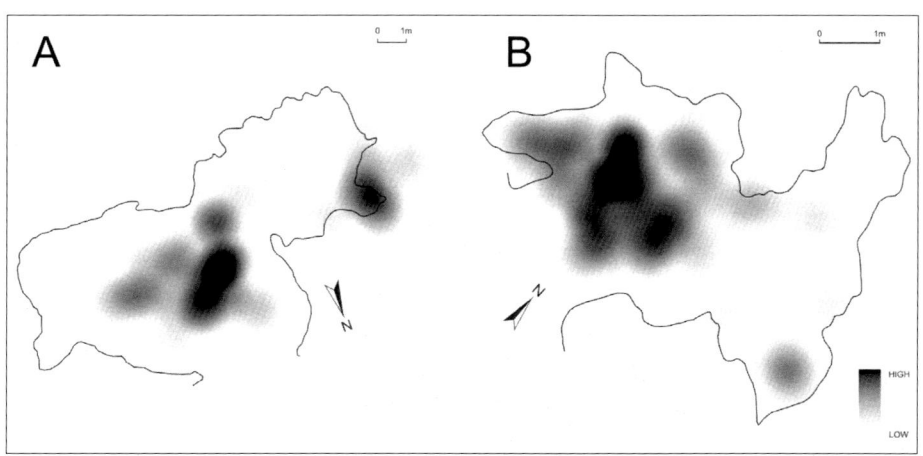

FIGURE 2. GLOBAL SPATIAL DISPERSION OF SKELETAL REMAINS (A – CDV; B – GRO).

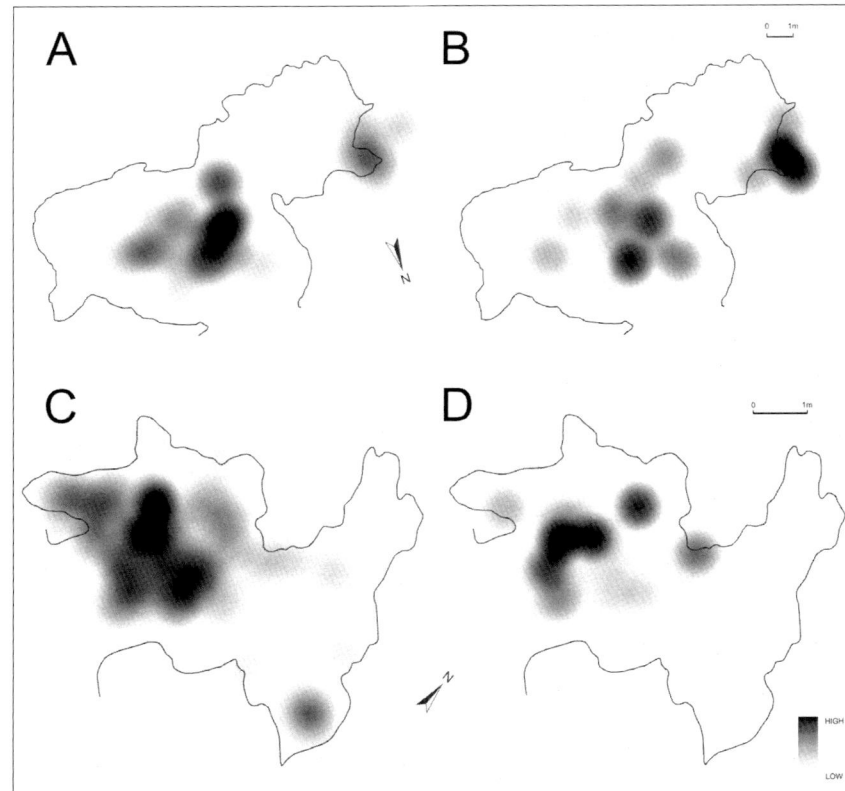

FIGURE 3. ADULTS *VERSUS* NON-ADULTS SKELETAL REMAINS DISTRIBUTION. TOP ROW: CDV (A – ADULTS; B – NON-ADULTS); BOTTOM ROW: GRO (C – ADULTS; D – NON-ADULTS).

remains distribution (Figure 3), density maps for CDV indicate that, although both clusters contained elements from both age-groups, adult remains were concentrated mostly in the main cluster, closer to the cave entrance, whilst the majority of non-adult skeletal remains were located in the secondary cluster. It would seem, then, that non-adult remains were mostly being deposited on a different area inside the cave than adult remains. The same comparison applied to GRO does not yield the same results, since both adult and non-adult skeletal remains cluster strongly close to the cave entrance; additionally, non-adult remains appear to be absent in the secondary accumulation at the deeper area of the cave.

Regarding specific skeletal regions, particular spatial patterns also arise. CDV shows a concentration of cranial and axial remains in the main cluster. Although we can attest their presence also in the secondary cluster, this smaller concentration of human remains is mostly composed of appendicular bones from both upper and lower limbs (Figure 4).

As for GRO, kernel density maps indicate that the secondary cluster is composed mostly of hand and foot bones (it is worth noting that cranial remains appear to be completely absent from this cluster). The remaining skeletal categories are much more clearly concentrated in the main cluster but, still, differential distributions of bone categories seem visible within it. First, cranial remains appear tightly packed in the central area of the cluster. Second, long bones also seem to have a particular distribution inside this cluster, with upper limb bones displaying a stronger concentration at its core, while lower limb bones appear to be more peripheral – the matrix corresponding to the latter shows them closer to the cave walls, besides revealing the presence of a clear concentration of lower limb bones inside a small niche, located to the left of the main entrance (Figures 5 and 6).

Final Remarks

Our results indicate that, although both of these burial-caves of the Nabão valley share some traits in terms of the distribution of human remains, they also exhibit several differences among them.

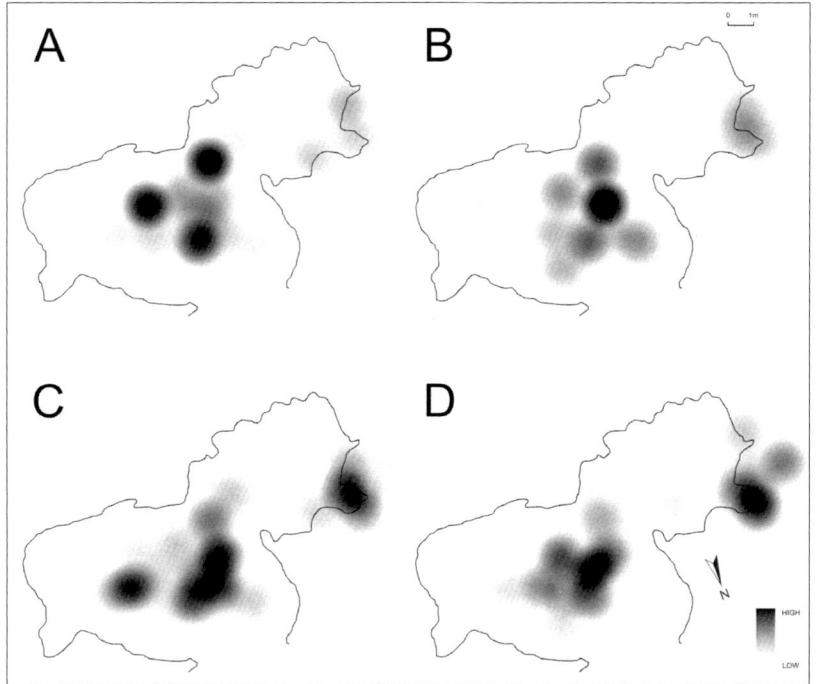

FIGURE 4. SPATIAL DISPERSION BY SKELETAL REGION AT CDV (A – CRANIAL REMAINS; B – VERTEBRAE; C – LONG BONES; D – HAND AND FOOT BONES).

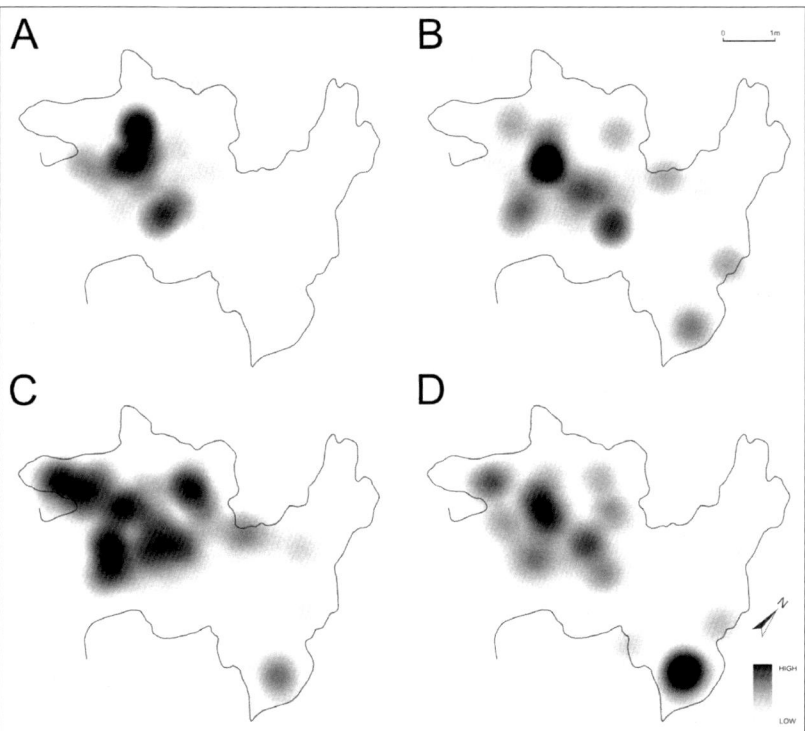

FIGURE 5. SPATIAL DISPERSION BY SKELETAL REGION AT GRO (A – CRANIAL REMAINS; B – VERTEBRAE; C – LONG BONES; D – HAND AND FOOT BONES).

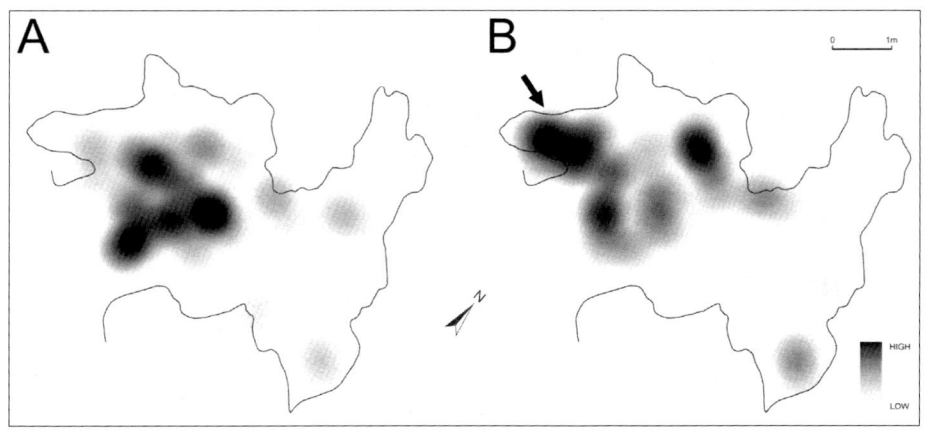

FIGURE 6. DIFFERENTIAL DISPERSION PATTERNS FOR UPPER AND LOWER LIMB BONES AT GRO (A – UPPER LIMB; B – LOWER LIMB; ARROW INDICATES CLUSTER OF LOWER LIMB BONES ON LATERAL NICHE CLOSE TO THE CAVE ENTRANCE).

It is not clear how different depositional areas correlate on each cave – did the smaller, secondary clusters correspond to areas where some bones were discarded during the manipulation processes occurring on the larger clusters? The fact that during osteological assessment very few secondary anatomical connections were identified further hinders the clarification of this issue.

Differences among both caves dispersion patterns may be revealing of discrete shifts in the funerary practices – and social/ideological rules governing them – performed by Late Prehistoric communities of the North Ribatejo. Two aspects could relate to this idea: (I) the apparent segregation of non-adults in CDV at the secondary cluster, seemingly non-existent at a later stage in GRO, which may indicate a change in the way younger individuals were regarded inside the community, as far as funerary treatment goes. Could it be that non-adults were being given a funerary treatment more similar to the one being performed for adult individuals in the late 4th millennium BC, when compared to its late 5th-early 4th millennia counterparts?; (II) the differing pattern of upper versus lower limb bones spatial dispersion in GRO, possibly reflecting specific post-depositional manipulation sequences which do not seem to be at play in CDV. A very clear case of this is the small niche, to the left of the cave entrance, almost exclusively dedicated to the deposition of lower limb bones.

This interpretation would converge with the hypothesis of a long lasting cultural tradition in the Nabão valley bearing a relation to the coastal Neolithic spread, which would be gradually impacted by the contacts with another tradition, further inland, related to the megaliths complex (Cruz 1997; Oosterbeek 1994, 2003; Tomé and Oosterbeek 2011). The slightly younger chronology of GRO, placing it closer to such proposed impact, suggests that the differential consideration of non-adults could correspond to times of intercultural relations, either as a consequence of new cultural approaches intake (in case the other tradition had no such segregation) or as a social adaptation mechanism (symbolic enlargement of the group through the 'emancipation' of non-adults, in order to resist to the outer influence that, as we know, ultimately would prevail).

The results presented here are, nevertheless, quite partial and further analytical developments should be considered. Statistical analysis may provide a deeper insight into the spatial dispersion patterns that became apparent from the present assessment.

GIS are certainly an important tool for the study of collective burials. Furthermore, the use of Open Source software allows for an inexpensive approach. This study demonstrates that, in the vast realm of analytical techniques allowed by GIS, the use of kernel density estimates may be a viable path in the study of prehistoric collective burials.

Acknowledgments

The authors wish to thank CIAS – Research Center in Anthropology and Health (Universidade de Coimbra) and CGEO – Geosciences Research Centre (UC/IPT), for the support given to the participation of several of us at the UISPP XVII Congress. The second author (CC) was supported by a grant from FCT – Fundação para a Ciência e a Tecnologia (Ministério da Educação e Ciência, Governo de Portugal) with the reference SFRH/BD/70183/2010.

References

Agosto, E.; Ajmar, A.; Boccardo, P.; Tonolo, F.; Lingua, A. (2008) – Crime scene reconstruction using a fully geomatic approach. Sensors. 8, p. 6280-6302.

Aldenderfer, M.; Maschner, H. (1996) – Anthropology, space and Geographic Information Systems. Oxford University Press.

Anemone, R.; Conroy, G.; Emerson, C. (2011) – GIS and Paleoanthropology: Incorporating new approaches from the Geospatial Sciences in the analysis of primate and human evolution. Yearbook of Physical Anthropology. 54, p. 19-46.

Baxter, M.J.; Beardah, C.C.; Wright, R.V.S. (1997) – Some archaeological applications of kernel density estimates. Journal of Archaeological Science. 24:4, p. 347-354.

Boaventura, R.; Ferreira, M.T.; Neves, M.J.; Silva, A.M. (2014) – Funerary practices and anthropology during Middle-Late Neolithic (4th and 3rd Millennia BCE) in Portugal: Old bones, new insights. Anthropologie. LII/2, p. 183-205.

Cascalheira, J.; Gonçalves, C. (2012) – Spatial analysis and site formation processes of the Mesolithic shellmiddens of Cabeço da Amoreira (Muge, Portugal). In Cascalheira, J.; Gonçalves, C. (eds.) – Promontoria 16 (Actas das IV Jornadas de Jovens em Investigação Arqueológica) Faro: Universidade do Algarve, p. 75-82.

Chapman, H. (2006) – Landscape Archaeology and GIS. The History Press Ltd.

Cruz, A.R. (1997) – Vale do Nabão: do Neolítico à Idade do Bronze. Arkeos 3. Tomar: CEIPHAR.

Dirkmaat, D.; Cabo, L.; Ousley, S.; Symes, S. (2008) – New perspectives in Forensic Anthropology. Yearbook of Physical Anthropology. 51, p. 33-52.

Djindjian, F. (1998) – GIS usage in worldwide Archaeology. Archeologia e Calcolatori. IX, p. 19-29.

Gaffney, V.; Stancic, Z. (1991) – GIS approaches to regional analysis: a case study of the island of Hvar. Ljubljana: Znanstveni Institut Filozofske Fakultete.

Field, J.; Petraglia, M.; Lahr, M. (2007) – The southern dispersal hypothesis and the South Asian archaeological record: Examination of dispersal routes through GIS analysis. Journal of Anthropological Archaeology. 26, p. 88-108.

García Sanjuan, L.; Wheatley, D.; Murrieta Flores, P.; Márquez Perez, J. (2009) – Los SIG y el análisis espacial en Arqueología. Aplicaciones en la Prehistoria Reciente del Sur de España. In Nieto, X.; Ángel Cau, M., eds. – Arqueología Nàutica Mediterrània. Monografies del CASC 8, p. 163-180.

Grove, M. (2011) – A spatio-temporal kernel method for mapping changes in prehistoric land-use patterns. Archaeometry. 53:5, p. 1012-1030.

Herrmann, N. (2002) – GIS applied to Bioarchaeology: An example from the Río Talgua caves in Northeast Honduras. Journal of Cave and Karst Studies. 64:1, p. 17-22.

Herrmann, N.; Devlin, J. (2008) – Assessment of commingled human remains using a GIS-based approach. In Adams, B.; Byrd, J., eds. – Recovery, Analysis, and Identification of Commingled Human Remains. Humana Press, p. 257-269.

Katsianis, M.; Tsipidis, S. (2005) – Trends and problems in archaeological GIS applications. In Triantis, D.; Vallianatos, F., eds. – CD-Rom Proceedings of the 2005 WSEAS International Conference on Engineering Education (Conference Session: Educational & Instructional Tools in History & Archaeology), Vouliagmeni, Athens, Greece, 8-10/7/2005.

Keeler, D. (2007) – Intrasite spatial analysis of a Late Upper Paleolithic French site using Geographic Information Systems. Journal of World Anthropology. III/1, p. 1-40.

Larmarange, J. (2013) – Mapping Demographic and Health Surveys (DHS): a method to estimate regional trends of a proportion. Extended abstract presented to the XXVII International Population Conference (Busan, 26-31 August 2013). Available at: http://iussp.org/sites/default/files/event_call_for_papers/Abstract%20prevR.pdf

Lock, G. (2000) – Beyond the map – Archaeology and spatial technologies. IOS Press.

Lock, G.; Stancic, Z. (1995) – Archaeology and Geographical Information Systems: a European perspective. London: Taylor and Francis.

Moscati, P. (1998) – GIS applications in Italian Archaeology. Archeologia e Calcolatori. IX, p. 191-236.

Oosterbeek, L. (1993) – Gruta dos Ossos (Tomar) Um ossuário do Neolítico Final. Boletim Cultural de Tomar. 18, p. 11-28.

Oosterbeek, L. (1994) – Echoes from the East: the western network. An insight to unequal and combined development, 7000-2000 BC. PhD Dissertation. London: University College.

Oosterbeek, L. (2003) – Megaliths in Portugal: the western network revisited. In Burenhult, G., ed. – Stones and Bones. Formal disposal of the dead in Atlantic Europe during the Mesolithic-Neolithic interface 6000-3000 b.C. British Archaeological Reports – International Series. Oxford. 1201, p. 27-37.

Sayer, D.; Wienhold, M. (2013) – A GIS-investigation of four Early Anglo-Saxon cemeteries: Ripley's K-function analysis of spatial groupings amongst graves. Social Science Computer Review. 31:1, p. 71-89.

Silva, A.M. (2002) – Antropologia funerária e paleobiologia das populações portuguesas (litorais) do Neolítico final/Calcolítico. Dissertação para a obtenção do grau de Doutor em Antropologia. Coimbra: Departamento de Antropologia da Universidade (policopiado).

Silva, A.M. (2003) – Portuguese populations of Late Neolithic and Chalcolithic periods exhumed from collective burials: an overview. Anthropologie. XLI, 1/2, p. 55-64.

Silva, A.M.; Crubézy, E.; Cunha, E. (2009) – Bone weight: New reference values based on a Modern Portuguese identified skeletal collection. International Journal of Osteoarchaeology. 19:5, p. 628-641.

Silverman, B. (1986) – Density estimation for statistics and data analysis. Monographs on Statistics and Applied Probability. London: Chapman and Hall.

Tomé, T. (2006) – Reflexos da Vida na Morte: Paleobiologia das populações do Neolítico Final/Calcolítico do Vale do Nabão – Gruta dos Ossos. Unpublished Master Thesis. Universidade de Trás-os-Montes e Alto Douro: Vila Real.

Tomé, T. (2011) – Até que a Morte nos Reúna: Transição para o Agro-pastoralismo na Bacia do Tejo e Sudoeste Peninsular. Unpublished PhD Thesis. Universidade de Trás-os-Montes e Alto Douro: Vila Real.

Tomé, T.; Oosterbeek, L. (2011) – One Region, Two Systems? A Paleobiological Reading of Cultural Continuity over the Agro-Pastoralist Transition in the North Ribatejo. In Bueno Ramirez, P.; Cerrillo Cuenca, E.; Gonzalez Cordero, A. (eds.), From the Origins: The Prehistory of the Inner Tagus Region. Oxford: Archaeopress, BAR IS, pp. 43-54.

Tomé, T.; Silva, A.M. (2013) – Práticas Funerárias na Pré-História Recente do Alto Ribatejo: Ponto da Situação. In Cruz, A.R.; Graça, A.; Oosterbeek, L. e Rosina, P. (eds.), 1º Congresso de Arqueologia do Alto Ribatejo – Homenagem a José da Silva Gomes. Arkeos, vol. 34. Tomar: CEIPHAR, p. 99-107.

Wheatley, D.; Gillings, M. (2002) – Spatial Technology and Archaeology – The Archaeological Applications of GIS. London: Taylor & Francis.